BRIAN MAY

THE DEFINITIVE BIOGRAPHY

BRIAN MAY

THE DEFINITIVE BIOGRAPHY

Laura Jackson

PORTRAIT

PORTRAIT

First published in Great Britain in 2007 by **Portrait Books**

**A CIP catalogue record for this book
is available from the British Library**

ISBN: 978-0-7499-5152-8

Text design by Goldust Design
Edited by Jinny Johnson

Typeset in Goudy Old Style by Palimpsest Book Production Limited,
Grangemouth, Stirlingshire

Printed and bound in Great Britain by
MPG Books, Bodmin, Cornwall

Portrait Books
an imprint of
Little, Brown Book Group
100 Victoria Embankment
London EC4Y 0DY

An Hachette Livre UK Company

www.portraitbooks.com

This book is dedicated to
David, my precious husband

PICTURE CREDITS

CONTENTS

ACKNOWLEDGEMENTS

Thanks to all those whom I interviewed: Benny Andersson; Michael Appleton; Simon Bates; Mike Bersin; Tony Blackman; Tony Brainsby; Sir Richard Branson; Pete Brown; Michael Buerk; Lady Chryssie Cobbold; Derek Deane; Simon Denbigh; Bruce Dickinson; Dave Dilloway; Wayne Eagling; Spike Edney; Joe Elliott; David Essex; Kent P. Falb; Eric Faulkner; Fish; Scott Gorham; Mike Grose; Jo Gurnett; Tony Hale; Bob Harris; Dr Tom Hicks; Geoff Higgins; Tony Iommi; Andy Jones; Mandla Langa; Gary Langhan; Jane L'Epine Smith; Professor Sir Bernard Lovell; Hank B. Marvin; Helen McConnell; Malcolm McLaren; Barry Mitchell; Mike Moran; Chris O'Donnell; Norman Pace; John Peel; Tony Pike; Nigel Planer; Andy Powell; Dr N.K. Reay; Zandra Rhodes; Sir Tim Rice; Sir Cliff Richard; Professor Jim Ring; Paul Rodgers; Richie Sambora; Joe Satriani; Tim Staffell; Sir Jackie Stewart; Michael Stimpson; Peter Stringfellow; Dick Taylor; Ken Testi; Malcolm Thomas; Bjorn Ulvaeus; Barbara Valentin; Brian White; Mike Winsor; Terry Yeadon; Paul Young.

Also helpful: *Birmingham Evening Mail*; *BBC Radio*; *Vox*; *Vintage Guitar*; *Evening Standard*; *The Times*; *Guitarist*; *Q*; *Guitar Player*; *Guitar World*; *Classic Rock*; *Daily Mirror*; *Uncut*; *Rolling Stone*; *Rock CD*; *Independent*; *Total Guitar*; *Record Collector*; *Mail on Sunday*; *Daily Mail*.

Special thanks to: David for all his support and encouragement, and Alice Davis and all at Piatkus Books.

1

STAR-STRUCK

Brian May is an intensely private person. As one quarter of Queen, for over fifteen years he strode the world's stage establishing his place as one of rock music's most distinctive and respected lead guitarists. Reassuringly dependable in an unstable profession, he forever fostered an outward air of calm and reason. Yet behind the scenes, in the late 1980s, he battled with debilitating personal turmoil and his depth of depression was once so acute that it drove him close to the brink.

Recovering, throughout the nineties he embarked on a successful solo career and in summer 2002, watched live by millions of television viewers around the globe, May provided one of the defining images of the Golden Jubilee celebrations by performing his own version of the national anthem on electric guitar, standing on the roof of Buckingham Palace.

Months after Freddie Mercury's untimely death in 1991, Queen disbanded, but their popularity has never waned. In late 2006, Queen's *Greatest Hits* became the UK's all-time best-selling album, relegating the Beatles' *Sgt. Pepper's Lonely Hearts Club Band* into second place. Brian May and Roger Taylor, as Queen, and fronted by vocalist Paul Rodgers, have returned to live performance, an event May has described as 'The Queen phoenix rising from the ashes again.' Music has been the professional mainstay of Brian May's life, and although he is a far from reluctant rock star, it was certainly not quite the stellar path planned for him by his parents.

Brian Harold May was born on 19 July 1947 in the Gloucester House Nursing Home at Hampton in Middlesex, the only child of Ruth and Harold May, a senior draughtsman with the Ministry of Aviation. Home was a three-bedroomed thirties semi in a comfortable middle-class neighbourhood of Feltham in Greater London. Only many years later would Brian discover that Freddie Mercury had lived a few hundred yards away.

Naturally inquisitive, Brian quickly showed that he had inherited his father's dexterity with his hands; he spent many happy hours making model toys. His education began at Cardinal Road Infants School before he moved to Hanworth Road Junior. Said Brian: 'I was pretty much an all-rounder there and enjoyed the science and English lessons. My favourite thing was rainy days, when we could stay inside to read comics.' He adored the comic-strip boys' hero Dan Dare and became an avid collector of the *Eagle*.

By the time Brian was six he was displaying an early liking for music and was often glued to the radio. His parents had enrolled him for piano lessons at a local music school and Harold decided to teach him to play the ukulele, on which he himself was proficient. Brian recalled: 'My father taught me about seven chords on the ukulele. When I asked for a guitar for my next birthday, I converted the chords from four strings to six strings. I made up chords.'

There was one snag, however, with the Egmond guitar he received – its strings were too high off the fret board. So father and son carved down its wooden bridge, making it easier to play. They also set out to give it the electric sound for which Brian had been craving. Copper wire wound around three little button magnets provided him with crude but effective pick-ups which he then fixed on to the instrument, making the acoustic sound electric once it was plugged into the family's wireless, which had to double as a makeshift amplifier.

Electrifying that guitar was not the only project on which the pair worked closely. They also built a four-inch reflector telescope so that Brian could indulge in another early passion – astronomy. The stars fascinated him. He was permitted to stay up to watch the weekly TV show *The Sky at Night*, presented with great panache by Patrick Moore. It made a huge impact on him. 'I was completely hooked,' he declared. 'It was something I knew I was going to be captivated by all my life.' Through his basic telescope Brian was excited to see, say, the rings of Saturn. He recalled: 'I remember getting up about 4 a.m. to see Jupiter, running out into the road trying to find a place where I could get a line on it with my telescope and actually seeing it with its moons and everything!'

Yet for all this enthusiasm, what Brian gravitated to most was music. Having persevered at the piano lessons long enough to pass Grade IV, by the age of nine he had had enough and gave up. Sometimes he would compose the odd song, but nothing serious; at this point he was very much finding his feet.

May recalled: 'The early fifties in England saw the beginning of electric guitar music as we know it and I grabbed at anything I could find. It was just magical and sent shivers up my spine.' He particularly adored American pop music and would play Buddy Holly and the Crickets, the Everly Brothers and Little Richard records over and over again. Gradually he grew confident enough to play along with them on his guitar, progressing in time from chords to picking out single notes. From an early age he had a very analytical mind, and in a remarkably short space of time he had dissected his favourite songs – finding the key to how each worked and why – and the perfectionist in him ensured that he kept at it until he had exhausted all their secrets. From then on, music would anchor his life.

In 1958, when he had turned eleven, Brian passed the scholarship exam that qualified him for a place at Hampton Grammar School, and it was here that his appetite for music really began to flourish; somewhat ironically, since the atmosphere was far from conducive as guitar playing was heavily frowned upon. 'We were forced to listen to classical music and told what to think of it,' May remembered.

Still, several boys fancied themselves as guitarists and, keen to learn from each other, would congregate at lunchtime to jam together. Recognised as having special aptitude, by the time Brian was in his second year he had attracted an early fan club, as one of his classmates in 2LA, Dave Dilloway, recalls: 'Someone in the corridor one day told me that there was a guy playing a guitar in the geography room, so out of interest I went to see. When I got there and looked in, Brian was sitting on a stool in the middle of a circle of school kids playing and singing Guy Mitchell's hit "I Never Felt More Like Singing the Blues", and I was really impressed.'

May and Dilloway became good friends and would often meet up at each other's house, armed with tape recorders, eager to experiment with sounds. 'It was all very basic, as was most equipment available in those days,' explains Dave. 'We mainly played instrumental material from the likes of Les Paul, Chet Atkins, the Ventures and the Spotniks. Brian had his original Spanish acoustic with its home-made pick-up and I had a home-made six-string electric guitar as well as a home-made bass. At this point, I used to tackle the lead guitar and Brian would play rhythm. We would record these two parts together on tape and then, while this pre-recorded track was played back, we would record on it again. This time, Brian would be playing my home-made bass while I played drums, by which I mean anything percussive we could find at home, including my mother's hat boxes. Meccano strips doubled for cymbals.'

As the fifties faded, a new addition to Brian's growing list of heroes and influences was the British group the Shadows, who had hit the number one slot in the UK singles chart in July 1960 with the instrumental 'Apache'. What captured May's attention, in particular, was the style and skill of their lead guitarist, Hank Marvin.

Hank Marvin reflects: 'With the advent of rock and roll, electric guitars came into their own. All you needed was a bass, drums, two guitars and a singer like Cliff Richard or Marty Wilde and you had a band. Plus, people were attracted to participate now, instead of just being onlookers. The fact that the guitar was so portable meant that with the addition of a small amplifier you could perform anywhere, any time. Not to be forgotten, either, was the image. The guitar's a cool instrument and very synonymous with white rock and roll. Think of Elvis. You didn't even need to be able to play the thing. It could just be a cool prop. There is no instrument like it. Just imagine trying to look cool blowing a trumpet with your cheeks all bulging and bloated!'

Brian May's burning ambition in 1963 was to leave behind the acoustic and branch out on to an electric guitar. Some of his friends had the new Gibsons and Stratocasters. One school friend, John Garnham, had a Colorama, which Brian would have given his eye teeth for, but while Ruth and Harold would have given their only child anything, they simply could not afford to buy him an instrument of this quality. Resourcefully, Brian and his father decided that they would build their own.

In August, work began in a spare bedroom. It took eighteen months to complete; to keep an exact record of its construction, Brian photographed and diligently logged every stage. The guitar they produced would become world famous in the years ahead.

First, Brian painstakingly carved the neck of the guitar from an antique solid mahogany fireplace that a family friend was throwing out, shaping it to perfection with a penknife. The body into which the neck was later fitted was made from a piece of oak, some blockboard and odds and ends. It was a long, laborious task but father and son were both patient and determined. A great deal of thought and imagination went into the construction and the design. Said May: 'I wanted it cut away more on the underside so I could genuinely get up to those top frets. We made everything totally from scratch with hand tools.'

Harold and Brian also believed that they had identified three common faults in conventional guitar making methods. First, the necks of many modern electric guitars tended to bend because of the enormous stress placed on the strings – by their calculations, a pressure of nearly 500 pounds. So they incorporated a steel truss rod into the neck, setting it at an angle to the tension through the neck and holding it in place with a steel bolt.

Next, their attention focused on the bridge. When the strings were tightened over it, repeated use of the tremolo arm sawed away at them and increased the risk of their snapping. Equally important, the strings failed to return to pitch after the tremolo arm had been used. Instead of the conventional bridge, therefore, they designed a set of small rollers over which the strings could tighten without inviting the same wear and tear. 'We tried various methods,' recalled Brian, 'including one with ball-races at each end of a cylinder, but the one which worked best was a milled steel plate rocking on a knife edge.' The tension of the strings was balanced by two valve springs which Harold found on a 1928 Panther motorcycle, and the arm itself was improvised from a bicycle saddlebag support, finished off with a piece of fat knitting needle.

Their ingenuity had not been exhausted. For fret markers Brian raided Ruth's button box, making off with the shiny mother-of-pearl ones which he cut down to size. He was forced, however, to buy the fret wire because he could not find anything else suitable, but this was reprofiled using jigs that Brian and Harold made up specially. When it came to the pick-ups Brian once again tried to make his own, to a similar design to that which had worked on the Spanish guitar, but he had to concede that they were less than satisfactory and so forked out £9.45 for a set of three Burns pick-ups which he modified by filling them with epoxy resin to stop them being microphonic.

The pick-ups themselves were important. Harold May once revealed: 'The secret of these pick-ups is in the position that each one is set, because this alters the tonal harmonic effect, and by some really clever switching, you can have any combination of twenty-four tones, and that is something that no guitar manufacturer has ever done commercially. When Brian plays that solo on "Brighton Rock", he is accompanying himself, using echoes.'

Together Brian and Harold had built a guitar that had tonal range and depth far exceeding those of most commercially available instruments at that time, and at a total cost of £17.45. The deep reddish-brown of the mahogany inspired Brian to call this treasured and remarkable instrument the Red Special. Unsurprisingly, he has built up a special bond with it. 'It is quite an emotional thing, playing the guitar,' he admitted. 'You need to be in contact with your strings because that's all you've got.' Hank Marvin explains: 'It's like another person you're embracing – an extension of your body, altering your shape. Some people abuse the instrument and act out a lot of violence. I don't know that it's erotic love, because you would have to be pretty perverted to feel like that about a bit of wood, but there is certainly a relationship between you and your guitar.'

In the early 1960s, Brian may not yet have decided that music was where his destiny lay – astronomy still fascinated him – but he felt its attraction strongly and knew that there was a vibrant local music scene out there. One of the most popular venues at this time was at Eel Pie Island in the Thames at Twickenham, where audiences were spoiled for choice in the quality of the bands to see live – the Rolling Stones, Fleetwood Mac and Cream were among the bands cutting the mustard there.

Getting to see these bands, though, was not always easy for Brian. There was more than the whiff of youthful rebellion in the air, centred around music. In March 1964, *Melody Maker* ran a headline that became the national catchphrase of the decade: *Would You Let Your Daughter Marry a Rolling Stone?* It was a social shift that spooked many middle-class parents, and Ruth and Harold May did not want their son to go gallivanting to these music havens in the evenings, preferring that he concentrate on his homework and stay at home. Their desire to shelter him may have been only natural but, feeling restricted, Brian made efforts to buck against it. Soaking up this surfeit of talent whenever he could, the teenage May was drawn most to guitarists Jeff Beck and Eric Clapton. Very quickly, the urge to form a band took root.

To date, Brian's experience in this respect had been limited to jamming with Dave Dilloway, although recently he had had his first taste of being inside a recording studio. Another Hampton Grammar pupil, would-be songwriter Bill Richards, had landed a music publishing deal. When he had to record a demo tape of 'The Left Handed Marriage' at Abbey Road studios in north London, Richards invited May and Dilloway along to provide instrumental backing. Says Dave: 'Brian played lead and sang and I played bass. Goodness knows what else we recorded, but it was good experience for us.'

Brian May's first band was an unnamed loose collection of musicians. He played lead guitar, Dave Dilloway handled bass, a friend named Malcolm provided the rhythm guitar, while another classmate, John Sanger, at one point drifted in on piano. Since no one knew a drummer, at first they made do without. Malcolm was soon replaced by John Garnham, whose Colorama Brian had once coveted so much. Garnham had other practical attractions.

He owned a proper amplifier, as well as microphone stands with mikes, and he also had the all-important advantage of having previous experience of performing live.

The line-up, though, was incomplete because they had no singer. Then one night, May and the embryonic band went to a dance to watch another local group perform. During the evening Brian noticed Hampton Grammar School pupil Tim Staffell at the back of the hall, softly playing harmonica and singing along. Brian crossed over to Staffell. The two got talking, found that they shared a love of music and soon they began to hang out together. Says Tim Staffell: 'There was a lot of music going on and we used to tour the different pubs and clubs to take stock of who was doing what. It all made a deep impression on us.'

Such was the impression that, fronted by Staffell, the band knuckled down to serious rehearsing at Chase Bridge Primary School in Whitton, next to the Twickenham rugby ground. This venue was made available by the local authority, which wanted to give the local youth somewhere to go to expend their energies. The discipline of regular rehearsals was exactly what the band had needed, and progress over the next several months was rapid.

Brian thoroughly enjoyed these evenings. He thrived on the way they bounced ideas off each other. In addition, they got to know one another better, and strong bonds developed. It soon became apparent, however, that they could not go on indefinitely without a drummer, so they placed an advert in the window of Albert's music shop in Twickenham. There was just one applicant, Richard Thompson from Hounslow, who was hired on the spot.

Just in time for their first fee-paying gig, at St Mary's church hall in Twickenham on 28 October 1964, they called themselves 1984, after the popular George Orwell sci-fi novel. The following month, 1984 played at Richmond Girls School, after which gig John Sanger left the band to go to Manchester University.

Tim Staffell recalls: 'We had a regularish gig at the Thames Boat Club on the riverfront at Putney. We used to play mainly on a Saturday night for no more than a few pounds, and for considerably longer than was average for bands too, often for as long as three hours. The set was peppered with schoolboy humour when I look back on it now, but it seemed to please the crowd at the time.'

There was also scant glamour attached to it. According to Tim: 'Equipment was always a problem, with home-made speaker cabinets and PA systems that were no more than rudimentary lash-ups, usually underpowered into the bargain.' Transport was a total hit-and-miss affair. John Garnham came to the rescue as much as possible with his tiny two-seater Heinkel bubble car. This bizarre-looking vehicle would be crammed with a hotch-potch of gear, with its roof removed so that chrome microphone stands could stick periscope-like out of the top. To get to gigs, Tim Staffell occasionally had to squeeze himself into the already overladen car, and even Brian managed to concertina his lanky body, already in excess of six feet, into this confined space.

For Brian, performing at local dances was far preferable to attending them. Throughout his teens, he would be steady in his romantic relationships with girls but although slender, intelligent and quietly spoken, he suffered from a distinct lack of self-confidence. Years later, he candidly confessed: 'I was very insecure. Whenever I did go to dances, I used to think: my God, I don't know what to do. I don't know what to wear. I don't know who I am!' He would look longingly at the band, wishing he was up there – more at ease with being on stage than having to ask a girl to dance. 'The guitar was my shield to hide behind,' he declared.

Having kept pace with his school studies, Brian was delighted when in February 1965 he was awarded an open scholarship in physics at Imperial College of Science and Technology in London.

By the time he left Hampton Grammar that summer, aged eighteen, his ten O levels had been supplemented by A levels in physics, pure maths, applied maths and additional maths. He was to study physics and infrared astronomy, with the ambition of becoming an astrophysicist.

Tim Staffell was now also in London, about to embark on a graphics course at Ealing College of Art. Dave Dilloway was set to read electronics at Southampton University. Brian, however, was determined that 1984 should continue to play gigs, as Dilloway reveals: 'Southampton was only an hour or so away and I had a motorbike then, so I came home at weekends. We would listen to material, decide what to learn, and go away and learn it, but if new ideas came to us while we were apart, we would write.' May and Staffell obviously found it easier to keep in touch and it was now that they began to write songs together, although at times this tended to be conducted in an atmosphere of semi-hostility as Tim's parents did not approve of this band nonsense.

It was an intolerance that was now mirrored in homes throughout Britain. Many parents' stomachs curdled on seeing their sons resplendent in floral-print, bell-sleeved shirts, lurid trousers and with a billowy curtain of long hair flying behind them. Dave Dilloway confesses: 'My mother used to hope that I would only go out at night so that the neighbours wouldn't see me!' Brian was as fashion conscious as the next guy and faithfully followed all the latest trends.

At the end of 1965, Dave Dilloway left Southampton University for an electronics course at Twickenham College of Technology, which meant that May, Staffell and Dilloway could once again practise properly, to better effect. With more regular bookings their experience was mounting and their repertoire widening all the time. Ever eager to experiment, Brian spent hours working out variations and trying out their own arrangements. As well as Rolling Stones, Yardbirds and Spencer Davis material, Beatles songs featured strongly at gigs, with May coming in on the three-part harmony sections of certain numbers.

'Sometimes Brian would sing lead on "Yesterday" and the audience always loved it,' recalls Tim. 'They would scream and bring the house down with their applause. It made me dead jealous, the rat, but he sang it far better than I ever could.' Brian's singing voice has a high register and often he and Tim would compete to see who could hit the highest note. May was candid: 'No competition. Tim always won!'

Although May felt at home on stage, he had no wish to be the showman in the band and was happy to stand left of centre playing his guitar with increasing speed and dexterity. 'His skill enabled us to play virtually anything,' says Dave Dilloway. 'Audiences recognised his unique talent even then. I don't know how many other bands ever tried to poach him away from us, but I imagine he had quite a few offers.'

By this time, visually Brian was beginning to carve the image with which he has become synonymous. His height and being as thin as a lamp-post set him apart anyway. His hair, which had gone through a Beatlesque stage in 1965, was now evolving into a thick mop of curls not unlike the bushy Afro associated with the American blues guitarist Jimi Hendrix; because of this Brian acquired the nickname Brimi.

Although the gigs themselves were stimulating and fun, they were rarely played in genteel establishments, and occasionally fist-fights broke out in the rowdy audiences. Of one night at a gig in Twickenham, Dave Dilloway recalls: 'I don't know why, but I remember looking out into the audience and thinking, fancy dancing with chairs like that, that's a bit unusual. Then I realised that a couple of guys were beating each other over the head with steel fold-up seats! They were ejected by the bouncers and we carried on playing through it all.' Trouble erupted again at the White Hart in Southall, a regular hot spot even though it was next door to the police station. That night, the rumpus resembled a Wild West saloon brawl.

Operating at a local level was one thing; gaining any kind of foothold on the ladder of success, however, seemed a distant prospect. Brian jumped, therefore, at the opportunity of entering a prestigious annual competition held at the Top Rank Club in Croydon. It was a national talent search, whose outright winner would secure a recording contract. Initial heats were by selection from pre-recorded material, so with the help of a college friend who owned a high quality tape recorder, 1984 put down three tracks in stereo. On the strength of this tape, the band secured a place in one of the heats.

The look they adopted that night was eye-catching. Tim Staffell wore a bold blue shirt with pink polka dots, while Richard Thompson was resplendent in a silver silk shirt, but Brian's style was inspired by old military uniforms which were all the rage at the beginning of 1967, and he had opted for a blue serge Royal Marine jacket that he had picked up at the Chelsea antique market.

The numbers 1984 performed included Jimi Hendrix's 'Stone Free', Buddy Knox's 'She's Gone', and 'Knock on Wood' by Eddie Floyd. They won their heat. The prize was a reel of Scotch tape and a CBS album each. They were not given a choice, just five albums to fight for among themselves. Staffell claimed the cream of the crop – Simon and Garfunkel's *Sounds of Silence* – while May made do with a Barbra Streisand album.

1984 did not go on to win the final and so never got the coveted recording contract. This disappointment was forgotten three months later when, on 13 May 1967, they played one of their most memorable support gigs ever at Imperial College. Topping the bill was Jimi Hendrix, on the brink of his breakthrough and generating great excitement. 'We were booked to play first for dancing in the small hall downstairs on that occasion,' remembers Dave Dilloway, 'and stopped when we knew Hendrix was due on in the main hall.' As they made their way upstairs and filed past the dressing room doors, Jimi Hendrix suddenly came out into the corridor and uttered to a dumbstruck Tim Staffell: 'Which way's the stage, man?'

With Jimi Hendrix that night was his close friend and mentor, Rolling Stone founder Brian Jones. A musical genius with a vibrant personality, in 1967 Jones was, however, struggling with all kinds of physical, mental and emotional problems and his fragile condition was all too apparent to anyone who met him in the flesh at this time. Dilloway says: 'Brian Jones came out of the dressing room behind Hendrix and went with him to the stage, where he stood quietly watching Jimi perform from the wings. I don't think I had ever seen anyone look so skeletal and ill as Jones did that night.'

Hendrix mesmerised May. Brian had become an early disciple when he had watched Jimi play support to the Who at a Brian Epstein show at London's Savoy Theatre, and been completely blown away, particularly by how the young American could make the guitar 'talk' – something May already aspired to. Brian recalled: 'This guy was so far in advance of everyone else. I went to see him a lot after that, wondering how he did it. I'd thought I was pretty good before I saw Hendrix!'

On the upside, 1984 seemed to be on a roll, for they were to complete their hat-trick of significant gigs with a support slot towards the end of the year at a star-studded event. Their participation in this had come about entirely by accident. While playing at the London School of Medicine they were approached by two pop promoters who had come along to see another band on the bill. The pair were on the lookout for someone to fill a single support slot left at a forthcoming all night event at Olympia. After watching the groups perform, they liked 1984 best. 'They chatted away to us for a while, then suggested we might like to do this gig. Naturally, we jumped at it,' admits Dave.

May set about working out which cover versions they should do, and decided to incorporate a song called 'Step On Me', which he had co-written with Tim Staffell. Now and then the promoters showed up at the band's rehearsals with suggestions on presentation. Brian was slightly wary. In his heart, he felt that 1984 was not going places and hardly qualified for the 'I'll groom you for stardom' routine. Nevertheless, when they were invited to the promoters' Soho office to be taken on a shopping spree in London's Carnaby Street, along with the others, he happily sidelined any scepticism.

The big night arrived on 22 December 1967. It was billed as 'Christmas on Earth', and the line-up featured Jimi Hendrix, Pink Floyd, the Herd, the Move, the Who, Traffic and the Animals. Although 1984, fifteenth on the bill, had been told they would not be announced on stage until near midnight, they arrived mid-afternoon and parked outside. After a long, frustrating wait, they finally got to play their set around dawn the next day. 'By this time, we were quite tired,' remembers Dave Dilloway. 'We didn't get a sound check or anything fancy like that. We were just pushed straight on and expected to play.' They had never before played on such an illustrious bill, to quite such a large audience, and certainly never through anything remotely resembling the bank of expensive Marshall equipment as was provided that night.

Their exhilaration was soon punctured when they came off stage to discover that thieves had ransacked their dressing room and made off with their wallets and valuables. On top of this, when they went dejectedly outside to load up their gear, they learned that all their cars had been towed away to the Hammersmith pound.

Early in 1968, Brian left the band. He needed to spend more time on his studies, and with finals looming at the end of his three-year course he could afford few distractions. He had been happy at Imperial College and some of his tutors had marked him down as someone likely to go places. Professor Jim Ring recalls: 'Brian was very likeable and friendly and an excellent student. At that time, at least in my mind, there was no suggestion of him becoming a rock star. To me, he was first and foremost a very bright physicist.'

It felt strange to May, though, to be no longer playing in a band. He still kept in touch with Tim Staffell, who stayed on in 1984 for a while and took over lead guitar duties as well as handling the vocals, but then he too left. The more time Brian and Tim spent talking about music, the more they realised how much they missed being in a band, and with a view to forming a new group they pinned an advertisement on the Imperial College notice-board asking for a 'Mitch Mitchell/Ginger Baker-type drummer'. Swamped with replies, the pair began to hold auditions.

Among the students drawn to that advert was a young man named Les Brown, who shared a flat in Shepherd's Bush with a dental student at the London Hospital Medical School named Roger Meddows Taylor. Roger was a drummer, and mad keen on joining a band.

Born on 26 July 1949 in the West Norfolk and King's Lynn Hospital in Norfolk, when he was eight he had moved with his family – his younger sister Clare and their parents, Winifred and Michael Taylor, a Potato Marketing Board employee – to Truro in Cornwall. Drawn from an early age to music, like Brian May, Roger started out on the ukulele before progressing to the guitar.

After practising in the family garage, along with some friends, Taylor formed a skiffle group called the Bubblingover Boys. It was an odd quartet that comprised two guitarists, himself on ukulele and a fourth guy playing a tea-chest bass. It was a short-lived venture and Roger was later brutally frank as to why the ensemble collapsed. He revealed that none of them could actually play. 'We just stood and twanged tuneless chords. It was dreadful,' he confessed.

By eleven, while at Truro School, he had joined the cathedral choir. The pressure of singing at three services every Sunday quickly put him off, although the voice training he received proved invaluable later, as he went on to play a vital role in the strongly harmonic style that would become the bedrock of so much of Queen's music.

In 1961 Roger, however, was given the beginnings of his first drum kit and realised that percussion was where his true talent lay. In his teens, he played drums in local West Country bands such as the Cousin Jacks and Johnny Quale and the Reaction – later known simply as Reaction – and cultivated a large following, but London was where it was at and he couldn't wait to get there in October 1967. Slim, blond, good-looking and bursting with energy, he had been turned on to Jimi Hendrix and had gone instantly psychedelic. Les Brown knew how avidly Roger had been scanning the music press for an opening with a band and told him about this IC notice-board ad.

Taylor got in touch, and May and Staffell went hotfoot to Shepherd's Bush to see him. Unfortunately, his drums were still at home in Cornwall and he only had a set of bongos with which to impress the pair. Brian and Tim had taken their acoustic guitars along and after rattling through a few tunes, they liked Taylor's evident skill and flair. Staffell states: 'I wouldn't actually say that we auditioned Roger, as such. It wasn't like that. It just became very obvious that Roger was dead right for us.'

May agreed, but he still wanted to know how the sound would knit together when everything was properly plugged in, and he made arrangements to use the college Jazz Club room so that the trio could have the chance to play for real. That session resolved any doubts. Tim reveals: 'The chemistry was spot on. It was clear right away that we would effortlessly evolve into a unit as equal partners. We had the same musical tastes, same sense of humour and fundamentally the same aspirations.' Individually their knowledge of the music business may have been sketchy, but collectively their ideas were strong and their determination that they would make a go of it gave them all the impetus they needed. Optimistically, they called their band Smile.

Brian was now in his element. Although he was approaching his finals, he made time to rehearse hard, was keen to perfect their music and style, and he wrote more songs with Tim Staffell. Tim confesses: 'For me, this was the start of really taking myself seriously with music. I wrote my first songs with Smile, some in collaboration with Brian, some alone.' Things appeared to be slotting neatly into place. They had even acquired a van now, courtesy of Pete Edmunds, an old school friend of May's who became their first roadie.

Creatively, it was a very fertile time in Britain; in particular progressive rock communicated itself vividly to true musicians. Andy Powell, lead guitarist with the progressive rock band Wishbone Ash, explains: 'The feeling was that post-1967, which is classed as a watershed year with the *Sgt. Pepper* album, the floodgates had opened and everything was up for grabs. There was no corporate rock. There was a great innocence and ignorance in us. We would draw on fifties jazz, folk music, Celtic music, R&B – anything that got the juices flowing. We had no qualms either about delving down alleys in search of inspiration and it got very eclectic, never mainstream.'

The strength and independence of this music hugely appealed to Brian May. He would vividly recall attending a massive open-air concert in Hyde Park and being mesmerised by Jethro Tull, another distinctive progressive rock band. He said: 'I was knocked out by Mick Abraham's guitar playing!' Life was moving fast for Brian, right then.

On 24 October 1968, at the Royal Albert Hall, he received

his Bsc (Hons) degree certificate from the Chancellor of London University, the Queen Mother. His parents were very proud of his academic achievements and privately hoped that he would continue with his studies, although they could not help but be aware of how important music had become to him. By now, May's focus was firmly fixed on launching Smile. The rehearsing was over and the band's first public appearance, in support of Pink Floyd, was due to take place in two days' time at Imperial College. It felt like an important beginning.

2

LEAN AND HUNGRY

In 1968, with a degree to his name and Smile showing potential, Brian's personal life was about to take a significant turn. Christine Mullen, known as Chrissy, was a student at the Maria Assumpta Teacher Training College in Kensington. Her flatmate, Jo, was dating Roger Taylor and when Jo took Chrissy along to one of Smile's gigs at Imperial College she was introduced to Roger's friend. Slender, with long dark hair, Chrissy had a pretty elfin face, and that evening there was an instant connection between her and Brian, though initially they settled for being just good friends. Chrissy was happy to rank among the growing circle which formed Smile's travelling support.

Unashamedly hyping themselves as 'The Tremendous London Band Smile', Roger Taylor was using his West Country music connections to secure the band weekend work, and they began to pull in considerable crowds at venues such as PJ's in Truro and the Flamingo Ballroom in Redruth. Brian's lead guitar skills dazzled audiences, but he barely registered the effect he was having. He was wholly concentrated on perfecting technique. To May, gigs were an opportunity not just to perform, but also to experiment with the sounds it was possible to create.

Although junketing about the countryside was a necessary evil to claw in cash, the band vastly preferred to play the college circuit which, in the late 1960s, had taken over from tough pubs and clubs as the main stomping ground for up-and-coming groups; it paid better, too. The London college circuit also made more sense because Smile primarily hung out in the Kensington area. There was very much a feeling of being in the right place at the right time, and by January 1969 Brian and his friends were spending most free evenings at a popular pub called the Kensington.

An important part of the fabric of Brian's life now was Chrissy Mullen. From being good friends they had fallen deeply in love. This romantic commitment went further than Brian had ever experienced and he found it hard to envisage life without her. The anchor of a stimulating yet stable relationship provided a solid platform from which he could try to further his ambitions.

One of those ambitions was for Smile to secure another major gig. It had been almost three months since their debut supporting Pink Floyd, and although they had recently played on a bill along with T-Rex and Family, nothing else was happening. Then in February they landed a slot supporting Yes at the Richmond Athletic Club and were also invited to take part in a concert organised by Imperial College in aid of the National Council for the Unmarried Mother and Her Child at the Albert Hall on the 27th.

The line-up for the Albert Hall gig included Free, Joe Cocker and the Bonzo Dog Doo Dah Band. May was staggered to discover that far from being stapled on to the bottom of the bill as they expected, Smile were actually placed above Free, featuring lead guitarist Paul Kossoff and vocalist Paul Rodgers. The event was to be compered by the influential DJ John Peel who, through his late-night radio shows, championed many a British or American underground band to which no one else would give airplay.

Initially, it did not go all right on the night for Smile. After they were announced at the Albert Hall, Brian and Tim ran on to the huge stage. Tim was short of some twenty feet of guitar lead and he didn't realise until he hit the first vital chord that his jack plug had been wrenched from its socket. An embarrassing silence ensued. On top of that, for some reason, he had opted to play this gig without shoes and as a result his feet ended up full of splinters from the stage. Ultimately though, Smile were pleased with themselves and they even had the excitement of receiving their very first review when one journalist referred to them as 'the loudest group in the Western world'. It was a pity he did not give them a proper name check while he was at it. Undaunted, Smile lived on the memory of the Albert Hall appearance for weeks, reminiscing endlessly about it with friends. Into that circle of friends at this time, Tim Staffell brought a striking looking young man named Freddie Bulsara.

Farookh Bulsara was born of Persian parents, Bomi and Jer Bulsara, on 5 September 1946 on the island of Zanzibar in the Indian Ocean. It has been said that Freddie was born a star. Certainly, his origins were exotic. After attending a missionary school run by British nuns he was whisked away to India where he went to St Peter's English boarding school in Panchgani, some fifty miles outside Bombay. It was here that Farookh became Freddie. Here, too, he studied the piano, loved to sing and formed his first band called the Hectics – an apt name since the ebony-eyed, dark-haired, skinny boy could not stand still for a second. He was full of restless, inquisitive energy and oozed originality.

Due to the political unrest in India in the early 1960s, the Bulsaras were among those who decided to leave the country. Packing up their household belongings, they moved to England, settling in Feltham, which was a culture shock for the highly charged Freddie. Already bright and experienced beyond his years, in appearance, accent and temperament he felt different in this neighbourhood and was treated as such. From the start, he suffered bigotry and was made the butt of constant ridicule and abuse. Freddie's response was a subtle form of attack. He played the Persian popinjay to the hilt and parodied himself ruthlessly, which took the sting out of his ignorant tormentors' tails, effectively robbing them of their fun. Brazening it out, though, took its toll and behind closed doors at home he became unhappy and insecure. He was desperate to fit in and yet was aware that he was different. The Bulsaras had stayed initially with relatives, until they moved into a small semi-detached Victorian house near Feltham Park. Just after his twentieth birthday in September 1966, Freddie enrolled at Ealing College of Technology in west London, on a graphic art and design course; he soon fell in with Tim Staffell.

Tim, Freddie and another student, Nigel Foster, spent a lot of time at college making music. Freddie's party piece was an over-the-top impersonation of Jimi Hendrix, miming wildly to his records while cavorting about pretending that his wooden ruler was an electric guitar. Tim reflects: 'Freddie was intuitively a performer. His persona was developing rapidly even in those days, linking his natural flamboyance with the confidence he acquired from his singing and, of course, it would later crystallise around his marvellous songs. Personally I think as far as being a star was concerned, Freddie was already in the ascendant. People responded to him.'

When Staffell introduced Freddie to Brian May, he certainly made an impact. Brian later stated: 'He was outrageous. He was always a star, even when he hadn't a penny to his name – very flamboyant. On the face of it, he was very confident but everyone has a soft bit inside – a little insecure bit.' This intuitive understanding came further down the track. Right then, all May could see was a very vibrant and irrepressibly colourful young man who, having once had a band of his own, was showing a distressing eagerness to muscle in on Smile.

That said, both May and Roger Taylor took to Freddie at once, even when he became frankly the bane of their lives at rehearsals. Said Brian: 'We used to more or less stand there and play. Freddie used to say: "It takes *more* than that. You should get out there and actually put it across with more force. If I was your singer, that's what I would be doing!"' Brian patiently tolerated Freddie's wildly imaginative suggestions as to how much he could spice them up, at the same time turning a deaf ear to his heavy hints that he be allowed to join Smile. If Bulsara had his way, he would up-end them all. He was as volatile as a stick of dynamite looking for a match. He gingered up everyone around him and became Smile's unofficial fourth member, squeezing his stick-thin frame into the already overcrowded van and travelling with the band to gigs.

On 19 April 1969, Smile played at the Revolution Club in London and after this performance they were introduced to Lou Reizner, who was involved with Mercury Records – an American label in the process of starting up a British arm. Reizner had been watching them all night and liked what he saw. When he asked Smile if they would consider signing with Mercury Records it seemed to be the dream break they had been yearning for.

The following month, Brian May, Roger Taylor and Tim Staffell signed a contract with Mercury Records and were whisked into Trident Studios in Soho to work with producer John Anthony. The whole experience overwhelmed the band and they truly felt that they were on their way. Staffell recalls: 'I had written a number called "Earth" and Mercury Records had us record this, with the B-side "Step on Me", which Brian and I had written back in the days of 1984.' When the label set the release date for Smile's first single as August 1969, they were ecstatic and it energised their Kensington cronies.

In that swelteringly hot summer those ranks were swelled with the invasion of a Liverpool band called Ibex and their manager, Ken Testi. His girlfriend was Helen McConnell, whose sister, Pat, was a fellow student of Chrissy Mullen's. Ibex were a three-piece band comprising lead guitarist Mike Bersin, bass player John 'Tupp' Taylor and drummer Mick Smith. They had piled into their rickety red van, quit Merseyside and, like many before them, headed to London in search of fame and fortune.

'Because my girlfriend was staying in a flat in Earls Court with her sister, at least we had somewhere to doss,' explains Ken Testi. 'Not long after we arrived it was Pat's birthday and we wanted to take her out for a drink. She was insistent that we went to the Kensington, down the road. There was nothing casual in her choice. She'd been going regularly to see a band called Smile, and she knew that the guys supped in that pub. The idea was that as we were a band and so were they, she would get Ibex introduced to Smile. None of us were fooled, though. Pat fancied Roger Taylor like crazy and she was just looking for a way of ingratiating herself with him! Anyway, she dragged us down there and that's what happened – Pat introduced us all.'

To Ibex, Brian May, Roger Taylor and Tim Staffell appeared to be very hip. 'They were all good-lookin' dudes, for a start,' says Ken Testi, 'and we felt like real northern hicks beside them. They actually had a record contract, too, and had just cut their first single. This seemed absolutely fabulous to us. They had a chap with them, who wasn't in the band, called Fred who was quiet and very reserved.'

Mike Bersin recalls that first meeting: 'We had a few beers together and a laugh. Brian made an instant impression on me. He's a gentle giant of a man, soft-spoken and kind and the most considering person I have ever known. What I mean is, if you asked Brian something like: "How ya doin'?" he would actually take time to think about it, then give you a detailed reply!' As a lead guitarist himself, Bersin was really keen to see and hear May play and was thrilled when later that evening they all decamped from the bar back to the McConnell girls' flat.

Mike Bersin's first surprise was when he saw Brian use a sixpence instead of the traditional plectrum. May had been using a coin for some time because, as he explained: 'It's got a round playing surface, obviously, and it's also serrated so, by turning it different ways you can get different sounds. When playing the guitar at high volume, you're looking for an extra bit of distinction, or attack, on the notes.' It is an idiosyncrasy that continues to intrigue budding guitarists.

Manager Ken Testi was also on high alert that night. He recalls: 'Suddenly Brian, Roger and Tim began to play us their songs and talk about what they were looking for. I knew immediately that I was in the presence of something extraordinary. They were playing remarkable stuff and Brian's technique was outstanding. It was a seminal Queen. They were special, and everyone watching them in the flat that night knew it.'

The two bands met up quite often after that and spent many a balmy summer evening supping warm beer at the Kensington pub. It was a time of sharing – sharing bands, flats, ideas, and above all sharing a great hope of making it in the music business. Roger Taylor had already made a conscious decision in that direction. After achieving the first part of his dental degree in August 1968, he had decided to take a year off and concentrate full-time on trying to become a rock star. He also had to keep the wolf from the door, however, so in summer 1969 he was ripe for Freddie's suggestion that to earn some much-needed cash they should take a stall at Kensington market.

The stall they got was in an avenue known somewhat depressingly among the traders as 'Death Row'. Ken Testi remarks: 'Years later, I had to laugh when I saw it referred to in Queen's publicity blurb as "a gentlemen's outfitters". The stall wasn't much bigger than a telephone kiosk!' At first, the stall was stocked with paintings and drawings courtesy of their Ealing art student friends, but sales were disappointing, so Roger and Freddie turned to selling clothes. 'They recycled bits of Victoriana, really,' explains Ken, 'silk scarves, some of which were of very fine quality, lace, stoles – that sort of thing.' Quickly, this endeavour began to turn a small profit.

Freddie, too, had been forced to come to a decision. It was patently obvious that he was not going to be allowed to crowbar his way into Smile, so he had turned his sights instead on to Ibex. Mike Bersin was the band's lead singer as well as lead guitarist and at times he found it hard to juggle both roles as well as he would like. So he raised no murmur when Ibex chose to audition Freddie to become its vocalist. Before the echo of Freddie's remarkable voice had died away, the verdict was unanimous; Bulsara was in. Freddie seemed thrilled, but Bersin says: 'We all knew that Freddie was desperate to join Smile but they weren't having any of it at that point. That's the only reason Freddie joined Ibex.'

With Freddie off his back, Brian could look forward in peace to the release of Smile's first single. Mercury Records released 'Earth'/'Step on Me' in August 1969, but only in America. It was not what the band had hoped for but they were not too dispirited because the label wanted them to record more tracks with a view to producing an album, and later that year more studio time was booked for them to work with producer Fritz Freyer. By this time, Brian and Tim had written several songs and were eager for the chance to record them properly. Staffell states: 'We cut quite a few tracks for that album including "April Lady" on which Brian did the vocals, "Polar Bear", "Blag", "Earth" and "Step on Me". Brian was happy with the results but Mercury

Records decided not to release the material. Funnily enough, the album did surface many years later in Japan. More for archive purposes than anything else, I guess.'

With matters not turning out in this quarter as anyone in Smile had hoped for, to dilute their deepening disappointment the band threw themselves into playing gigs. By now they had enlisted the aid of the Rondo booking agency in Kensington High Street, which represented the band Genesis and for which Tim Staffell had done some graphic work. Smile were still in demand at Imperial College, and Ibex manager Ken Testi, with whom they had kept in touch, was proving to have really useful contacts in the north of England.

Memorably, that August, Testi arranged for Ibex to play a gig at the Bolton Octagon Theatre, then play the next day at an open-air festival in the city's Queens Park. May was to join them for the open-air gig, travelling up separately by train. Ken remembers: 'By now when Ibex went to gigs, more often than not Brian, Roger and Tim would come too, along with assorted girlfriends and whoever else could squeeze into the van. I did all the driving. I'll never forget those Bolton gigs. There was this guy, Richard Thompson (ex-drummer with Brian's school band 1984), who worked as a driver at Heathrow Airport. Quite illegally, we borrowed his Transit van and started to pick up everybody who was coming to Bolton. "Tupp" Taylor wanted us to pick him up in Piccadilly and by the time we got there the van was crammed with people up front, while in the back they were playing guitars and singing, making a hell of a racket. I stopped the van just long enough for them to roll up the shutter and let John jump in. As soon as the shutter shot up everyone in the street was gaping at all these hippies banging hell out of their guitars.'

It turned out to be a day of imagery. Mike Bersin clearly recalls getting ready for that Saturday lunchtime gig: 'We had decided to dress up a bit more than usual that day. My mum had made me a gold lamé cloak, which I felt obliged to wear, although when the time came I felt a right twit in it. Freddie stood out a mile, although in those days he had only one outfit. All he had to his name was one pair of boots, one pair of trousers – admittedly white satin – one granny vest, one belt and one furry jacket. In the theatre dressing room, Freddie stood for ages twitching at himself in a mirror. Eventually, I yelled at him: "For God's sake, Freddie, stop messin' with your hair!" To which he happily tossed back: "But I'm a star, dear boy!" He meant it, too!'

That evening, Brian was due to arrive. Says Ken Testi: 'I was meeting Brian off the train at Lime Street Station, so again we all piled into the Transit van. In the back was Pat McConnell and a few of her friends. Freddie had his girlfriend Mary Austin on board, Roger was there and, of course, all of Ibex. In those days, you could reverse a truck right through the front entrance of the station. I reversed up the ramp and told everyone to be quiet. I mean, we had no insurance, the van was in effect stolen and we didn't want to draw attention to ourselves. So I was looking in the rear-view mirror watching what I was doing, and what did I see? Not only a police constable but a high-ranking officer with braid everywhere on his uniform and a stick under his arm, and they were approaching the van. I was trying to look cool while hissing at everyone to keep absolutely silent. There was a knock on the window and I rolled it down saying: "Yes, officer, what can I do for you?"

'"Are you waiting for the London train, sir?" one of them asked. I was trying to stop my knees from knocking, convinced that everyone in the back was breathing too hard, but I managed to squeak that I was. Well, next thing, the braided officer told me that I had his permission to reverse right on to the platform. Two railway porters hurried off to pull back the corrugated gates and I backed this hot Heathrow Airport van along the platform, flagged all the way by these two coppers!

'By this time, I was sweating and I was scared stiff that when Brian arrived his reaction would give us all away. Everyone in the back kind of knew what was going on, and you could have cut the atmosphere with a knife. Well, the train pulled in and all the passengers emptied on to the platform. Brian stepped off the train and, God, he was good! He sussed the situation in a second. As bold as brass he strode confidently, guitar case in hand, right up to the van, passed the policemen without blinking an eye, and got in beside me at the front, as if he was a VIP being picked up. Then we drove off, but it was a very long time before any of us let our breath out!'

These visits north tended to be memorable for various reasons. Helen McConnell recalls: 'Once, Brian was staying at my family's house in St Helen's. He wasn't used to the strength of northern beer and he'd had a few, so we left him to sleep it off. He was sitting in front of the hearth with those long legs of his stretched up above the coal fire, and after a while my mum went dashing into the room because there was this awful stench of burning rubber. The thick soles of Brian's boots were melting and the dozy soul hadn't even noticed.'

For a while, Ibex put an end to the endless trips up and down the motorway. Nothing tangible was happening for them in London, so they thought they would stay and work the rife music scene in Liverpool. When they were free, Brian, Roger and Tim would travel up to join Freddie at his digs, which consisted of a big bedroom above the Dovedale Towers Banqueting Halls in Penny Lane. The mother of one of their friends, Geoff Higgins, was catering manageress at the Dovedale and would often put up Geoff's friends.

Ken Testi was running himself ragged for Ibex. He revealed: 'The worst was when we had all been down in London for a spell and I had hitched up to St Helen's because I had decided to look into going to college there. I had just arrived when Mike Bersin rang to say that the band had a booking for the following day and to ask if I could come back to get them and bring them up in Pete Edmunds's van. I grabbed a sandwich and hitched straight back to London, arriving late. Then, very early the next morning, I went round to Imperial College for the gear. There was a music room there on the third floor that had a tower at one end with a spiral staircase. The equipment was stored at the top. Freddie was the one designated to help me, which was unfortunate because while I humped all the heavy stuff time after time down this spiral staircase to the van, I think Freddie only managed one music stand, a tambourine and a few drumsticks, but never mind. One never expected too much manual from Freddie. Brian and Roger were coming up just to groove, because this was Freddie's band and they wanted to support him.'

That gig was at the Sink in Hardman Street, a basement club below the Rumbling Tum. As the Sink was not licensed to sell alcohol, before they went on stage they nipped along to a nearby pub. En route, they suddenly encountered a gang of skinheads. To this breed of thug, with their shaven heads, braces and bovver boots, hippies made excellent Saturday night punching material.

The incident remains vivid to Geoff Higgins: 'It was outside the Liverpool Art College. Round the corner came this gang of skinheads and I thought "Aw naw!" There was about seven of us and whole lot more of them. We were dressed in velvet trousers and frilly shirts and you did not dress like that in Liverpool then. We looked a right bunch of poofs! All skinny, frail, and cowards to a man. I was just wondering what would happen next when Roger, quick as a flash, bluffs that he's a black belt in judo and the law said he must warn them of this first because if they

31

ignored his warning and got hurt, it was their own lookout. My head was in my hands by this time. I thought: bastard Taylor! He's going to get us all bloody massacred. I hissed at him: "You don't try it on with scouse skins, you idiot!" But it worked. I don't know whether they believed Roger or whether they were just amused at his hard neck, but they left us alone and walked away. We were all shivering with fear.'

About the performance itself that night, Ken Testi recalls: 'I don't remember all that much about it because I napped on and off, but I do know that Brian and Roger got up and did a couple of guest spots with Freddie joining in. Freddie already knew all of Smile's stuff.'

Taking close stock of Freddie that night, May chalked up how well the singer was developing. Just as Freddie had deep respect for Brian's musicianship, so the guitarist admired Freddie's inimitable panache and the style and strength he brought to every ounce of his performance. Having his home base in Liverpool was not to Freddie's taste, though, and by September he returned to London in time to graduate from Ealing Art College with a diploma in graphic art and design.

For Brian, September also marked a change. Now in his second year as a postgraduate student, he was able to pursue an avenue in astrophysics on which he had set his heart for some time. Earlier in the year, he had seriously considered joining Professor Sir Bernard Lovell's research laboratory at Jodrell Bank in Cheshire. It was an honour even to have been invited. According to Sir Bernard Lovell: 'We would normally interview around forty students every year for postgraduate studies at Jodrell. About ten per cent are invited to come here for a one-year MSc or a three-year PhD course.' Lovell believed that, with Brian's existing astronomical work he was a prime candidate for their select list. 'I was sorry when he rejected our offer,' he admits.

Brian had turned Jodrell Bank down in favour of accepting

an invitation from Imperial College's Professor Jim Ring to do a PhD as part of his research team studying zodiacal light, a subject which already fascinated May. Professor Ring explains: 'I started research into zodiacal light when I was at Manchester University. Ken Reay was a student of mine, just as in turn Brian became a student of Ken's. I recruited from the top ten per cent of the cream of the brightest graduates. I had joined Imperial in 1967 and Brian was one of the first research students I selected. Jodrell Bank was, I suppose, a rival to us but Brian chose to join my team.'

May's involvement in astronomy was a source of admiration among his friends. Mike Bersin confesses: 'You couldn't help but be impressed by the guy. I mean, on top of being a great guitarist, he was well up with this astronomy lark.' While Ken Testi adds: 'Later on, we used to think it awfully grand whenever Brian was gone for long spells to the observatory in Tenerife.'

There was nothing grand, however, about the state of their accommodation in London by late 1969. Forever cash-strapped, Smile, Ibex and an assortment of friends threw their lot in together in a flat in Ferry Road, Barnes. Mike Bersin recalls: 'It was only supposed to house three people, so when the land-lady came calling for the rent, we would all hide in the bedroom. At one point, we ended up pushing the three beds together to make one great big bed and we all slept in that – girls as well. At times, we tried all sleeping sideways to see if that was any more comfortable – it wasn't! The flat itself was pretty hideous. Besides the odd chair, there was just one red plastic sofa which had holes in it with the stuffing sprouting out all over the place.'

Despite the dire conditions, it was a time of great camaraderie. An ex-resident had left behind an old bashed acoustic guitar on which Brian would strum away. It was in a poor state, but with perseverance May managed to coax some decent tunes out of it.

Says Geoff Higgins: 'I was asleep one morning on the grubby chaise longue and woke up to find Brian sitting looking out of the big stained-glass window at one end of the room, softly playing the Beatles number "Martha My Dear", complete with bass line and everything. This was on that battered gut-strung guitar which no one else could play. I thought: I don't believe this.'

Mike Bersin admits: 'Brian quite often used to show me bits on the guitar. Once, he taught me a special way of playing the G-chord, which gave a wonderful sound. That chord was perfect for checking your tuning too, which at that time was a huge thing to me. Brian favoured the VOX AC30 amp – that is a 30-watt valve amp with speakers. It looked like a black suitcase with control knobs on top but it gave out a lovely rich, warm tone. In the late sixties, everyone went for Marshall stacks but Brian swore by his two VOX AC30s. I think his very distinctive sound came seventy per cent from his brilliantly unique Red Special and thirty per cent from the VOX amps. In style at this time, there was a very classical influence in Brian's approach to rock. Yet he had the blues feel of a five-note scale, as opposed to the full thirteen notes in a run which you get in classical playing.'

At this dingy apartment Brian, Freddie and Roger would regularly rehearse harmonies in what was grandly called the breakfast room. Bersin also used to watch May alone composing songs at the kitchen table. 'I thought then that he was a special songwriter. Years later, when Queen were famous and Freddie had established himself firmly as a frontman, I always felt that Brian was perhaps one step back from the limelight but that he always had a lot of nice things to say.'

As the decade drew to a close, some mad times were had by all. Geoff Higgins reveals: 'At Kensington Market we would get marijuana mixed with jasmine tea, and then take it in turns to separate the grass from the tea. One day, "Tupp" Taylor took it home and hadn't the time to separate it. Now, in those days,

Freddie would not go near dope but he didn't know that it was still all mixed up and made himself what he thought was a pot of jasmine tea. When we got home, Freddie was smashed out of his head. He had a Frank Zappa album, *Only In It For The Money*, and on one track there is a noise like a stylus scraping across a record, but it's meant to sound like that. Freddie was busy wheeling around the room, arms flapping, and he had put on this album. When it came to this bit, he thought somebody had scratched his precious album and went flying across the room, throwing himself on to the turntable to check the LP. He was clean out of his box that day.'

When Freddie later learned what had happened, impishly he could not wait to try it out on someone else as unsuspecting as he had been. His chance came shortly afterwards when the police, summoned by annoyed neighbours, arrived late one night to break up a particularly noisy party. Freddie appeased the officers with tea and cakes that were laced with marijuana. The cops left feeling that they had handled the disturbance well, unaware of what lay in store for them once the effects set in.

Life was not a barrel of laughs, however, for Brian. At the end of 1969, Mercury Records had arranged a showcase gig for Smile at the Marquee Club in Wardour Street, London, playing support to the group Kippington Lodge. The crowd that night did not take to them and the band left the stage dejected. All round, in fact, their association with the record label was beginning to look doomed.

More than that, Brian quietly harboured serious doubts about Smile making it, and at the start of the 1970s he felt the band was entering its death throes. He also found that he had to give more of his time and attention to his work at Imperial College than to his music. In addition to doing research for his PhD, Brian gave tutorials two half-days a week and there were now plans for him to join his supervisor, Ken Reay, on a trip to build an observatory in Tenerife in the Canary Islands.

By late February 1970, no one in Smile was laughing. Tim Staffell recalls: 'It understandably suffered from a lack of finance, as most student bands did at that time, but we had played some notable gigs and had supported some very big names. We'd also had a good time doing it. I think, I would say that at our worst we may have been a little shaky, but at our best I'm sure we were quite worth the admission price.

'To be honest, I was growing tired of rock played loud. I went to audition for Colin Petersen's band. Colin had been drummer with the Bee Gees and while I was not one hundred per cent convinced that I was doing the right thing, I did like the quieter style that the new band offered. Possibly, it also had something to do with what I was writing at the time. My songs seemed as if they might fit into that context more successfully. Whereas I left Smile for my own reasons, in one sense I was moving out of the way, and the evolution of Queen was a natural and inevitable outcome.'

Soon after Tim Staffell's departure, Mercury Records dropped Smile, which was not entirely unexpected by Brian May or Roger Taylor. Relations with the label had been stale for some time and besides, their original contract had only been for one single, which had been fulfilled.

Brian talked incessantly now with Roger about the direction of their musical future. Ibex had changed its name to Wreckage but Freddie had never felt that this outfit was his vehicle to stardom and so he, too, was ripe for a move. The trio debated the issue intensively, but it was inevitable that Brian, Freddie and Roger would gel into one band. In addition to their individual talent, they were firm friends and they shared the same white-hot burning ambition to become a major force in rock music. They knew they could do it – it was just going to take planning and a great deal of hard work.

3

NOW OR NEVER

In spring 1970, for Brian, forming a new band took second place to his scientific activities. Along with Professor Jim Ring and Ken Reay, he travelled to Tenerife to set up an observatory on the slopes near the 12,000ft Mount Teide – the dormant volcano that dominates the island and resembles a lunar landscape. Brian was thrilled at the prospect.

'We built a prefab hut of aluminium which we lived in as well as using it as a lab,' explains Professor Ring. 'I was the project group leader, so I used to apply for all the grants that I possibly could to finance their work. Brian was responsible for maintaining all the equipment and was there for much longer spells at a stretch than I was, or even Ken Reay.'

Ken Reay recalls: 'I vividly remember the first time we flew to Tenerife, which involved a one-night stopover in Casablanca. We had arrived in the Canaries and were walking through the shopping centre in the capital, Santa Cruz. At this time, Brian always wore the same thing – blue jeans, very flared, with tiny bells sewn all around the bottom of each leg, a black velvet jacket, which was all the rage then, and his hair was long and curly. Don't get me wrong, he didn't look weird. Remember, this was the fashion in the early 1970s, but over there I guess he looked a bit of a bizarre character. We were walking along, talking of Casablanca which, combined with the way Brian looked, must have sparked off the incident which followed because, suddenly, this American guy, who had obviously been listening to us, leaped in front of Brian, grabbed him tight by the lapels and gasped into his face: "Where do you get your stuff, man? I *must* have it!" We got the shock of our lives. The best of it is, in all the time I knew Brian, he never touched drugs, but that American clearly thought differently and was not about to let go!'

It was on Brian's return to London in April from this first scientific trip that he, Roger and Freddie set out to find a bass player for their band. Taylor solved the problem by roping in Mike Grose, a former member of Reaction who was also co-owner of PJ's in Truro. Says Mike Grose: 'Smile used to play at PJ's now and then. Sometimes there was a bit of friction between Roger and Tim Staffell but nothing serious, just squabbling really. Anyway, one night they had turned up for their gig and Tim had quit so I stepped in and played. That was the first time I met Brian. That guitar of his has a fingerboard on it like silk. Lightly touch it, and you're there. He was a tremendous player even then, far ahead of anyone I had ever seen or heard. Since then, of course, a lot of guitarists have copied him but in those days he was so damned original. A few weeks later, Roger rang and asked me to join the band. They didn't yet have a name for it but it was going to consist of Brian, Roger and Freddie. The timing was just right for me. PJ's was under a demolition order, so I took up the offer and went to London to stay with them in a flat in Earls Court.'

For the four to meld together they had to knuckle down to serious rehearsals and here May's connections at Imperial College were crucial. Ken Reay explains: 'I used to book lecture theatres in the physics block for Brian and the band to practise in free of charge. As a tutor there I could do that, so Brian would bring along a constant flow of forms for me to sign.'

Mike Grose picks up: 'As well as practising twice a week at

Imperial College, Brian, Roger, Freddie and I often used to sit out in the garden at the flat tossing ideas about. Quite a bit of songwriting went on there too, especially by Brian and Freddie. Songs like "Keep Yourself Alive" and "Seven Seas of Rhye" were emerging even then. In fact, almost all the songs which later turned up on Queen's debut album got their first airing in that garden.'

According to Grose, the name Queen came up for the first time one day as they were jamming in the garden. 'I remember that clearly,' he maintains, 'and at the same time there was also an idea for them to adopt a very rude logo – Freddie's influence, of course!' Mike saw Roger and Freddie as being two extremely live wires who sparked off one another. The more reserved May would observe and absorb. 'When Brian did speak, though, it was always worth listening,' Mike adds.

Naming the band Queen gave rise to serious debate among the four. Naturally, its camp overtones had to be considered. Yet it had an appealingly regal quality. It was also short, universal and easy to remember. May mulled over the name before asking Ken Reay for his opinion. Reay was blunt: 'I told him it sounded extremely camp to me. I didn't need to be told that it was Freddie's idea, but I wouldn't say Brian had too much trouble with it. He seemed more amused, than anything, at the risqué connotations. Above all else, he obviously saw it as a good move to call themselves that.'

With hindsight, Mike Grose wonders why Freddie's attachment to naming the band Queen didn't tell him something but he says: 'Freddie was a super guy and we went out drinking together a lot, yet I didn't have a clue that he was gay.' That was not unique to the bassist. Freddie quite obviously enjoyed the company of women, he had a steady girlfriend and, as others would later attest, his homosexuality was not something he generally flaunted when out socialising.

The four were still wrestling over the name when they played their first live gig together, on 27 June 1970 at the City Hall in Truro, when they were billed as Smile anyway. 'The reason for that,' explains Mike Grose, 'is that Roger's mother was in the Red Cross in Cornwall and he had promised a while back that Smile would play at a charity event they were organising. As Smile was now defunct, Queen went in its place.

'The hall held about eight hundred people, but only a quarter of that number turned up. Nobody knew who we were, obviously, which was perhaps just as well since we were awfully loose that night – more like rough, to be brutally frank. We had practised hard, but the real thing is not the same as rehearsing in some lecture theatre. We also had quite complicated arrangements worked into our repertoire, and when you write your own music you tend to change those arrangements a lot. One of us remembered a song one way and someone else remembered it another way. I'm not saying we were bad as such, but let's put it this way, we didn't expect to be asked back.'

They had, however, played their first gig and had left a lasting impression. Instead of opting for the casual rock look of denim jeans and T-shirts, they had dressed in silky smooth black and white costumes which, with the addition of junk jewellery dangling from their necks and wrists, were guaranteed to set them apart. The strength of their visual impact was some consolation but the band was unhappy that they had not yet performed officially as Queen. Freddie was restless on another front; he felt that he needed to change his name. Countless performers had done this in the past, but Freddie's reasons seem fairly deep-rooted.

The name Bulsara tied him firmly to his Persian ancestry and he would always be careful later during interviews to avoid any reference to his Asian background. His parents' religion and culture represented a world from which he had been distancing himself for some time. Although his name change was not intended as a slight to his family, he preferred to close the door on Farookh Bulsara and to reinvent himself as someone who was synonymous with glamour, fame and strength. For this, he delved into Roman mythology and chose Mercury, the messenger of the gods. As from July 1970, he insisted he be known as Freddie Mercury.

Brian, meantime, continued to balance his music with his academic studies and was still giving tutorials. At these classes he would demonstrate in the lab and wander among the students, helping with problems and answering questions. 'He was a very good teacher,' says Professor Jim Ring, 'very sympathetic and popular with the students.'

It was not enough for May, though. He was increasingly frustrated at Queen's lack of progress. He believed that he had learned from Smile's experience with Mercury Records and he felt it was high time that they tried to get record companies interested in this new outfit. Freddie had similarly itchy feet. Although the sight of him mincing up and down Kensington High Street every Saturday swathed in feather boas looked to the uninitiated like nothing more than Freddie just being Freddie, behind this apparently facile ritual lay a calculated intent to bump 'by accident' into certain influential people in the record business who could help them.

Reluctant to cradle all their hopes in the hands of Providence, Brian arranged a gig to take place in Lecture Theatre A at Imperial College on 18 July. The audience would be made up of personally invited record company executives, with close friends of the band in the audience to provide moral support and to help impress the businessmen with their enthusiasm. The gig proved how much the band had developed but, unfortunately, nothing else came of it.

One week later, they again played PJ's in Truro, only this night billed for the first time as Queen. That gig turned out to be the last for Mike Grose. 'I left Queen because I had had enough of playing, basically. I had got to that point. We weren't earning anything to speak of and we were living in squalor. I just didn't want to be a part of it any more. Brian had another year of studies to go and so did Roger, and I thought, to hell with it. I knew I would regret leaving because I knew in my bones that they were going to make it.'

Mike Grose's replacement was Barry Mitchell, who joined Queen in August. Says Barry: 'That summer in Cornwall a friend of mine met Roger, who told him that his band was in need of a bass player. My friend gave me a number to ring and, as a result, Roger asked me to an audition at Imperial College. The audition was very friendly, just a blues jam really, and I got the job straight away.'

Barry, though, never felt that he quite fitted in. 'To a certain degree, I always felt an outsider. It wasn't them. It was me. I guess it was because they were all so very well educated that I felt out of it, which is my own fault. Also, the three of them were obviously buddies. Having said that, Brian was the friendliest by a very long way. He was approachable and went out of his way to try to help me become a part of the band. Freddie, on the other hand, was very deep.'

Mercury was, generally, something of an enigma to those around him. Geoff Higgins recalls: 'Freddie would ask me along to Kenny market saying: "Come and help me sell something today, for fuck's sake," and when I was there some of his friends would turn up. They were all as effeminate as him, but at the time we mostly thought they were just larking about.'

Ken Testi opines: 'In these touchy times it's hard to find the right words to describe Freddie without offending someone, but it was common then to see him behaving in a very affected manner. He certainly displayed all the qualities we attribute to gay people but then again, he and Mary had become a fixture in a relatively short space of time, so it was hard to tell. To be honest, no one took that much notice. There was too much else of more importance going on – like having fun.'

Freddie's flamboyance gave rise to some way-out ideas when it came to performing, which frankly alarmed Queen's newest recruit. Barry Mitchell recalls: 'He would have had us all wearing women's clothes and I wasn't having any of that! Freddie wasn't as out-rageously camp as he later became but it was still there in those days. He would paint his nails, curl his hair with heated tongs and everything. When I saw him at that game, I thought, wait a minute, what's goin' on 'ere then?' Barry believed bands ought to be dirty and sweaty and not tarted up, but he had to concede that Queen got far more work than any band he had previously been part of.

Barry Mitchell's first stage appearance with Queen was at Imperial College on 23 August 1970. This gig was meant to be their springboard to fame, and Freddie had employed a dress-maker friend to run him up something special to wear. Following his rough guidelines, she had made him a black figure-hugging one-piece outfit boldly slashed to the navel, with a wings effect at the ankles and wrists. Freddie proudly dubbed it his mercury suit and had a white version made up as well. From the start, Queen were determined to be seen as different from the run-of-the-mill groups, but the success they sought was still a way off.

In September, Brian returned to Tenerife with Ken Reay, but now he was finding it much harder to leave his musical life behind, even for a short while. Ken confirms: 'Brian was forever talking about Queen and showing me photographs of them in their stage clothes. He would fish out his acoustic guitar and if we weren't working of an evening he sat outside on the steps of the observatory and played. It's laughable now, but I used to listen to him and think to myself, that boy will never make it. It just goes to show how much I knew!'

That month, the rock world that Queen were so desperate to enter was stunned by the shocking death from drugs of one of its brightest stars. Barry Mitchell recalls: 'It was on 18 September. I arrived at the flat to meet the others and had just walked in when Freddie, very pale-faced, asked: "Have you heard? Jimi Hendrix is dead." God, the stunned feeling was immense. He had been our idol, and we were all absolutely shattered. Freddie and Roger closed their stall that day as a mark of respect, but by night we were still in a state of shock, so at rehearsal, as our own tribute, we played nothing but Hendrix numbers for the whole session.' Over in Tenerife, Brian took the news of Jimi Hendrix's sudden death just as badly.

Once May was able to return to the fold, Queen were keen to acquire as many gigs as possible. Their friend Ken Testi, who was now studying at a Merseyside college where he was social secretary, invaluably stepped into the breach. Says Ken: 'There was a public call box at the end of Freddie and Roger's row in the market, and I would phone them there to tell them that I had fixed them up with a gig. Sometimes it took forever to get an answer, then whoever did pick up the receiver had to run like hell to tell Freddie or Roger to come quick before all my money ran out. There was no other way of contacting them. Fred told me they were ready, and I promised I'd try to book a few gigs at a time to make it viable for them to come all the way to Liverpool.'

One weekend at the end of October 1970 stands out for Geoff Higgins and Barry Mitchell. The first gig was at St Helen's College of Technology, and Higgins recalls: 'Queen were using the college kitchen as a dressing room and Freddie had poured himself into the tightest velvet trousers I had ever seen. There was a seam up the back of each leg, like in ladies' nylons, and he was going berserk trying to get them to lie straight. Eventually, he asked Ken to get him a big mirror, so he nipped off to the fashion department and returned with a full-length one. Well, Fred started writhing and twisting furiously, struggling to straighten these seams and he flatly refused to go on stage until he got them right, no matter if it made the band very late.'

When they finally prised Mercury away from the mirror to perform, it was all hardly worth it. Higgins reveals: 'They were playing progressive rock, which was a complete no-no in Liverpool, so they were flogging a dead horse trying to serve up that music that night.' They were to perform the same set the next evening, but the excitement of the venue overrode any doubts left over from the night before. 'When I fixed up this Hallowe'en gig at the Cavern, Queen were thrilled,' remembers Ken Testi. The omens were not good, however. Barry Mitchell's amp chose that night to die, and when he plugged in his guitar to another band's equipment, it promptly exploded.

Barry reflects: 'For all the Cavern's reputation, it was nothing but a dingy basement, and with so many people squeezed into it that night it became a cauldron, with their sweat literally making condensation run down the brick walls. Yet, undeniably, it had something. It is quite an amazing place.'

Early in the New Year, Barry Mitchell quit Queen. 'I had had enough of never having a shilling in my pocket,' he says. 'Also, we were more or less performing all of their own compositions, and I wanted to play different music as well. Freddie's girlfriend, Mary Austin, said to me: "It's a shame you're leaving now. You're just getting to know them," which was true, because I had begun to hang out with Roger, but it wasn't enough and I had made up my mind.' Barry played his final two gigs with Queen in January 1971.

It seemed that Queen could not hold on to their bass players. A guy named Doug was hired to fill the gap temporarily but two gigs later he began cavorting about on stage in a mad manner and was duly jettisoned. That last gig with the excitable bassist at Kingston Polytechnic, on 20 February, was in support of two leading progressive rock bands, Wishbone Ash and Yes. Wishbone Ash's lead guitarist, Andy Powell, remembers Queen's performance, and in particular Brian's, very well.

'That was the first time I heard him play,' Andy recalls, 'and his tone immediately grabbed me. Brian has his own style and sound, so you can always tell his work. Even in 1971 he had incredible finesse, amazing fluidity. A little later, Queen became a glam-band but at that time what they were doing was similar to us. Although, having said that, they did have that edge that was a bit more mainstream. I think you could tell that they would not stay playing progressive rock for long.'

A former Kingston Polytechnic student, Tony Blackman, also recalls that night: 'Two things have stuck in my memory. The first is that although Queen, whom nobody really knew at this time, were supporting Wishbone Ash and Yes, amazingly they did not come over in any way as second rate. Also, their image stood out. Dressed completely in black, their clothes were skintight and there was no doubt about the fact that they were going out of their way, particularly the singer, to project an effeminate image. That kind of thing just was not done in those days, but Freddie was flaunting it.'

Queen's on-stage confidence, however, was undermined by their frustration at not having found the ideal bass player. They made determined efforts to see other bands, in the hope of spotting the right person to replace Barry Mitchell. It eventually paid off when May and Taylor went to a dance held at the Maria Assumpta Teacher Training College in Kensington, where Brian's girlfriend Chrissy Mullen was still studying, and were introduced to John Richard Deacon.

Born on 19 August 1951 in the St Francis Private Hospital, London Road, Leicester, to Lillian and Arthur Deacon, an insurance company worker, John was a quick, intelligent boy whose main hobbies from a young age were music and electronics. He began playing the guitar at the age of seven; newly a teenager he formed his first band, called the Opposition, and by seventeen was active on the local band circuit. Deacon was also a conscientiously committed student and, in June 1969, he left Leicester's Beauchamp Grammar School with eight O levels and three A levels in maths, further maths and physics – all A passes – which secured him a place at Chelsea College of Technology, part of the University of London, where he began a degree course in electronics in October of that year.

He retained his love of music, though, and caught as many shows as he could, including a Queen concert. Queen struck no particular chord with him, other than the fact that on the poorly lit stage that night the four members clad in black had appeared more like spectral figures. In early 1971, it was a different story when he heard that Queen were looking for a bass player. His flatmate, Peter Stoddart, knew Brian May and it was through Stoddart that John Deacon met them that night, with the express purpose of offering his services. Brian could not believe his luck. Along with Roger and Freddie, he invited John to audition for Queen at Imperial College a few days later.

May, Mercury and Taylor were bowled over by Deacon's obvious musical skill and his knowledge of electronics; with their past experience of faulty equipment, this was no small consideration. Plus, his placid manner appealed. Similar in temperament to Brian and the opposite of Freddie's and Roger's exhaustive vibrancy, he seemed to promise to balance the band. So, in late February 1971, the Queen line-up was finally complete.

Once again, months of intensive rehearsing were needed so that by summertime they would be ready to go looking for bookings. Brian had to miss much of this preparation because his astronomy work took him back to Tenerife, this time with a fellow research student, Tom Hicks. Says Tom: 'Our job was to look at dust in the solar system, which entailed carrying out experiments and observing for time spans of between one hour and all night, depending on the time of year. The hut – known as ZL, for zodiacal light – had one room that we used as a kitchen and two bedrooms with bunk beds. The fourth room was the lab where all the instruments were. Some of our equipment was quite crude in many ways. We used one device called a coelostat which was really no more than a set of mirrors that directed light through a hole in the wall into the laboratory.'

Typically, Brian and Tom would spend six weeks at a stretch at ZL. 'We'd go out ideally before a full moon,' explains Tom, 'and set everything up. Then we would start once the full moon was past. At first, we would be working for two hours, then three, then all night. At the dark of the moon you could work from 10 p.m. to 11 a.m. and, at times, we got very disoriented. We'd be having bacon, eggs and beer for breakfast!'

The generous research grants that Professor Jim Ring managed to obtain for them meant that they could take time out to enjoy themselves a little when they were there. Sometimes, Brian and Tom would trek down to the coast or take trips up the extinct but still smoking volcano to peer into its bowels. Says Hicks: 'Brian used to produce this cheap little Spanish acoustic and proceed to thrash out all these wild rock chords on it. It was very strange hearing hard rock on a Spanish guitar. Brian wasn't around a lot with Queen when they first started up because he was out in Tenerife so much, yet I would swear that what he was playing ended up on their first album.'

While in Tenerife, they were given support and assistance from the University of La Laguna, in particular by Professor Francisco Sanchez Martinez and Dr Carlos Sanchez Magro. 'Carlos took Brian and me out for a meal one night and afterwards Brian was driving back,' recalls Tom. 'Their roads in those days were very primitive. They just had one new motorway. Suddenly, we saw these lights coming fast straight at us. We were driving up the motorway the wrong way! Thankfully, there were no barriers at the sides and in a split second Brian sawed the wheel, pulled us on to the rocky verge and cut the engine. We had escaped by a whisker!'

Being supervisor to both students, Ken Reay would join them there for spells and the three of them built a Fabry-Perot Interferometer which they used in their work. 'Brian was the one most involved in building this,' states Ken. 'It was also Brian who was heavily into carrying out the observations, data reduction and recording. He put in a lot of hours.'

Returning to London, Brian swapped his cramped lodgings at ZL for a minuscule bedsit in Earls Court which had to house not only a bed but also his precious AC30 amps and piles of academic books. If he was in the room, only one other person could hope to stand up. There was a phone on the landing for communal use and the kitchen was part of an old corridor, partitioned off.

On 11 July, an Imperial College audience saw Queen play their second gig with John Deacon on bass. Deacon was unsure what reaction to expect, since Queen had played so often at the college with other bassists, but it was a good night, made even better when record producer John Anthony, who had worked with Smile two years earlier, turned out to have been in the crowd. As he was leaving, he promised to give them a call.

It was the lack of money that most weighed the band down. Roger Taylor registered for a degree course that would make him eligible for a grant and, in autumn 1971, he enrolled at North London Polytechnic to study plant and animal biology. Brian had recently stopped giving tutorials at Imperial College and, although his fees had been modest, he still missed the cash.

Taylor rustled up what they grandly termed a Cornish Tour for August and September. It became an eventful trip. There were near nightly arguments with pub landlords over the volume at which they played, fees had to be wrested from reluctant hands after some performances and, taking exception to the 'dodgy' way Queen looked, on occasions some of the locals could turn nasty. Once, a posse with its blood up piled into an old banger and gave chase after Queen had fled a rowdy pub in their van. Roger's local knowledge meant that the band managed to shake off the mob in the labyrinthine narrow country lanes. Exhilarating as such escapades were, Queen saw themselves as being a cut above this level.

'We wanted to be the fulfilment of the kind of band we wanted to see on stage. We would look at the Who and the Beatles, and we wanted to create that kind of excitement. We wanted people to feel wrung out by the time a Queen show was over,' revealed May.

Brian still felt strongly that their best chance of moving upstream lay in persuading the music moguls to come and see how good they actually were. It had failed before, but again he arranged a private performance at college. He invited representatives from several London-based bookings agencies. Many showed up on the night but disappointingly no bookings were forthcoming.

By this time, Ken Testi had returned to London, where he ceaselessly attempted to encourage booking agents to take an interest in Queen. The band appreciated his efforts, but their first real break came via Terry Yeadon, a friend of Brian May's, who, in autumn 1971, was involved in setting up a new recording studio in Wembley called De Lane Lea.

Says Terry: 'I was a disc jockey in Blackburn in the mid-sixties and then came to London to work at Pye Recording Studios at Marble Arch as a maintenance engineer. In about 1969 a mutual friend asked me to come and see Brian May play, so I went to one of Smile's gigs at Imperial College. I thought they were pretty good. We got chatting and Brian asked if there was any way Smile could get some recording done. Pye knew nothing about it, but along with Geoff Calvar, who was a disc-cutting engineer, I recorded Smile on the side. We recorded two tracks, "Step on Me" and "Polar Bear", and Geoff did acetates. At that point, Brian asked if I would like to get involved with them but I was busy at Pye and made all sorts of excuses not to.

'Come 1971, I had moved to De Lane Lea and Geoff and I were putting together this new complex in Wembley. We had built three studios but thought we had a problem with isolation, that sound was being carried through the air-conditioning ducts and such like. We were carrying out tests like firing pistols and shotguns and recording in the next studio to see if it picked anything up, but we weren't satisfied and reckoned that what we really needed was a rock band. There is nothing to compare with a rock band playing at full blast! By a happy coincidence Brian tracked me down again right then and told me they had a new vocalist and a full-time bassist. That's just what Geoff and I had been looking for and so we worked out a deal.'

Terry Yeadon first put Queen into the biggest studio, which could hold up to 120 musicians. He states: 'There was just them set up in the middle. Brian took along his AC30 amps but they were no good for our purposes. We needed more power and De Lane Lea hired a whole load of Marshall stacks. Queen played, while Geoff and I were in studios two and three testing. The problems with new studios are endless, especially to do with acoustics, and so testing took a while. When it came to recording Queen's demos, we did that on four-track in studio three, which is the smallest and was always going to be the rock studio.'

Queen felt in seventh heaven. Not only could they record with the latest equipment for free, but they had the chance to meet the people whom they had been dying to come into contact with for so long. They eagerly set to work with producer/engineer Louie Austin and, despite many hitches, in the end created a demo of four of their own compositions: 'Liar', 'Keep Yourself Alive', 'The Night Comes Down' and 'Jesus'.

51

It gave them a great spur. Their future *had* to lie in music and increasingly they each now had little time for anything else. Brian was committed to yet another trip to Tenerife but was aware that he was withdrawing from the academic scene, and that Queen now took precedence in his heart and mind. Around November, for the regular income, Brian took up a full-time teaching post at Stockwell Manor School, a co-educational comprehensive serving the north Brixton area.

He was a popular teacher. In his stylish clothes, with his long hippy hair and fine-boned, almost vulnerable good looks, he became a magnet for schoolgirl crushes. For the boys? Brian recalled: 'They never knew at the time that I was in a band and used to say: "Hey, you should play in a group, sir!"' That said, these were not sedate middle-class kids from cushy homes politely open to expanding their minds, and it was tough to get the restless pupils even to stay in their seats, let alone to pay attention. Brian found maths stimulating and he strove ingeniously to make the dusty subject fun, to engage the children's interest. 'I used betting on horses to teach statistics, for instance,' he once recalled.

Not everything May tried, however, had the desired effect. He has vivid memories of his attempt to teach his pupils the difference between rectangles, pentagons and hexagons. 'I had the idea of letting them cut up coloured paper. The staff said: "Are you seriously going to take scissors into the second form?" Half an hour into the lesson, they were all attacking each other with scissors. There was blood and paper everywhere!' No one was seriously injured, but it had proved to be a valuable lesson to the teacher.

At the end of 1971, Queen were still being allowed the use of the De Lane Lea studios, which was immensely important to them. They remained convinced that the vital link they needed to the record companies would stem from working there. That faith proved justified one day when, as they were playing, the studio received a visit from John Anthony, who six months previously had promised to ring Queen, and Roy Thomas Baker, engineer at the then highly influential Trident Studios. After the session, both men were happy to accept a demo tape. Norman Sheffield, co-owner of Trident, listened to the tape but was not prepared to do anything more than say that he found it interesting.

Undaunted, Queen again enlisted the aid of their friend Ken Testi to take their demo tape and try their luck with it around the various London-based record companies. Says Ken: 'It was high time. For too long, Queen had not seemed to be going in any real direction. So I got out the Yellow Pages and started looking up likely labels. I tried making appointments over the phone and largely got the heave-ho, but some did agree to see us.' According to Ken Testi's diary those record companies included CBS, Decca, Island, A&M, Polydor and MCA. It was a thankless task. Many turned the band down without even letting Ken beyond the reception desk. 'I have a record of the names of all those people who told Brian and me that Queen were no good,' adds Ken.

In the New Year, one record label sat up and took notice. Tony Stratton-Smith, head of Charisma Records, liked what he heard and wanted to sign Queen. He put a deal on the table but, despite their frustration, Queen turned it down. First, the money on offer was not a lot and they desperately needed to replace their equipment. Then there was the fact that Charisma was a small label and Queen felt that they could benefit from having big muscle behind them. They liked Tony Stratton-Smith and appreciated his interest, but he did not have the right resources, in their opinion, and that made them shy away. It has to be said that it took guts to turn down what could have been the only record deal they were ever offered.

Queen continued to have high hopes of engaging Trident Studios' interest. Certainly, Norman Sheffield had not forgotten them but he needed to see them perform live before he would consider making a commitment. Propitiously, the band were booked to play at a hospital dance in mid-March 1972, and at Roy Thomas Baker's urging, Norman's brother and business partner Barry Sheffield went along to weigh them up. That night Queen were in their element, the audience was enthusiastic, and any reservations that Barry had harboured evaporated. He offered them a contract with Trident Audio Productions on the spot. Two months later, however, nothing had been signed.

May, Taylor, Deacon and Mercury gave a lot of thought to understanding just exactly what they wanted at this stage. Keeping as much control as possible over their destiny was important to them, and as a result Queen made certain stipulations about the terms of any agreement: they wanted three separate contracts, individually covering publishing rights, management and recording. Trident were unused to this, but considered Queen worth accommodating, and agreed to draw up the necessary documents. Still, they remained unsigned.

Trident did set about kitting the band out with new equipment and instruments, with the exception of Brian, who refused to part with his Red Special, and a full-time manager, American Jack Nelson, was employed to handle their daily affairs.

Brian watched these developments with quiet optimism. He felt so close to everything they had been working towards for seemingly an age – nothing else mattered now. He had long since drifted away from work on his PhD, which to his supervisor seemed a vast waste of his talents. Ken Reay states: 'We did still keep a desk there for Brian for a while, and occasionally he would drift in and do some work, but music was tugging him away all the time. It is a real pity that he didn't just give it that little extra push. I read the manuscript of his thesis and helped with corrections. His work was of very good quality. If he had submitted a final version he would have got his doctorate and become Dr Brian May.'

According to Brian May, his thesis *was* typed up and waiting to be bound. 'I showed it to my supervisor,' he recalled, 'who told me I should spend another couple of months on it, which I did. When I took it back and he started going on again, I thought: this is as far as it goes.' Years later, May further reflected: 'I don't think my discipline was good enough to be a good astronomer. Professional astronomers take their observing trips very seriously. Mostly, I wanted to go outside and gaze at the stars.'

It was a similar story at Stockwell Manor School where Brian had been teaching all year. Mike Winsor, science teacher there at the time, clearly recalls: 'Brian was obviously contemplating a full-time career in music. He was a conscientious teacher, a likeable colleague and he had very good relations with his pupils, and some of the staff thought he really ought not to throw that away. I remember Mr Simon, then head of the maths department, who was an old-fashioned teacher nearing retirement, vigorously counselling Brian one lunchtime to consider *very* carefully the wisdom of leaving the teaching profession with "its prospects, security and pension" and taking a real risk in a notoriously unpredictable business like music. I was forcibly reminded of this years later when Brian, along with the rest of Queen, was cited in the *Guinness Book of Records* as being one of the highest salary earners of that particular year!'

Brian's parents also had their qualms. Said May: 'From my upbringing, I was taught that you had to put your education first. All the pressure on me was to keep on the studies and not to go off and play.' Brian has since conceded that his father, Harold, in particular had great difficulty accepting this decision to give it all up for rock music. Brian revealed: 'To my dad, it was the worst thing he could imagine. He thought I was abandoning all my education to go off and try to do something that he didn't regard as a proper job. It was difficult for him.' Brian fully appreciated the sacrifices his parents had made to ensure that he got a good education but he stated: 'The call was too strong to ignore. I remember thinking that if I don't go into music at this point full pelt, then the door will close for ever. I *had* to do it.'

4

BAPTISM OF FIRE

By autumn 1972, Brian had given up his PhD course, Roger had graduated in biology, John had gained his degree in electronic engineering and Freddie turned his art diploma to good use by designing a special logo for Queen, which incorporated all of their birth signs and befitted the band's grandiose image. Then, on 1 November, Queen at last signed with Trident Audio Productions. The band would record for Trident, who in turn would procure the best recording and distribution deal they could wrest from a major record label. Trident were taking a chance. No other independent production company to date had taken on full responsibility for a rock band. After some stiff negotiation the company also agreed to start paying a weekly wage of £20 to each band member.

Five days later, Queen played a gig at the Pheasantry Club in Chelsea's King's Road. Trident enticed as many record company executives as they could to attend. Technical problems with their equipment, however, threw a spanner in the works and although John Deacon's electronics expertise rescued the band from total disaster, when they came to play their nervous tension showed.

Recording for Queen's first album was completed at the end of November but it had not been conceived under the greatest circumstances. They had been allocated down-time – meaning that they could only use the studio when no established artiste required it – and although Trident professed themselves pleased with the album, the band were unhappy with the mixes, even before it was discovered that one track had inadvertently been overdubbed on to the wrong backing tape. Along with record engineer Roy Thomas Baker, Brian insisted on being given time to rectify this error and to tidy up the recording in general, with Queen having a little more control over the general sound. By January 1973 the album was finally ready, but still they had no record company to press and distribute it for sale. In the end it was Ronnie Beck, an executive of Feldman Music Company, who was crucial in getting Queen to the attention of the right person.

Roy Featherstone, one of EMI's top executives, had been wading through the piles of audio tapes offered to him at the annual Midem festival in Cannes in the south of France, but had found nothing to excite him. Then Ronnie Beck suggested he listen to the Queen tape – Featherstone was blown away. Working on the old maxim that nothing makes someone jump faster than to think that a rival is after the same product, Beck spun Featherstone the tale that a couple of other record labels were showing keen interest in Queen. Featherstone cabled Trident, urging Queen not to sign a thing until he had had the chance to speak with them.

The timing was sweet. Queen had just landed a special session of the BBC Radio 1 programme, *Sounds of the Seventies*. This meant exposure of a kind that they had hitherto only dreamed of. The session was recorded at the broadcaster's Maida Vale studios with producer Bernie Andrews, and went out on air on 15 February 1973. The listeners' response was so positive that EMI did not dither, and signed Queen in March. The deal was for the UK and Europe but while his bandmates were ecstatic, Brian quietly nursed a kernel of concern – enough to guard against getting carried away.

With this recording contract sewn up, in April Queen

performed a showcase gig at the Marquee Club for the purpose of impressing Jac Holtzman, managing director of Elektra Records in New York. Visiting London, Holtzman had expressed an interest in signing the band and Jack Nelson had promised him a live performance to help him make up his mind. With so much riding on that single gig, it would have been easy to blow it, but that night Queen excelled and Holtzman went away well satisfied; Queen's coveted US contract was effectively in the bag.

Throughout the spring, bolstered by the upturn in their fortunes, Queen were blossoming. Experimenting with their stage clothes, they used dramatic make-up to accentuate their features. The clever use of white and ultraviolet lighting added to the overall uniqueness of their shows. They had several pet stomping grounds but in Liverpool they had acquired a cult following, with hordes of fans imitating them by showing up for the gigs dressed in all black or all white.

In the early 1970s, the British music scene was a kaleidoscope of conflicting styles. Progressive rock and sixties psychedelia had given way to folk rock and teen heart-throbs; hard rock was mutating into heavy metal. By 1973, however, glam rock had gathered momentum, with the likes of Wizzard and Slade dominating the charts. May kept tabs on the latest musical shifts and trends but primarily he concentrated on Queen's first album.

The band had become immersed in the design of their first album cover. Enlisting a photographer friend, Doug Puddifoot, they set to work in Freddie's flat, where between them they kicked around a variety of ideas. Photography interested Brian and that day he experimented by stretching a sheet of coloured plastic over the camera lens and having the band's photograph taken through that, which produced a weird, distorted effect. In the end, though, the band's favourite was a Victorian look with sepia tinting against a maroon oval background. For the back cover, they rustled up some old snaps, tentatively considering a collage.

It proved to be a tiresome exercise, however, because Mercury rejected any photograph that he felt did not flatter him. Some called it pure vanity. Later, with the cushion of his fame, others reflected fondly on Mercury's pure professionalism. Finally, they submitted all their ideas to EMI for consideration.

Next, they were required to select which track should become their first single. They decided on 'Keep Yourself Alive', penned by Brian, with 'Son and Daughter', another May composition, on the B-side. It came out in Britain in early July, and Trident promised that European release would quickly follow. The record received mixed reviews from the music press. With no yardstick to go by, Brian did not know whether to be pleased or not. He had no idea what lay ahead with rock critics.

What May did know was that the real importance lay in securing widespread radio play. So it was all the more disheartening when, although the single was sent out to all local, regional and national radio stations for inclusion on their playlists, none except Radio Luxembourg picked it up. Licensed commercial radio stations would not appear for another few months and BBC Radio 1 – which therefore enjoyed a monopoly of the pop airwaves – rejected Queen's debut single five times on the trot. Unsurprisingly, 'Keep Yourself Alive' shrivelled and died chartwise.

Queen's eponymous debut album followed in mid-month and, given the way the single had sunk, it was now vital to scare up national exposure. EMI circulated the usual white labels – early pressings of an album in a plain paper sleeve, which carry no band name or record label – with the usual publicity release. One of the best rock programmes on British TV at this time was the BBC's *The Old Grey Whistle Test*, and EMI sent the album to it, unfortunately without the back-up PR material. Had it not caught the attention of the programme's producer, Michael Appleton, it too could have vanished into oblivion.

'We used to get sent loads of white labels,' recalls Michael Appleton. 'They are highly prized nowadays and were actually of top-class cut. One day, this white label arrived on my desk on its own – nothing with it. I listened to it and liked it so much that myself and Bob Harris decided to use it on that night's show. In those days we played tracks accompanied by our own visualisations. We played "Keep Yourself Alive" along with a cartoon of the President Roosevelt Whistle Stop tour. We said on air that this was a really good track from a really good album, but we had absolutely no idea who it was by or where it had come from and that same night, I think during the transmission, someone from EMI frantically got in touch and told us it was their white label of the debut album of a band called Queen.'

Whistle Test presenter Bob Harris vividly recalls first listening to Queen. 'I absolutely loved it,' he says. 'I especially thought "Keep Yourself Alive" was wonderful. Personally, I was very enthusiastic about them.' The band's association with *The Old Grey Whistle Test*, and Bob Harris in particular, became a strong one that spanned several important years, providing Queen with valuable exposure.

'*Whistle Test* concentrated on sound first and foremost rather than vision,' explains Michael Appleton, 'which was peculiar to us in broadcasting in those days, and I think Queen appreciated that and reciprocated by being very professional to work with.' The flat-out enthusiasm of *The Old Grey Whistle Test* team was fine for the band's morale, but was not reflected by every rock critic. *Melody Maker* said of this debut album: 'Queen are either the future of rock or a bunch of raving poofters doing a poor piss-take of Black Sabbath.'

Privately, Queen themselves had qualms. Each member was very conscious that because it had taken two frustrating years to get their material out on release, what had once been innovative and fresh could now look stale and reactionary to prevailing trends. 'By the time the album came out, we felt it was so old-fashioned,' admitted May, 'and we were really upset about that.'

Initial sales were also a lot slower than anyone had hoped for. May has recalled how he and Mercury began regularly catching a number nine bus to go together to Trident's office to find out what was to happen next with their album. Trident plugged on and booked Queen into Shepperton Studios in Middlesex, to make their first promotional film, for what they hoped would be worldwide distribution. They also enlisted the PR services of Tony Brainsby, who in mid-1973 was one of Britain's top publicists.

'My first impressions were of Freddie. He was strong-willed, gregarious, very ambitious, charming and striking,' says Brainsby. 'He was also such a raving poofter that I could not believe my eyes! He wore skintight red velvet trousers, had black varnish on his fingernails, long hair and, of course, all those teeth. God, was he touchy about his teeth! He never allowed himself to be photographed smiling and would automatically cover his mouth whenever he burst out laughing.'

According to Tony Brainsby, there was an unusual quality to the entire band. 'Of all the groups I have handled, I would say only two made an instant impression on me,' he explains. 'One was Thin Lizzy, and Queen was the other. They knew what they wanted and knew that they would be big. It was just a question of finding the way. In my experience, that's not normal but it is a huge advantage for a PR consultant when a group has that depth of belief in themselves. It was also that edge that was going to make them stars.'

Catching one of Queen's live gigs at a London polytechnic only confirmed Tony Brainsby's professional instincts about the band. 'They were playing standing on the floor for that gig,' he recalls. 'What I mean is, there was no stage and the band were at the same level as everyone else, which can be quite a disadvantage, but Queen were remarkable that night, and I knew what I was seeing was real talent.'

A profitable working relationship began between them. Says Tony: 'It was always a group, and from the start we were all made very conscious of the importance of treating them equally. With Brian's guitar sound and Roger's high falsetto voice, each one had a Queen sound to add. In those days, Freddie was a very inwardly aggressive and angry man in the sense that he knew he should be a star and he wasn't – yet. It's not a side of him that too many people were allowed to see, but it was definitely all the way through him. He felt that stardom was his by rights, and he was extremely frustrated at the time it seemed to be taking for him to reach it. He had an incredible need for acceptance. When I bumped into him in the mid-1980s, he had mellowed enormously, but ten or twelve years before it was a very different story and that aggression, that energy, was what gave him the fight.

'Yet although Freddie's voice was unique, Queen's identity struck me right from the start as coming from Brian May and his incredible guitar sound. Brian was always very quiet and extremely modest – a rather intelligent guy too, of course. It was Brian who gave me the chance to create Queen's first major press because of his Red Special. It was a great angle. Here we had not only a brilliant guitarist but someone who got all those sounds out of a home-made guitar, for God's sake! It was a heaven-sent instant introduction into all the important music magazines, and made a great talking point that started to get Queen noticed.'

In summer 1973, Britain was plunged into economic crisis. A miners' strike led to a series of enforced power cuts and the country was put on a three-day working week. It was a bleak time for everyone but, determined to look forward, Queen were hard at work in the studio creating their second album, this time not operating on down-time.

Round about now, too, Brian's former astronomy colleagues Ken Reay and Tom Hicks had submitted to the Monthly Notices of the Royal Astronomical Society the paper on which they had all jointly worked. Says Tom: 'Brian had done a lot of the early work, then Ken and I continued when he drifted away. So when we submitted the paper to the RAS, it was in our three names. Papers have to be refereed by other scientists, who make comments on the work, and if they decide that it is good enough to be published they accept it – and they did. We were delighted.'

In early September, Elektra Records released *Queen* in the US. The album attracted enough radio play for it to enter *Billboard*'s Top 100 Chart, an achievement for a new British band, but once again the single 'Keep Yourself Alive' failed to ignite interest.

It became clear to Jack Nelson that Queen needed to be seen on tour. They were not headlining material, but securing a good support slot was vital. Arranging support work is rarely straight-forward. Often, an established band will not risk being upstaged by too good a support act but, equally, a mismatched bill makes an audience undesirably restless from the start, which benefits no one. Nelson turned to Bob Hirschman, who managed Mott the Hoople. Because he had never seen Queen perform live he proved hard to persuade but, in the end, Jack secured Queen the task of backing Hoople on their upcoming UK tour.

'Before that tour with Mott the Hoople,' recalls Tom Hicks, 'Queen played a warm-up gig at Imperial College. It was a free concert for the physics students and I went along to see Brian. I was knocked out by the difference in their playing, and it was deafening too – the loudest band on the planet. I tell you, you heard it through your chest that night and that's not a joke!'

The 23-date Mott the Hoople tour, which included a quick raid across the border into Scotland, kicked off on 12 November at Leeds Town Hall. Throughout, Brian's virtuosity literally made audiences sit up and take notice, for by clever use of echo on his guitar he created the impression that two guitarists were duetting, which caused many people to swivel in their seats as they searched in vain for the other guitarist.

Queen's first true taste of life on the road, playing every night in a different city, was an invigorating experience. For Freddie, the adrenalin was still pumping when the first gig was over. Instead of getting some sleep before heading to Blackburn the next day, he sought out a bit of nightlife, as one now famous nightclub owner, Peter Stringfellow, recalls: 'I first met Freddie when he came into my Cinderella Rockerfella club in Leeds, and I thought he was a really nice bloke, obviously not a megastar yet and so he had no entourage surrounding him. He sat at my table, and we had a laugh and a few drinks. I had a Polaroid camera and asked if I could take his photo. As I say, Freddie was not yet a star, but what a performance it turned out to be! I thought to myself: this guy is certainly different!

'I went through two packs of film before Freddie decided that one shot was all right to keep. He promptly insisted on destroying the others. His vanity was out of all proportion, but the way he scrutinised each photo and discarded it until one came out just right I suppose, with hindsight, was a lesson in professionalism. Apart from that, we had a good night. I had absolutely no idea that Freddie was gay then. There was nothing in his behaviour to remotely suggest it but I would say that was the first and last time I had a truly enjoyable evening with him. Later on, whenever he came into a club he was always completely mobbed.'

The only crowds Queen saw in those days were turning up to see Mott the Hoople, but with each gig their confidence was growing. There were no passengers in Queen, though it must be said that with Roger Taylor hemmed in behind his drums, and John Deacon and Brian May being naturally retiring, the onus was heavily on Freddie Mercury to electrify each performance. It is something that he would perfect to a fine art, but even in these very early days Queen were beginning to draw their own reaction, as Tony Brainsby confirms: 'I also handled Mott the Hoople, and both bands had met for the first time in my office when it transpired that they were to go on the road together. That tour was one hell of an experience. You came out of gigs just breathless with it all.'

The tour ended on 14 December at the Hammersmith Odeon in London, which was the night that Brian's parents first saw him perform with Queen. They were astounded at the response their son, and the band, elicited from the hundreds of young people corralled in the theatre.

Elated by the experience and at having established a strong rapport with Mott the Hoople, Queen's performances were exceptional enough to leave their audiences wanting more, but though the six-week tour had proved a success, the music media either criticised Queen or ignored them. Tony Brainsby holds forthright views on this subject. 'Queen were accused of being a hype band,' he states, 'and the reason for that was that their management put a lot of money behind them and I got them a lot of press coverage, concert bookings, interviews, etc. If you're a success too quickly, you are automatically accused of being a hype band even if, as in their case, you're bloody good. What people forget, too, is that Queen had a big following even before they made hit records. When you're getting fan mail and phone calls at that stage, you know you've got something special on your hands. The quirky thing is that the vast majority of their early fans were mums. There was one really old lady, in particular, who was so besotted with them that she would write and ring all the time!

'The music press saw Queen, particularly with Freddie being the way he was, as an easy target. You get some journalist who wants to make a name for himself and he'll latch on to an easy band to attack. In those days, of course, it was considered essential to have the music press on your side. Papers like *Disc, Melody*

Maker and *NME* were far more important and influential than they are today. It is my belief that they felt Queen were in danger firstly of being too big and secondly of achieving it too quickly, and that is why they went for them. Of course, it hurt the band. Brian was always extremely anxious about their press image and what was being said about them, but they were also extremely excited when good things happened – like the first time there was a pop poster of them in, say, *Jackie* magazine, which used to be a landmark in any band's career. So it was not all bad.'

As to why Queen elicited such a poor response from the music press, DJ Bob Harris suggests: 'It possibly stemmed from their inability to label Queen and they took their own inadequacy out on the band. When Queen were huge and they still attacked them, it was the same old thing. The British press love to build 'em up and knock 'em down. They just do not or cannot recognise achievement and leave it at that. You sometimes get the feeling that they feel duty bound to smash holes in people. Part of it, of course, stems from a worry that they could be accused of sycophancy if they constantly admire anyone's work.'

After the stint with Mott the Hoople, Queen played four more gigs to the year's end; the final performance of 1973 took place on 28 December at Liverpool's Top Rank Club in support of 10cc. It was the last show Ken Testi was to book for Queen. Ken recalls: 'By then I was working in a shop in Widnes. Brian had phoned to ask if I wanted to become Queen's personal manager. Naturally, I was thrilled and I asked what the money would be like. I hated having to ask because, for myself, I wouldn't have cared but I had a mortgage to meet. Everyone in Queen was now getting £30 a week, and I was offered £25, which I thought was good, but I had to say no.

'It was everything that my life had been leading up to and I had to turn round and refuse but on that money I could not make the payments on the house, and I also had to look after my mother and sister. One can't live on what-might-have-beens but I regretted it for years afterwards.' When Queen turned up at the Top Rank Club they discovered that a local band called Great Day was also on the bill; among its line-up was Ken Testi. It was a good night.

That Liverpool show ended Queen's most successful year yet, and on the strength of the UK tour Mott the Hoople invited them to be support on their tour of America. For Brian, 1974 began with health problems. At the end of January, Queen were to headline at two gigs at a three-day open-air music festival in Melbourne; like the others he had to have the appropriate inoculations. Almost immediately he became feverish and his arm began to swell up dangerously. It was quickly discovered that the needle used on him had been dirty and, consequently, he had developed gangrene. During the first crucial days, it was touch and go whether he would lose his arm.

Apart from the obvious worry this caused, it also meant that rehearsals for their first headlining foreign gig suffered. To Queen, the festival seemed doomed at the outset. They took a passionate interest in dramatic stage lighting, and now that resources were less tight they could indulge this to better effect. Proud of a new specially designed lighting rig, they had it transported to Melbourne along with the rest of their equipment. Because the apparatus was complicated to use, they took over their own crew to operate it, which unfortunately upset the local technicians. On arrival Queen also sensed a general air of resentment that an unknown British band had been chosen to headline in preference to home-grown Aussie groups; this grievance was only aggravated by the imported lighting-rig operators.

On top of concern that Brian's arm would be too weak to last a performance, Freddie developed an ear infection. The antibiotics prescribed him were so strong that he began to feel increasingly drowsy as the day progressed. As they waited backstage for their cue to go on, he found it hard to psyche himself up for the show. Out front, the audience began a slow handclap, and as Queen prepared to take the stage the compere did not help when he introduced Queen as 'stuck-up pommies'. As soon as the band launched into the first number, Freddie was disoriented when his ear infection made it impossible to hear himself sing. Conscious of the huge disappointment this show was becoming, the rig then gave out just when it was dark enough for the lights to be seen at their best. Sabotage was the suspicion.

Instead of buckling, however, Mercury pushed himself to the limits to perform, May battled valiantly with an extremely painful arm and Deacon and Taylor focused on the music. By the end of the performance, their grit had paid off as the crowd's hostility had been neutered and no one was more surprised than Brian when, after the last note rang out, they were greeted with a healthy roar from the audience demanding an encore. It never happened. Before Queen could obligingly strike up, the compere rushed on stage and within seconds changed the crowd's collective mind to shout, rather, for one of their own home-grown bands.

The sting of humiliation was complete the next day when the Melbourne press slated Queen right royally. It was the last straw. May's arm was still worrying him and Mercury's ear infection had worsened, sending his temperature soaring. Queen cancelled that night's performance, ignoring the wrath of the promoters, and boarded the first plane home. On the long flight, Brian had plenty of time to nurse his aching arm and to reflect morosely on just how much the whole fiasco had cost them. Not only had they had to pay their own return air fares but the experience itself, so early in their career, had been painful in every way. Resiliently, May later maintained: 'None of us thought it was disastrous. We just thought – one day we'll be back, and we were.' Clearly, though, Queen could have done without bad relations with the Australian press adding to the hostility from the British media.

Even as individual music press journalists disparaged them, the music magazines themselves produced annual polls that showed the growing strength of Queen's popularity at street level. In February, *NME* readers placed Queen second to Leo Sayer as the Most Promising Newcomer. That same month, Elektra released 'Liar' as the second single from *Queen*, which sank without trace. All eyes now turned to the release of the next single, scheduled for later in the month.

By now Ronnie Fowler, head of EMI's promotional department, had entered the fray. Impressed with Queen's sound, Fowler plugged the band wherever he went. The ambition of every new band was to appear on BBC 1's prestigious Thursday night programme, *Top of the Pops*. One Tuesday evening Fowler received a call from the television show's producer, Robin Nash. David Bowie's promo clip for 'The Jean Genie' had not arrived in time for that week's show and he asked Fowler to suggest a replacement. Fowler offered Queen.

Unfamiliar with the band's work, Nash requested to hear a demo, which he liked, but as artistes in those days mimed to special backing tracks, the demo was useless. EMI and Queen seized their chance when that night Fowler persuaded Who guitarist Pete Townshend to relinquish some studio time and allow Queen to record the necessary tape. At the BBC studios the following day, they pre-recorded their slot for transmission the next night.

During the long 24-hour wait for their debut appearance on the nation's premier pop show, Ronnie Fowler received a visit from an irate Steve Harley, lead singer of Cockney Rebel. Harley had heard about the coup that Fowler had engineered for Queen and he was said to be furious. He was under the impression that this was exactly the kind of opportunity that Fowler had promised to put their way. In his annoyance, Steve Harley gave Fowler a piece of his mind. He saw Queen as being leap-frogged over Cockney Rebel and demanded that Fowler get his band on *Top of the Pops* the following week.

Among music's many myths, there are different versions of what took place, but publicist Tony Brainsby has vivid memories of the general tetchiness between the two bands. He says: 'In later years, I handled Cockney Rebel and there was certainly a strong rivalry there. Both were newly emerging from EMI at this time, both vying for chart positions and attention. I am pretty sure that it would not have worked if I had had both bands on my hands at the same time.'

On 21 February 1974, Queen appeared for the first time on *Top of the Pops*, performing 'Seven Seas of Rhye' – a single that had not yet been officially released. That evening Brian, Roger, John and Freddie congregated on the pavement outside an electrical goods shop window, waiting to watch themselves through the glass on the bank of display televisions inside.

'Seven Seas of Rhye' showcased Mercury's weakness for swirling crescendos and fantasy lyrics. It fades incongruously at the end into a sing-a-long of the English ditty, 'Oh I Do Like To Be Beside The Seaside', which Ken Testi recalls recording back in 1973. He says: 'I joined in on the reprise at the end of "Seven Seas of Rhye". So did Pat McConnell and a whole bunch of us. I recall an awful lot of reverb, and Brian played the stylophone on it, but it was done in one day and we were all totally pissed at the time.'

With the momentum begun, next day Ronnie Fowler and Jack Nelson went all out to capitalise on the previous night's national exposure by hitting BBC Radio 1 with white label copies of the single, which EMI rush-released on the 23rd. Around this time, songs topping the UK singles chart included such lightweight froth as 'Tiger Feet' by Mud, Suzi Quatro's 'Devil Gate Drive', and Paper Lace's cringe-making ballad 'Billy, Don't Be A Hero'.

Queen's 'Seven Seas of Rhye', being of a vastly different ilk, swum against the tide. By the second week of March, nevertheless, it peaked at number ten.

By now, Queen had turned their minds to their forthcoming first UK headlining tour, and had started to consider what they would wear. The days of raiding the clothing stalls at Kensington Market and relying on help from seamstress friends to run up stage clothes on the cheap were over. The time had definitely arrived to enlist a professional. They chose zany top fashion designer Zandra Rhodes.

'They came to me, I think, because they had liked some of the outfits I had designed for Marc Bolan,' says Zandra. 'At the time, too, I was seen as a very colourful bird of paradise with my bold make-up, freaky hair and flowing scarves, and I think they were drawn to that imagery. My workshop in those days was an absolute death trap in a brownstone building in Paddington, which had a winding rickety staircase with a low ceiling leading to it. Brian was very sweet. He is so tall and I have this clear mental image of him stooping right over to save braining himself on the low ceiling as he and Freddie tramped up to see me.'

Having safely negotiated the stairs, May and Mercury discovered there was a price to pay for their desire to shine on stage. 'Well, obviously they had to try things on,' explains Zandra, 'and so they both had to strip off in front of me and my machinists. We were used to it, but they weren't! Poor guys, they were *so* shy – especially Brian.'

Zandra turned out some truly stunning outfits, indulging freely in yards of sumptuous satin, silk and velvet, all beautifully embroidered in minute detail. She recalls: 'Everything was very positive in those days. What's called the seventies' style is really late sixties' fashion. We had thankfully evolved from the dreary miniskirt into fabulously free-flowing skirts, flares and loads of scarves. Colour was vital, too.'

One of Mercury's outfits in white satin with a glorious pleated-wing effect would become world-famous, but although Freddie had arrived fired up with his own ideas, he was happy to be guided by the professional. Says Rhodes: 'Even if someone has had wonderful artistic training, it does not always follow that they know best, and Freddie was always extremely appreciative of what I did, which was lovely, as was Brian. Queen's look was very much part of their success and has always been important to their whole make-up, in conjunction with the music.'

Brian stated: 'The image and concept of the band were there from the beginning. I remember going to see David Bowie at the Rainbow Theatre very early in his career. I was really excited about what he was doing but apprehensive, because I was still afraid people would think we were jumping on the bandwagon.'

After intensive rehearsals, Queen's first headlining UK tour began on 1 March 1974 at the Blackpool Winter Gardens. Topping the bill was very different from playing support. It was quite hard going, especially for the first couple of gigs, because May's arm was still hurting him and they did not have a support band. Then a Liverpool group, Nutz, joined them for the remaining dates. This tour saw the birth of the audience's habit of singing 'God Save the Queen', while awaiting the band's arrival on stage. Later, Queen closed their shows with the national anthem.

With the success of 'Seven Seas of Rhye', everyone fixed on the launch in early March of *Queen II*. Its most distinguished physical feature was its innovatory white and black sides instead of the traditional A and B, and for Brian May personally there was much to like about this album. 'It was the fulfilment of an ambition for me to start using the guitar as an orchestral instrument,' he said.

Queen's aim was to create music that had the power of head-bending rock but the sophistication of a tapestry of textures, embracing harmony and melody. May reflected on how surprisingly few people recognised what Queen were doing initially. Within a fortnight, *Queen II* cracked the UK Top 40.

From previous experience, no one in Queen seriously anticipated glowing reviews but neither did they expect the music press to savage them. One reviewer had described their debut album as 'a bucket of stale urine', and it was difficult to imagine plummeting from that. This time they were accused of lacking depth and feeling, were even denounced as 'the dregs of glam rock'. The fans disagreed and nightly came away from gigs thoroughly exhilarated. At the critical point of live contact between band and audience, Queen were thriving, which was essentially what mattered most to them.

Keeping this in mind, Queen concentrated on perfecting their art. The meaty, mesmeric bass work from Deacon and the driving surge of Taylor's drums, coupled with May's powerful lead guitar and Mercury's vibrant flamboyance, pumped adrenalin straight off the electrified stage into the faceless throng crowding the gloom beyond the footlights.

Occasionally that adrenalin spilled over in negative ways. After a gig at Glasgow University, their next appearance of the tour was on 15 March at Stirling University. All went well with the actual performance and the first three encores. However, when Queen refused to return for a fourth, a small section of the overheated audience grew ugly. Within minutes, a rash of fights had broken out. The police were called and Queen had to be locked in a kitchen for their own safety, while in the hall a pitched battle raged. Two members of the audience were injured and two members of the road crew required hospital treatment – one for cuts, the other for concussion.

With the press tagging the band with lurid headlines, Queen performed on the Isle of Man at the Palace Lido, where they courted controversy again when in Douglas a party spun out of control. Making a low-profile exit off the island the following morning, they were quickly cheered by the news that *Queen II* had scaled the album charts to reach number seven. Furthermore, their first album, until now lethargically received in the charts, had managed to hitch itself up on the back of its successor's popularity to a semi-respectable number forty-seven.

Although press accusations of inciting riots were unwelcome, there is no doubt that the coverage helped to publicise Queen's existence. By the tour's end, their shows were regularly sold out and fans were becoming vocal in their adulation. This new adulation was going to Freddie's head, and during the day of their final gig, on 31 March at the Rainbow Theatre in London, a row erupted in the band.

In the afternoon, Freddie began behaving like a prima donna during the sound check and it was enough to goad the normally patient Brian into calling the singer an old tart. Unused to May losing his temper, Mercury took the attack to heart and stormed off. At first his absence was treated as a joke, but as time went on the other three started to worry. Acting on a hunch, Brian turned up the volume on the mikes and began taunting at the top of his voice: 'Freddiepoos? Where are you?' Before too long, Mercury burst furiously back into the theatre and after glaring silently at each other, the band got back to work.

Although they shared a determination to succeed, May has admitted that in these early days the band had very little idea of what kind of long-term future they could hope to have in the notoriously fickle music business. Their first ambition had simply been to make a record and have something tangible that they could say they had done. Having achieved that goal, their next aim had been to play some of the concert venues that were familiar to them. One of those venues was certainly the prestigious Rainbow Theatre, and so that night's gig was a culmination of their latest dream.

Before a capacity crowd, it turned out to be one of Queen's most memorable gigs. Sound engineers had experimented ambitiously with the theatre's acoustics, while Roger Taylor poured beer on top of one of his drums, so that each time he struck it, it sent up a wild, frothy spray. It made not a blind bit of difference to the sound but it looked great, as did Mercury in one of Zandra Rhodes's extravagant white costumes. It was the first time Queen had headlined at a major London venue and the sheer panache of their performance was enough to silence some of their fiercest critics, if only for a time.

5

DIZZY HEIGHTS

In April 1974, Brian was eager to quit Britain for America, where Queen were to tour as support to Mott the Hoople. Apart from the odd European gig and their recent trip to Australia, Queen had not yet had the opportunity of winning over an overseas audience. The US market was massive, and it was vital to make their mark. It sounded like it could be fun, especially with the bonus that they got on so well with Hoople, but they must have been aware that with *Queen II* having newly struggled to reach number 83 in America, from Elektra's point of view they had a lot to prove.

At gig after gig, unsurprisingly, people did not recognise their songs and Queen's stage image was not what US audiences expected – Freddie Mercury pirouetting and posing in clingy costumes did not fit the stereotype of heterosexual rock. Gradually, however, the crowds took to Queen's music and diffident acceptance grew warmer as each night progressed.

Life on the road was tougher than they had been used to. The travelling distances between cities were obviously much greater than in Britain and nothing seemed to go smoothly. On 1 May, Queen were set to perform at the Harrisburg Farm Arena in Pennsylvania, where on arrival they discovered that the American rock band Aerosmith were also due to appear. A row broke out between the two support groups as to who should be first on stage. It grew quite heated and Brian, tired of the squabbling, wandered off backstage. There, he met Aerosmith's lead guitarist Joe Perry, who was also fed up with the bickering. Since neither man gave a damn who got to play first, they left the others out front to get on with it and opened a bottle of Jack Daniels to christen their acquaintance.

The two guitarists found a good rapport and they liked the smooth-textured Tennessee whiskey even better. By the time agreement was reached on that night's line-up May and Perry could scarcely stand straight, never mind play. Some desperate sense of self-preservation kept Brian from crumbling and he later maintained that he had played the entire performance from memory. Next day, he was stunned to be told that he had come out of his customary shell and had injected his playing with fiery, spicy action. Joe Perry became a life-long friend but from then on May followed two golden rules – to pile on the action and to avoid drinking liquor before a gig.

Three weeks into the tour, however, Brian ran into real problems. Queen played six nights at the Uris Theatre in New York and halfway through he began to feel unwell. Although worried, he kept quiet about it at first. He had never felt like this before. On 12 May, their final night in New York, he collapsed. On the assumption that it was exhaustion, he was strongly advised to rest.

Queen were looking forward to appearing next in Boston but when Brian woke up in the Parker House Hotel there he knew that something was dreadfully wrong. His whole body felt like lead and when he dragged himself to a mirror he was shocked to discover that his skin had turned a ghastly yellow. A doctor was called urgently. The others waited anxiously, worried about Brian's health and concerned that they may have to call off the Boston gigs. In fact, they had to cancel the whole tour, for Brian was diagnosed as suffering from the potentially dangerous, certainly contagious illness hepatitis.

Dispatched back to Britain, Brian was hospitalised, while all those with whom he had been in contact were immunised against the virus. The infection was attributed to the dirty needle with which Brian had been inoculated for the Australian tour, and which had already nearly lost him his arm due to gangrene. Now, no one could be sure that he would ever fully recover from the hepatitis. Brian was most concerned that he had let the band down.

While he was confined to bed he turned his time to good use by writing songs, for Queen were due to start recording their third album. Early in June the band went to the Rockfield Studios in Monmouthshire to rehearse, to pen new material and to lay down backing tracks. Having convinced himself that he was fit, Brian joined them but he kept disappearing to be sick. He couldn't eat and felt thoroughly drained.

Sticking to their schedule, Queen next began work at Trident Studios. For roughly three weeks, all went well. Then suddenly Brian collapsed again. This time, he was rushed to King's College Hospital where he underwent an emergency operation for a duodenal ulcer. The band had been due to tour America in September. Now, again because of Brian's need to convalesce, those plans had to be scratched. Brian was devastated and this time feared that the band might consider replacing him.

Aware that May was an inveterate worrier, Freddie Mercury often visited him in hospital to put his mind at rest. Superficially jokey and quick to clown, privately Freddie was something of a mother hen to the others in the band. For years he had proved to be a trusted confidant to friends and he could just as effectively heal a row within Queen as cause one. When it came to health, he was acutely conscious of Brian's needs. In response to press queries about the band's reaction to their abortive US tour, Mercury stated: 'Brian has got to look after himself in the future. We all want to make sure something like that never

79

happens again. I tend to worry about him a lot because he'll never ask for anything if he's not feeling well.'

When Brian regained his health and strength, it transpired that his brush with illness had afforded him the chance to see Queen from the outside; the different perspective excited him very much and when he got back into the studio he threw himself into finishing off songs such as 'Brighton Rock' and 'Now I'm Here', a number with which he had tussled unsuccessfully prior to being hospitalised. Now, it knitted effortlessly together.

Working with the band was Gary Langhan. 'I was tape operator and assistant at Sarm Studios,' explains Gary, 'and Queen had chosen to finish off their new album there. My first meeting with Brian was when we were mixing the track "Now I'm Here". Brian is the ultimate professional, but he finds it *so* difficult to make a decision. Part of my job was to make sure that everything in the studio was working okay and that everyone had what they wanted, which included getting refreshments. Time and again, Brian wouldn't be able to make up his mind whether to have tea or coffee, so you can imagine what it was like when it came to working on tracks! There is one thing, though. When it came to records, once he'd made a decision it was always the right one.'

While Queen put the finishing touches to their new album at Sarm Studios, *Queen II* earned a silver disc. It had sold in excess of 100,000 copies during its first six months of release. This heralded an upsurge in media interest that the band greeted with caution considering the journalistic treatment meted out to them thus far. Said Brian: 'I still had the naive belief that if you opened your heart to the press, they would be fair to you.'

It had also been over six months since their only hit single, and they had to decide which of the new tracks should be extracted first. This time, Roger Taylor had contributed a track, John Deacon made his songwriting debut with 'Misfire', and

'Stone Cold Crazy' was the first number to be credited collectively to Queen. Brian made four contributions, while the rest were Freddie's and it was one of his songs, 'Killer Queen', that was released in October 1974 and peaked at number two in the UK charts.

'Killer Queen' was in a category all of its own, yet it was held off the top by David Essex. The year before, the cheeky-faced Essex had portrayed the fictional doomed rock star Jim McLaine in the Puttnam/Lieberson film *That'll Be the Day*. His hit, 'Gonna Make You a Star', was his first number one and it resolutely refused to give way to Queen's latest single.

Says David Essex: 'Funnily enough, "Killer Queen" is my favourite Queen record. Everyone knows now that they were a highly innovative band, but it was obvious even then. I would say that Queen were probably the best British band to come out of the seventies. With their stacked-up voices and guitar work, "Killer Queen" was extremely well produced and very clever.'

This view is endorsed by Oscar-winning lyricist Sir Tim Rice: 'I hadn't particularly liked "Seven Seas of Rhye" at first, although I got to like it better when I knew the band, but it was "Killer Queen" which really turned me on to Queen. The composition of its lyrics was quite sophisticated, particularly for its time. I have absolutely no doubt about Freddie's immense talent as a songwriter.'

Mercury was proud of what he dubbed the 'bowler hat, black suspender belt number'. 'People are used to hard rock, energy music from Queen,' he observed. 'Yet, with this single you almost expect Noel Coward to sing it.' With a number two hit to their credit, the public assumed that Queen had hit the big time, but although 'Killer Queen' was a turning point in their career, they were still impoverished, as evidenced by the state of their living accommodation. The illusion of success had to be maintained, though, and for this Mercury's great gift for exaggeration came in useful. Without a scrap of modesty, Freddie would crow: 'The reason we're so successful, darling? My overall charisma, of course!'

As Zandra Rhodes reflected, a large part of Queen's initial success lay in their look – an amalgam of appearance and props. As well as elaborate costumes, all four wore their hair long. At a college dance one night, Mercury had been struggling with an ancient microphone stand when its heavy base had suddenly fallen off. Left with only the top half of the chrome shaft, he had realised that it wasn't only much lighter to manoeuvre, but easier to move suggestively over his body and face. By the time he performed 'Killer Queen' on *Top of the Pops*, twisting the shiny rod skywards, his fingertips groping their way sensually up its length, this had become as much his hallmark as his long black feathercut hair and scoop-neck leotards.

The question arose though: were Queen a glam rock band, or not? At first, they came in for criticism over the homosexual over-tones they exuded – Freddie was fond of sliding his shoulder up against Brian May's right side, apparently deriving an ambiguous pleasure in the process. At the height of the glam era, Mercury was not the only one promoting a bisexual image, but whereas the band Sweet were taken to be joking, Freddie's intentions were less clear.

To Queen, image and material were different concepts. Considering the general calibre of songs released by glam bands, it is inconceivable that these could seriously be equated with the sophisticated yet uncluttered composition of 'Killer Queen'. Gary Langhan states: 'No way for me were Queen glam rock. For a start, there was a far greater content to their records. I spent *days* with Brian working on the harmony structures and the guitar solos for "Killer Queen". It was extremely meticulous!'

As far as May was concerned, such care paid off, although initially he had had reservations about releasing it as a single.

He has admitted: 'When we put out "Killer Queen", everybody thought it was very commercial and I was worried that people would think that we were doing something light.'

The single's success gave Queen a good springboard from which to launch a 19-date UK tour, commencing on 30 October. Undeterred by their experience down under, each performance included an impressive light show, with a fireworks display. Fans adored it, but music press critics denounced it as pure theatrics. May was at last fully recovered and went all out to prove it. Experimenting with ambitious stagewear only rivalled by Freddie Mercury's, he rushed back and forth across the stage playing guitar better than ever and mirroring the enthusiasm of the fans who had now started charging to the front in their desperate attempts to make close contact with the band.

At Glasgow's Apollo Theatre in early November – just as their third album, *Sheer Heart Attack*, was released – fans were chanting and waving, directly below the footlights. In a second's mistiming, Mercury got too close, and in a flash a sea of hands pulled him off stage and into the hysterical mob. Security guards plunged in and retrieved him, breathless and frightened, but unharmed. In the ensuing melee, however, fights broke out resulting in a few split heads and damage to several rows of seats. Queen had originally been booked to play one date at London's Rainbow Theatre in mid-November, but such was the demand for tickets that promoter Mel Bush had to hastily organise a second night. Queen left for Gothenburg soon afterwards to commence the sell-out European leg of their tour.

Rolling Stone later said of this new album: '*Sheer Heart Attack* is, like its two predecessors, a handsomely glossy construction. If it's hard to love, it's hard not to admire. This band is skilled, and it dares.' Although it was difficult to deny Queen's increasing popularity – voted by *Sun* readers as Britain's Best Live Act of 1974 – their old adversaries continued to confront them. It got to be a no-win situation. Queen remained wary of talking to journalists, who they felt were out to trap them. The British press, in turn, took this lack of compliance as further proof of Queen's conceit.

By the end of 1974, it was not only with the press that Queen's relations were strained. In late December, after taking Europe by storm, they returned home to begin long and largely frustrating meetings with Trident over money. Their salaries had more than trebled by the time *Sheer Heart Attack* was released, but still the band felt that this was nowhere near commensurate with their success.

At this point, they were all living in insalubrious conditions. Home for Brian was a depressingly dingy room behind a steamy boiler room in the basement of a rambling house in Queens Gate, South Kensington. Freddie's bedsit was so damp that fungus hung off the ceiling, and water constantly streamed down the walls. John Deacon was engaged to be married to his long-time girlfriend Veronica Tetzlaff, and felt they ought to be able to afford better accommodation. It did not seem right to any of them that they were forced to exist in such spartan conditions. In addition, they worried that they could not pay lighting and sound companies – the mounting debts were affecting them greatly.

This kind of plight was not peculiar to Queen – many acts in the Top 20 were, in reality, in dire financial straits, but Queen had no intention of standing still. When they began to suspect that a long stalemate could set in with the Sheffield brothers, they hired music business lawyer Jim Beach to examine their contracts for a way out of their association with Trident.

Relieved to hand over the problem to someone else, in January 1975, Brian took off to relax in Tenerife. In the middle of the month 'Now I'm Here', the fourth single from their latest album, was released. In early February, Queen's first headlining tour of

America and Canada finally kicked off with a gig at the Agora Theater in Columbus, Ohio, and Tony Brainsby fully understood why the band were nervous.

'Queen's effect on America had been slow,' he admits, 'but this happened with most bands. It goes back to the sixties, when US bands couldn't get arrested in their own country. Only British bands counted and, I think, come the seventies, that it was a backlash of this; that Americans, in simplistic terms, got their own back by being downright cool to any English band.' In Queen's case, their image continued to create an extra stumbling block. American rock audiences still preferred no-frill jeans and T-shirt machismo to Queen's foppish finery.

During the flight, however, the band reminded themselves that 'Killer Queen' had reached number five in the US charts, so there ought not to be real grounds for concern. They were right. The US rock critics scorched them, determined to compare them unfavourably with Led Zeppelin, but tickets for each gig sold like hot cakes and several extra dates had to be quickly arranged to meet demand. The pace became crazy – at times they played two shows in one day; inevitably within the first three weeks Mercury developed problems with his voice.

Coming off stage at the end of the second day's performance at the Erlinger Theater in Philadelphia, Freddie was in such pain that a throat specialist was brought in from the University City Hospital to examine him. He was suffering from voice strain but the doctor suspected he was also developing throat nodules. He recommended that the star not sing, but it was advice Mercury ignored. 'I'll sing until my throat is like a vulture's crotch!' he vowed inelegantly. Next night he went on stage in Washington but it was obvious he was struggling and he came off in agony.

The following morning, while Freddie consulted another specialist, the rest of Queen waited anxiously for the diagnosis. May could have been forgiven for feeling that they were jinxed in America. Problems with his own health had cut short their first assault on the country and prevented their second from taking place at all. Now, on their third attempt to win over US audiences, it was Freddie's turn to be laid low.

It transpired that Mercury was suffering from severe laryngitis and he was ordered to rest. With no option, this time he gave in and the next six gigs were cancelled. When the shows did resume, however, it quickly became obvious that the rest had not been long enough and Freddie relapsed, resulting in yet more cancellations. The remainder of the tour was conducted on this stop-start pattern, with the final date in Portland on 7 April having to be cancelled at the last moment. Because of the tour's erratic nature, it was hard for Brian to assess its impact.

During this tour, Queen had come into contact with show business manager Don Arden. Impressed by Queen, Arden head-hunted them with promises of lucrative deals if he could be their manager. Moves to break free from Trident were proving to be frustratingly slow, but Don Arden claimed he could change all that if the band would allow him to contact Norman Sheffield direct. Queen agreed, and at first it appeared to have been the right decision. Norman and Barry Sheffield agreed to let Queen go, and Brian, Roger, John and Freddie all signed a letter that authorised Don Arden to act on their behalf.

By mid-April, Brian took a brief holiday with the others in Hawaii, before tackling their debut tour of Japan. He relished the challenge, but all the optimism in the world could not have prepared him for the reception Queen received in Tokyo. Pandemonium broke out among the 3,000-strong crowd of teenagers cramming the airport to greet them, as they screamed themselves hoarse under the uncomprehending gaze of the airport security guards. May was thoroughly bemused. He could not believe that all these kids were actually chanting for Queen. 'We couldn't take it all in,' he revealed. 'It was like another world.'

Brian May is easily one of Rock's most distinctive figures. Pictured here on stage in 1986.

Complete conviction and a shared determination to succeed propelled Queen into rock music in the mid-1970s: Rockfield Studios, 1975.

In the early 1970s, Brian became a teacher for a while, but music always had a stronger pull on him.

In a Zandra Rhodes outfit, May cut a romantic figure onstage.

The costumes for the 1984 'It's a Hard Life' video allowed the band to exercise their fondness for the flamboyant.

By Live Aid in 1985 Queen had become one of the world's biggest stadium rock bands.

Brian found it hard to watch Freddie's health deteriorate. By the late 1980s Mercury's illness was beginning to show.

With Roger Taylor and Freddie Mercury's mother, Jer Bulsara, Brian celebrates Queen's induction into the Rock and Roll Hall of Fame in New York, March 2001.

Guns n' Roses guitarist Slash and May in action at the Freddie Mercury Tribute Concert, held on Easter Monday 1992 at Wembley Stadium, London.

Frontman Paul Rodgers joining Brian May and Roger Taylor has allowed the Queen phoenix to rise again: in concert at the Carling Academy Brixton, London, 28 March 2005.

The first concert, in Tokyo's Budokan Martial Arts Hall on 19 April, was a sell-out; the hysterical scenes at the airport paled into insignificance compared with the delirium exhibited by their audience that night. Brian recalled: 'They said: "The audience will be very quiet, but don't worry!" This was the start of something new in Japan. It's still with us in various ways.'

Although the band's amps were working at full blast, their music was completely drowned out by the screams – finally the crazed crowd lost control and rushed the stage. In the stampede, normally sturdy seats began to buckle and collapse under the sheer weight of the lunging bodies. For Queen it was a shocking, though strangely exhilarating, sight. Sensing that they were dicing with disaster, Freddie stopped the show and appealed to the frenzied fans to calm down. It took a while, but eventually it worked.

Queenmania spread throughout the whole twelve-day tour to Nagoya, Okayama, the ancient city of Kobe and beyond. Japan was the first country to recognise Queen as a major force in music. Off stage, their hosts treated the band with enormous deference, showering them with expensive gifts. Brian came to believe that all this unvarnished adulation brought out a new strain of confidence and made them a shade more extrovert in live performance. On their final night – again at the Budokan – the band came on stage for their encore, dressed in traditional Japanese kimonos. The delighted audience went berserk at the compliment.

Someone who fully understood the impact that Japan had on Queen was Bay City Roller guitarist Eric Faulkner. That March, Britain had witnessed the peak of Bay City Roller mania when the Scottish group seized the number one spot with 'Bye Bye Baby'. Love them or loathe them, there was no denying the delirious mass adulation that these tartan-clad lads commanded. Says Eric: 'Japan is like a separate planet for bands. The press hysteria stories precede you, and by the time you arrive they are ready to swallow you whole! It is an unforgettable experience.'

As for the mania, Faulkner freely concedes: 'Of course you enjoy it, but if it gets to the mania pitch you have to take it with a very big pinch of salt. If you believe it, you will go clean off your head. It's a strange world. You end up looking out at it from the inside – that is, if you can see past the wall of bodyguards.'

Queen's first taste of Japan instilled in them a fascination for the country's culture, as their publicist can vouch. 'They were all smitten,' says Tony Brainsby, 'couldn't wait to buy all things Japanese. Freddie, though, was the most affected in the long run. He once spent all his Japanese royalties on Japanese antiques and artefacts – and why not? It had been such a thrilling time for them. Japan was the first country to fall. They made it big there, before making it big in their own country. So, of course, it made a huge impression on them.' When they returned to Britain at the beginning of May, both 'Killer Queen' and *Sheer Heart Attack* topped the Japanese charts. The album was also a hit in America.

Back home, the band busied themselves with work on their fourth album. They had all benefited from their recent experiences and the new material, reflecting this stimulus, looked to be the most promising yet. Brian ceaselessly sought new ways to extract ever more sophisticated sounds and effects from his guitar. Queen resisted falling back on the synthesisers favoured by many bands at this time, and Brian May with his Red Special was rapidly becoming the envy of many of their peers.

In summer 1975, two musicians acted on that impulse. The group Sparks, fronted by former child models Ron and Russell Mael, had enjoyed a handful of chart hits and the pair approached Brian in the hope of luring him into their band. May was flattered by the proposition, but was not remotely tempted to quit Queen.

By autumn, Queen were working hard in six different recording studios. Equally intensive were the continued attempts to release the band from Trident. In August, severance agreements were finally prepared for signature. EMI would be given more direct control in the publishing and recording fields, while Queen were free to seek new management. The downside was that they had to cough up £100,000 in severance fees to Trident, plus the rights to one per cent of album royalties. Brian May observed: 'We effectively had to trade the first three albums' sales up to that point for our future.'

Queen were broke again. A planned American tour had had to be called off due to the upheavals, and with such discord around rumours circulated that Queen were about to disband. It wasn't true, but they did urgently need new management as Don Arden's offer had fallen through, leaving the band to think again.

They compiled a short-list of names, one of which was John Reid, who managed Elton John. Reid's initial reaction was not encouraging but he agreed to a meeting. Apart from Queen's conviction that they would be superstars, at this point to an objective observer they were simply an impressive live act with a couple of hits and healthy album sales to their credit, which made them better than many and not as successful as others, but something attracted John Reid and by the end of September 1975, he had become Queen's new manager.

John Reid's first act was to hire a day-to-day personal manager for Queen, a former colleague named Pete Brown. Says Pete: 'That was me for the next seven years. I would go everywhere with them, to recording studios, gigs, out on tour – the lot. I can always remember Freddie saying: "I decided that John Reid was the right person for the job of our manager the moment he fluttered his eyelashes at me!" Seriously, Queen really were in dire need of help then. Their finances were in a total mess.'

Developments moved fast under John Reid. Along with Jim Beach, he addressed the problem of where to find the substantial sum owing to Trident. Before the November deadline expired, he had persuaded EMI to provide it as an advance against future royalties. Having secured this, he threw a party at the London Coliseum where, in a blaze of publicity, Queen received a shed-load of gold and silver discs in honour of record-breaking sales of 'Killer Queen' and their first three albums.

Their fourth album, meanwhile, was very much in the making. Pete Brown recalls: 'Once, three of them were working in three different studios at the same time, which had never been done before.' The new material was also innovative. One of Brian May's contributions, 'Good Company', had a unique 1920s sound to it and was the product of some considerably intricate work. The richness of the arrangements in twenties' dance tunes intrigued Brian and he had often thought of attempting to create that effect on guitar. That notion had returned to him when 'Good Company' had come to him one day as he sat playing the ukulele. Going for it, he created a wind section for the song by getting trumpet, clarinet and trombone sounds out of his guitar. He made a meticulous study of these wind instruments first and said: 'To get the effect of the instruments (on guitar), I was doing one note at a time, with a pedal and building them up.'

Another of his notable compositions at this time was ''39', in which he indulged in a little science fiction storytelling. Conceding that most songwriters, subliminally at least, reflect their personal feelings in lyrics he felt that in this number he could detect a growing awareness that he was seeing different lifestyles from a changing perspective. The raucous rock world he was standing on the fringes of was so vastly removed from the steady way he had been raised and he knew that inevitably it would change some of his outlooks.

There was depth and complexity in all the material crystallising in the studio, and by October the band had unanimously agreed that the track they boldly wanted to be their next single was a composition of Freddie's called 'Bohemian Rhapsody'. The boldness of the choice lay not so much in the lyrics – rather, in the fact that in its uncut state the song was a virtually unheard-of seven minutes long, and distinctly operatic. John Reid was flabbergasted. Pete Brown states: 'A lot of us thought Queen were quite mad considering this track as their single. I tried to dissuade them, saying it was far too long, and privately John Deacon agreed with me, but Brian, Freddie and Roger were emphatic. They felt very strongly that they needed to establish their credibility and they completely dug in their heels.'

Record producer Gary Langhan remembers that resistance well: 'I suppose you could call it arrogance, but only in that it stemmed from total belief in the number. Their attitude to it being twice the usual time slot allocated to each record on radio was: well, if that's the case then DJs will just have to have one less record on their playlists that day. I was standing at the back of the control room the day "Bohemian Rhapsody" was completed and I knew I was hearing the greatest piece of music I was ever likely to hear. There are two feelings you get in your body about a new number. One's in your head, and that one can fool you time and again. The other is in your stomach, when you *know*. That time, it got me right in the pit of my stomach. Queen knew it too.'

John Reid may have admired Queen's determination to defend their professional integrity but as their manager it was his job to try to avert possible disaster. No one in his position could have felt anything but anxious in the circumstances. Initially, he tried to persuade Queen to edit the song down. Getting nowhere, he realised the depth of their faith in the number, so with his blessing the record went to press.

One story has Freddie Mercury going to see Kenny Everett, a

DJ friend he had cultivated a few years earlier, taking with him an advance copy of the disc to see what he thought of it. Brian May's memory, however, is that Kenny came to the playback. Either way, on discovering how long it was, privately Everett had reservations that any radio station would respond well to it but as soon as he heard the single, those doubts evaporated.

'Bohemian Rhapsody' had not yet been accepted by Capital Radio, but the renegade disc jockey was not renowned for abiding by the rules. Pete Brown laughs: 'Kenny was great! For two days he played "Bo Rhap" on air, practically non-stop. He would say: "Oops, my finger's slipped!" and on it would come.' Everett 'accidentally' played 'Bohemian Rhapsody' so often that the station's switchboard was jammed with callers wanting to know when could they expect the new single to be released.

Kenny Everett's agent, Jo Gurnett, confirms: 'Kenny was hugely instrumental in getting Queen airplay for "Bohemian Rhapsody". He was incredibly enthusiastic about the record and played it all the time at home, too.'

Tony Brainsby recalls: 'Everybody now says: "Oh! What a great record!" but Kenny Everett was the only person brave enough to play it at first. It was the kind of record that would either go to number one and make Queen, or it would die a death and be their epitaph. My first reaction was, hey, good number, but who the hell is going to play it? It's ridiculously long and what on earth is Freddie playing at with this opera bit in the middle? I mean, let's face it, it just wasn't what was going on at the time. Queen realised it was a risky move but underneath it all they were astute enough to take a chance with it. Other records were nice and safe and regulation length. This was stunning and a whole EP on its own, but we were sure radio would block it.'

At the end of October, 'Bohemian Rhapsody' was officially released. For four years Queen had skiffed in and out of musical styles, never quite being progressive, never quite being glam rock, picking up experience, absorbing influences and always carving a new path that defied definition. Now, the remarkable marriage of rock and opera knocked the music industry sideways.

In 1975, no one was ready for a ballad that had involved almost two hundred vocal overdubs, and that segued into complicated multi-tracking harmonic operatics before exploding into gut-busting hard rock. Incomparable to anything else, it was Queen's most positive statement yet and it provoked an equally positive reaction; you either loved it or loathed it, and decades later people still try to fathom the meaning of its complex lyrics. Brian May has remarked: 'It was Freddie's baby. He never explained it and I think he was right not to.'

The grandiose pomp of the song squares with Mercury's love of drama and passion, but it is worth considering if perhaps there were other forces at work. In 1969, when he had innocently made himself that tea laced with marijuana, friends testified to Mercury's total avoidance of drugs. Six years on, his horizons had broad-ened through travelling and meeting new people on tour. His exposure to drugs and drug-taking had also increased. Before long Freddie was known to be using cocaine, which had to have started around the mid-seventies. Is it possible that his early experiments with cocaine coincided with writing this song? He would not have been the first performer to believe that drugs unlocked the mind and released his best work.

Whatever influenced 'Bohemian Rhapsody', its effect on the public was polarised. One Midlands radio station poll in the mid-eighties would reveal that the single topped both the Best Ever Record and the Worst Ever Record categories. In 1975, reviewers were split in their response but what did prove unfounded was the fear that radio would not play the single in its entirety. Demand for it was so great that it received massive exposure on the airwaves.

The phenomenal impact of 'Bohemian Rhapsody' had journalists clamouring for interviews. This time, to tackle Mercury's resistance to talking to the media, Tony Brainsby adopted a new strategy. He explains: 'By the time Queen started to get themselves a name, Freddie began doing just the major interviews. He became a commodity only to be brought out when the big guns were around, like national newspapers, NME front cover, that sort of thing. When they were interested, then I could talk him into doing interviews. Later, Brian and the others became cover material, but in those days it was very much Freddie who was the focus. When Fred did do an interview, mind you, it wasn't that the people got close to him, because he treated these sessions the same as performing. He would put on a big show for the journalists and photographers, and be wonderfully colourful and camp.'

As it happened, there was not a lot of time to fend off the media, for Queen were to embark on a lengthy UK tour in mid-November. 'Bohemian Rhapsody' was rising up the charts from its starting point of number forty-seven. Top of the Pops was the obvious next step but the song's highly technical make-up ruled out live performance. Director Bruce Gowers, who had previously filmed Queen at the Rainbow Theatre, was approached to make a promotional video.

The concept of pop promos had hardly moved on from when the Rolling Stones would play on a beach and people off-camera would lob boulders down a hill behind them. What Queen had in mind was different. Having already booked time at Elstree Studios for pre-tour rehearsals, on the morning of 10 November 1975 they put their ideas into practice. What they produced took four hours to shoot, cost £4,500 and required one day to edit. The result was semi-psychedelic and eerily dramatic; when premiered on Top of the Pops ten days later, the prototype hard-rock video promo was to change the face of pop-music marketing for ever.

Captivating the record-buying public's imagination 'Bohemian Rhapsody' would top the UK singles chart and go platinum, selling in excess of 1.25 million copies in Britain alone. It made its mark too among Queen's peers, as Abba stars Benny Andersson and Bjorn Ulvaeus both recall. Says Benny: ' "Bohemian Rhapsody" took rock and pop away from the normal path. Its sheer originality completely matched Queen's originality.' Bjorn recalls: 'I was very green with envy when I heard "Bohemian Rhapsody" for the first time. Queen were very inspirational to both Benny and myself. With "Bohemian Rhapsody", we felt that they were going in the same direction as us – towards a more theatrical, dramatic sound. And, of course, to Benny and me "Bohemian Rhapsody" was another spur on the road that would eventually lead us into musicals.'

Both Abba and Queen became renowned for their studio craftsmanship, for producing intelligent music and for writing songs of which one hallmark was the effective use of harmonies. Bjorn Ulvaeus reveals: 'People can't normally hear the complexity of the harmonies in a song. Certainly in the case of some Abba songs, they sounded simple when they were actually quite complex. With "Bohemian Rhapsody" you could not mistake the brilliant harmonies.'

However, amid the gasps, sighs and envy in the music world, there were the odd dissenters. DJ John Peel once reflected: 'I liked Queen when they started out, although I have to admit they are not one of my favourite bands. I took the mickey out of them one night on *Top of the Pops*, and quite soon afterwards something appeared in a newspaper saying that Freddie Mercury and Roger Taylor were going to punch me out if they ever saw me. Thankfully, they never did but, seriously, when they first appeared I thought that they were unique and sounded like nothing else ever had. Most people came to class "Bohemian Rhapsody" as the beginning of Queen – but for me, it was the end of Queen. After that, they became too bombastic in style for my taste.' Brian May held his own view: 'What we actually became was successful. It's not cool to be successful in England.'

Someone else who had a mixed reaction to 'Bohemian Rhapsody' was Dick Taylor, an original member of the Rolling Stones, later lead guitarist with the Pretty Things and a friend of Freddie Mercury's. He declares: 'I think it is great now. I mean, it's a classic. You can't argue with it, but at the time, I kind of fell in and out of love with it. The first time I heard it, I thought, blimey! That's a bit over the top, but that was Freddie and he was so bloody good at it!'

The day after that TV debut, the album from which 'Bohemian Rhapsody' had been taken, called A Night at the Opera, was released. Many bands come to consider a particular album as marking the peak of their creativity. Perhaps Brian May classes A Night at the Opera as Queen's pinnacle for, years later, he looked back on this album and declared: 'This can be our Sgt. Pepper!'

6

TANTRUMS AND TRIUMPHS

Queen were on a high as they toured all over England. Then, after a gig in Newcastle in December 1975, they were heading across the border to meet their Dundee Caird Hall date when the bubble of euphoria burst as their coach was stopped on the motorway by the police. 'To put it bluntly, they were looking for drugs,' recalls personal manager Pete Brown. 'An ex-member of the crew who had been given the sack by the PA company, not Queen themselves, had decided to get back at the band. So he had anonymously tipped off the police, claiming that Queen were all high on drugs. It was a load of rot but the cops mounted this enormous roadblock, sealing off every exit route. It must have cost them a fortune. I well remember the silent anxiety that some silly sod in the entourage might have something, however small, on him but no one had.'

For Pete, who was responsible for ensuring that the band kept to their timetable, the biggest worry was the potential delay that this night-time drama could cause. 'During all the time I worked with Queen, they had never cancelled a show, and I was more concerned about that than anything else,' he admits. 'The cops hauled us all in – the PA company, the lights, the lot – for searching. It was obvious that they thought they had a real scoop. They treated us okay, I guess because they must have realised fairly early on that it was all a hoax. They rifled through the whole bus – noses into the ashtrays and everything – and could not come up with so much as a joint. In the end, their disappointment was so strong as to be almost laughable.' The police eventually released them, furious with whoever had wasted their time and caused them acute embarrassment.

The furthest north Queen ever played in Britain was a gig in mid-December at the Capitol Theatre in Aberdeen. By this time, it looked as if 'Bohemian Rhapsody' would hold on to the top slot long enough to be that year's Christmas number one, a distinction much fought over. Towards the end of the tour, the band had a few days off and Pete Brown recalls going to the Brighton Dome with them to see Hot Chocolate, fronted by singer Errol Brown: 'We had all gone to see Hot Chocolate perform. They were a great band and their number "You Sexy Thing" was sitting at number two. Afterwards, we were all in the restaurant of the hotel we were staying at when suddenly Errol burst in, headed straight for Brian and Freddie and roared at the top of his lungs: "You bastards! My main shot at a Christmas number one! You bastards!" God, it was so funny!'

On Christmas Eve 1975, Queen returned to the Hammersmith Odeon in London for a performance that was televised live by *The Old Grey Whistle Test* and picked up for simultaneous broadcast on BBC Radio One. Three weeks before, *A Night at the Opera* had been released in America, while in Britain it had already gone platinum. The day after Boxing Day, it too hit the top slot in the UK album chart, making this the band's most successful year to date.

For the first time Brian felt that while they might not know where their career would take them or for how long, at least they were definitely going up. There were forward moves in his private life, too, when at the beginning of the New Year he and Chrissy Mullen set a wedding date. They had been together for seven years and for a lot of that time had been inseparable. Queen had always placed a big drain on the time they could spend together, and now that the band's career was clearly set to soar those demands were sure to increase drastically. In the next four months alone, they were to plough through three major tours all over the world. Since their concert commitments slowed down for a while after April, the couple decided to marry in May.

As Chrissy began her preparations for the big day, Brian knuckled down to serious rehearsals for the first of those tours – a 32-date trip around North America. Confidence was high. They had already mopped up a heap of awards at the UK music press annual polls, and 'Bohemian Rhapsody' was sitting for the ninth consecutive week at number one in the charts. In mid-January 1976, Queen flew to New York, and as the aircraft's wheels touched down at Kennedy Airport, the only prayer May needed to send up was that no one would be taken ill this trip.

A week after their arrival they opened to a rapturous reception at the Palace Theater in Waterbury, and everywhere they went now fans mobbed them. Despite the increasing dubiety surrounding Freddie Mercury's sexual preferences, on stage his style, especially in America, had become more macho. With his slinky build, luxurious dark hair and lively, wicked eyes, women found him incredibly sexy, although they were wasting their time. They could prove determined in their pursuit of him, as the singer learned the hard way. One day in New York, as he stepped on to the kerb into a frantic gaggle of girls, his scarf was grabbed at both ends and pulled tight. He could have been choked to death had it not been for the swift intervention of his companions. What amused them most about the incident was Mercury's subsequent outrage at the damage done to his precious silk scarf.

During their four-day stay in New York, Brian discovered that

Mott the Hoople's frontman, Ian Hunter, was recording at Electric Ladyland Studios with producer Roy Thomas Baker. He, Freddie and Roger went along to catch up with their two friends and inevitably got down to jamming. All three ended up playing and singing backing vocals on the track 'You Nearly Done Me In' for Hunter's forthcoming second solo album, *All American Alien Boy*.

While abroad, news reached Queen from back home that they had an unprecedented four albums in the UK top thirty at the same time; even *Queen* had reached number twenty-four, two years after its release. Inspired by this success, at gigs Mercury took to toasting their loyal subjects with brimming flutes of champagne. Behind the scenes, however, it was not all moonlight and roses. Pete Brown has his own vivid memories of this tour, particularly of the stopover in Chicago.

He reveals: 'Wherever we went, when the time came to move on it was my job to settle the hotel bills. We had been two days in Chicago and were heading to St Louis, but when I tried to use the Queen credit card they said that it was overextended. What made it worse was that it was a Sunday and no banks were open, and I still had to organise their luggage and transport to the airport. Getting anxious, I argued with the desk clerk, insisting he would just have to take it now and the band would sort it out later, but he wasn't having it. I didn't know what to do and started to turn away when suddenly the guy pulled a gun on me. I can't remember if I actually threw my hands up, but I certainly froze and said: "Easy, mate! I've got all the time in the world." Eventually I managed to get the promoter down to the hotel and he paid cash, but it meant that we had missed the flight.'

That US tour ended in mid-March, and a week later they kicked off their second assault on Japan – a shorter stint this time. May and Mercury had taught themselves a smattering of the language so that between numbers they could communicate in some small way with their audiences. The fans loved them all the more for the courtesy.

Queen's globetrotting took them next to the Antipodes. This first tour of Australia, kicking off at the Entertainments Centre in Perth, was important to them. Wary of their reception after their disastrous Aussie debut two years before at the Melbourne festival, they were also exhausted. They had been on tour for nine weeks already and Mercury, in particular, was feeling stressed. When they reached Sydney to play the Hordern Pavilion, events turned ugly.

'It was all because when we arrived we discovered that to get to the theatre it meant going through a huge fairground,' Pete Brown explains. 'Well, from one look at the set-up, it was obvious that there was no way you could drive through the crowds of people, so I asked the band to get out of their respective cars and walk. Freddie's immediate response was: "My dear, I can't possibly walk anywhere!" and he point-blank refused to leave the limo. We had to drive through at a snail's pace so as not to injure anyone, and Freddie acted up with the champagne all the way. Needless to say, your average male Oz didn't much care for this, and the catcalls started, shouts like "Pommie pussies" and worse. They lunged angrily at the windows, sticking two fingers up at those inside, and banged with clenched fists on the passing cars.'

When the cavalcade reached the Pavilion safely, despite the fact that his own arrogance had caused much of the trouble, Mercury took his temper out on Pete Brown. 'When Freddie wanted to be, he was very tough,' Pete reveals. 'He often made me cry during the years I worked for him. This time, when we got inside he was in such a cold rage that he picked up a big mirror and literally smashed it over my head. Then he ordered me to find a brush and shovel to sweep up the glass, at once.'

Mercury once blamed the constant pressures of fame for his temperament. His growing reputation for throwing things at people was, he stressed, very unlike him. Certainly Pete Brown must have known other, better sides of Mercury, for he held no grudge against the star for this latest abuse, maintaining: 'You see, it was the humiliation he had suffered. He just had to take it out on someone, and that time it was me. I understood.'

By their final gig at Brisbane's Festival Hall on 22 April, there was good reason to celebrate. The tour had been a great success. This time, when their Quantas Air flight took off for London, both their single and album topped the Australian charts, marking their first major breakthrough there.

Brian had more reason than the others to be happy just over a month later, on 29 May 1976, when he and Christine Mullen married at St Osmund's Roman Catholic Church in Barnes. John Deacon was already wed to Veronica Tetzlaff, and Roger Taylor remained the committed bachelor. Freddie Mercury, although still close to Mary Austin, was grappling with some serious inner battles that he would continue to fight for several more months. The band gave all four a sense of continuity, though. Taylor once called reverting to Queen work as 'like coming home to mother', and here something had changed, too.

Queen's first five singles had been written by either May or Mercury, but this time around John Deacon had come up with a melodic ballad, 'You're My Best Friend'. Released in mid-June, it gave the band a number seven hit. That summer, Brian got down to working on songs for their new album, which they hoped to release before the year's end. They called this 'routine time', when they individually wrote songs that they would then argue hotly over in the studio. This way of working produced lively debate and, at times, stubborn resistance, but they all considered it constructive.

The urge to perform live, however, was never dormant for long, and Queen were growing restless just when Richard Branson, founder of the Virgin Group, came up with an exciting proposition. 'I had had the idea to try to stage a free open-air gig in Hyde Park, which would promote a few bands at the same time,' says Richard. 'The problem was, I wasn't in a position at that time to finance something like that, so as I already knew Roger Taylor, I approached him thinking that perhaps it might be an idea if Queen put it on. I also thought that Queen might *really* break as a result of that kind of exposure. Having been to the Rolling Stones' Hyde Park concert in 1969, I remembered just what a special kind of feeling a huge free gig like that generates.'

Queen agreed, and were eager to arrange the gig for the following month – which was hardly feasible, but Richard Branson worked through the many stipulations laid down by the Metropolitan Police and the London Parks Committee, gradually pulling the pieces together. He says: 'When I had all the necessary clearance and the project was a goer, I handed it over to the Queen management to take from there.'

The date was set for 18 September, which worked in well with Queen's arrangements to play two gigs earlier that month. The first show took place during the annual Edinburgh Festival at the Playhouse Theatre, when they were supported by Supercharge. 'Ask anyone who was there at the Playhouse that summer,' Pete Brown maintains, 'and they will tell you it was a great experience. It's hard to explain, but it had a profound effect on everyone in Queen.' One of the considered highlights was when Queen performed a new hard-rocking number of Brian May's called 'Tie Your Mother Down'. It had the audience off their seats and jigging in the aisles.

The second concert was in Wales, at Cardiff Castle. Billed as 'Queen at the Castle', the outdoor gig came at the end of the worst drought in Britain for years. Reservoirs had dried up, arid riverbeds were cracked, and in some towns street standpipes were back in operation, but as the twelve-thousand-plus crowd assembled that night, the rains poured down as support acts Frankie Miller's Full House, Manfred Mann's Earthband and Andy Fairweather-Low played their sets. By the time Queen appeared, the ground was a quagmire and the audience was soaked through.

At Hyde Park the day was baking hot as around 150,000 people converged on the area, bringing confusion to London's congested traffic system. Capital Radio was covering the event live, with commentary from DJs Kenny Everett and Nicky Horne; the compere that day was BBC Radio One's Bob Harris. Beside his professional association with Queen, Harris had developed a close friendship with the band. He says: 'They were very bright and their overview was always keen. They were never an exploitative band either. Queen genuinely cared very much for their fans.'

The support acts that day at Hyde Park included Steve Hillage, Supercharge and Kiki Dee. Bob Harris recalls: 'Supercharge's lead singer was a rather overweight fella and I remember he came storming on in a costume like one of Freddie's ballet dancer outfits – not a pretty sight! Kiki had just had a number one hit with Elton John for six consecutive weeks called "Don't Go Breaking My Heart", and I know she had been desperately hoping that Elton could come and perform it with her there, but he had other commitments and couldn't. So that night, she sang the number to a cardboard cut-out of Elton on stage instead. Queen came on just as it was getting dark. People had been amassing since midday and by mid-afternoon, when you stood on the stage, you could see the crowd literally stretching to the horizon line. The mass of humanity was an incredible sight.'

Greeting this mass of humanity with the words: 'Welcome to our picnic by the Serpentine', Freddie Mercury, in a black leotard scooped to the navel and with ballet pumps on his feet, launched into a high-energy rendition of 'Keep Yourself Alive'. 'You could *feel* the anticipation,' remembers Bob Harris. 'When Queen had walked on, to the strains of "Bohemian Rhapsody", the audience went wild and Queen gave one hundred per cent throughout, but then they never had that throwaway quality that some bands have. The light show was incredible, too.'

When the roar for an encore was deafening, Queen were desperate to oblige. At concerts, Freddie frequently taunted an audience with the battle cry: 'This is what you want? This is what you're gonna get!' Only, that day the police saw to it that no one was getting anything more. Prior to the event they had laid down a strict set of dos and don'ts, and as the schedule had overrun by thirty minutes they threatened Queen with instant arrest if they tried to go back on stage. To emphasise their seriousness, they pulled the plug on the power supply, momentarily plunging the park into pitch darkness. Richard Branson recalls: 'It was a vitally important gig for Queen, and a turning point in their career.'

After several weeks of solid work, their new album, A Day at the Races, was released mid-December. A month earlier, Mercury's ballad 'Somebody to Love' had been selected as Queen's next single. Kenny Everett's saturation airplay of the number catapulted it to the top of Capital Radio's chart, Hitline. When it was officially released, however, it stopped just short of giving Queen the satisfaction of a second national number one.

By the end of 1976, Brian and Chrissy had bought a comfortable house in Barnes, John and Veronica moved into a house in Putney, while Roger went one better – opting to purchase a luxurious country house in Surrey, set in acres of garden and woodland. Freddie Mercury, meanwhile, having battled with himself for a long time, now felt that he had to sacrifice his relationship with Mary Austin for stronger desires. That he deeply loved Mary was not in dispute, and that he felt impelled to redefine their life together did not mean that he was less devoted to her, nor, time would prove, she to him. His decision now though led to an unusual coexistence. While Mercury pursued the gay life he craved, Mary Austin went on to make other relationships.

The break with Austin was a huge relief to Mercury, and so began a period of promiscuity that lasted for at least five years. Freddie boasted that his enormous sex drive led him to bed hundreds, not an unusual claim in rock, though the bragging usually refers to female groupies. After an evening's partying on the gay scene, Mercury would select whoever took his fancy. He wanted sex with no strings, and around dawn would leave a club for home, with his conquest in tow. It appears that he wasn't fussy, and for someone whose artistic sensibilities were becoming increasingly refined, he could go extremely downmarket. This period also saw a marked increase in Mercury's use of cocaine.

In January 1977, when Queen embarked on their most extensive US tour yet, they arrived in Milwaukee to find the country experiencing the lowest temperatures of the century. Joining them on the bill was Thin Lizzy, fronted by Phil Lynott and featuring lead guitarist Scott Gorham. Their manager was Chris O'Donnell, and he remembers landing this support slot.

'Thin Lizzy had themselves been due to tour America,' says Chris, 'then one night Brian Robertson got involved in a fight at the Speakeasy Club. Some guy had been going to break a bottle over Frankie Miller's head and Brian had thrown up his arm to stop the bottle. It shattered, badly cutting his hand. Obviously, he couldn't then play the guitar. So I sped off to America to see if there was some way I could salvage the situation – some way we could keep Lizzy's new album alive. It was there that I got a phone call out of the blue from Howard Rose, who was Queen's US agent then, asking me if Thin Lizzy would support Queen. Lizzy had been a big fan of Queen's since their conception, and I could not believe our luck at being offered the slot.' Brian Robertson's place would be taken by Gary Moore.

The trip was a revelation for Chris O'Donnell. He declares: 'There were definitely times when Thin Lizzy played Queen off the stage. I felt that, good as they were, Queen were now so stylised that the slightest thing going wrong threw the whole perfect balance right off. Whereas Lizzy were so hungry and raw that by contrast they had this unpredictable energy on stage, and it showed. Having said that, they were a great package.'

Thin Lizzy's lead guitarist was the easy-going, irrepressible Californian Scott Gorham, and he recalls the tour with deep affection: 'This was Lizzy's second tour of America. Before, we'd never toured with a British or European act – always American bands – and there's a whole different mentality there, especially with Queen. Once you get to a certain level in the rock world, it changes some people. A lot of bands get paranoid. They become obsessed with not letting the support act upstage them. They won't give you a sound check, a decent PA or anything, because they want to really keep you down. We didn't get any of that with Queen. They moved in right away and said: "Here's the PA. Now, you'll need sound checks and lights, and what else?" Queen and Lizzy had this attitude that we had set out as a British attack to conquer America.'

The two bands got along very well. Says Scott: 'I think it was partly to do with the fact that the bands were so very different. Lizzy was a sort of punk band with street cred, whereas Queen were very polished and sophisticated. I always think "pompous" is a really unkind word to use to describe their music, but it was certainly grand – so you see there was no competitiveness on that score.'

They had some great and eventful times. Scott reveals: 'One

night I was on stage, playing away, and in the heat of it all this thing whizzed past my face, just missing me by a fraction to thud into my amp behind me. I looked round and saw it was a lemon. I took a second and thought: is there a hidden message behind this piece of fruit here, or what? I mean, why not an apple or a lettuce? Why a lemon?

'We did our set and Queen went on. I went out front to watch them and all of a sudden, from the same direction of the audience, a hail of about a dozen eggs went up in the air aimed right at Brian. Suddenly, Brian's skating about on raw egg and he lands right on his ass! I started to laugh real hard, then stopped myself. I thought: what are you laughin' at? You got lemoned! I couldn't work out which was worse – an egg or a lemon. Anyway, I looked into the audience thinkin' there's a guy somewhere in there with a whole salad bar just waitin' for us. We may not be getting paid much, but hell we'll sure eat well. This was in one of those mega-dome places, too, and what could Brian do but get up like nothing had happened, but he was wearing his flowing white top. Uh-uh, not any more. Man, I'm talkin' *yella!*'

Scott Gorham has equally vivid recollections of Mercury: 'Yeah, well Fred was a real different kinda guy for me. Thin Lizzy were one hundred per cent a politically incorrect band and I mean, all down the road, you know? For a start, we were all completely homophobic and we didn't know how to treat this Freddie Mercury, until we met him and discovered that he was a lovely guy. He wasn't at all how we had imagined, especially with our ready-made prejudices, but Fred had a personality that was strong enough to win just about anybody over, and that's what he did with Thin Lizzy.'

Touching on the homophobia, Chris O'Donnell says: 'Despite having a name like Queen and their frontman being the way Freddie was, it was very much a boys' band. The gay element on stage just wasn't there now. They played hard rock, and Freddie never came away with any of those familiar effeminate gestures.

Off-stage was another matter and, I suppose, it was one of the hardest aspects for Freddie to be living one lifestyle on stage, which was so much at odds with his private life.'

The two worlds, however, were not always so distinct, something for which Scott Gorham can vouch: 'Hell, no! We played one gig at the massive Winterland in Frisco, which is a city kinda known as having a big gay community. We were first up and I'm blastin' away and rushing about the left-hand side of the stage, thinking I'll go and mess with the audience on the right. The spotlight all the time is chasin' me, and I get over there and look up, and there's like five hundred of the gayest guys I've ever seen, man! They were wearing sequinned hot pants, satin jump suits, huge floppy hats with waving ostrich feathers and they're jumpin' off their seats, chuckin' feather boas in the air. As soon as I arrived at their side, they all started lunging at me shoutin': "Yeah! Shake it, boy!" Geez, man! I'm thinkin', whoa there buddy. I'm not real ready for that kinda contact! And I'm already makin' a beeline to the furthest left I can find! But if you could've seen Fred on that tour, he was just kickin', man. When Queen weren't going down particularly well, he worked his ass off to ensure they still ended up with two or three encores.'

Beyond the camaraderie, there was a kind of rivalry. Thin Lizzy already had a reputation for wildness, and their concerts were frequently violent. It had been quite clear from the first night that they would challenge the headliners by virtue of the sheer energy they created. 'We were out there to make Queen earn their money,' admits Scott. 'We were also out to win fans. Sure, we wanted to kick Queen in the ass – it makes you a better band – and we set out to make it as rough as possible for them to follow us. Man, once we were up there we wanted to blow those guys off the stage!' Brian recognised the threat and welcomed it. Not that long ago, Queen had tried their utmost to upstage Mott the Hoople.

During an arduous gig, in the midst of an equally strenuous

tour, Freddie Mercury would gain the stimulus to keep going from sources other than his own adrenalin. Of this tour, Scott Gorham says: 'I never actually saw Freddie doing drugs that trip. He wasn't throwing it about and making it a problem. He was very discreet.' It had been a different story before the tour began, though.

Gorham recalls: 'I was recording at Olympic Studios at the same time as Queen, and I met Freddie in the lobby, and he had had a few hits. He said: "Hey, Scott, can you do me a favour?" I replied: "Well, yeah." Freddie asked: "Can you come up and check out what we're doing upstairs. I really want you to listen to Brian's guitar sound. I think it's great, but he doesn't like it. Come on up and give us your opinion." By this time I'm saying: "Well, I'd rather not. I mean, the world's full of critics – who needs another?" But Freddie just had that persuasive thing, so I went, and it sounded great.

'Anyway, by this time Fred had had a few more snorts and was really goin' at it. In fact, that was the first time I saw Freddie take cocaine. I guess that's what was making him buzz the way he was, coz he started saying to Brian about me: "Hey! Isn't this a handsome guy? Couldn't he have a great career on his own without playin' the guitar – just on his looks alone? Hey, Brian, don't ya think?!" He kept on and on and I'm winking at Brian, taking it all as a joke but Fred was real loose and pestering Brian bad now, so to please him, Brian finally agreed.'

On the US tour, in early February, Queen played the prestigious Madison Square Garden in New York, when the capacity crowd adored them as much as they loved performing there. This, they felt, meant that they were now in the big league. Scott Gorham agrees: 'The building's not much in itself but you know, you're there. It's Madison Square Garden – you've made it!'

Pete Brown confirms: 'Queen always set themselves goals. To play Madison had been a goal and they had sold out. It was a terrific night and afterwards they were delighted with themselves until somebody piped up that Yes had headlined three nights running. That was all it took. Freddie leaped up and roared: "Right, that's it! Five nights!" – meaning, Queen wouldn't rest until they had bettered three consecutive nights at the Garden.'

This kind of fierce rivalry was not confined to vying with other bands. It was also prevalent within the group. Pete Brown reveals: 'They were always *very* tough on each other. No one got away with a thing. In various ways, they were all at one point pushed by the others into things that individually they did not feel right about but would agree to because it was part of being Queen. Their standards were the highest I'd ever known. They encouraged each other all the time, drove each other relentlessly. If Freddie wanted to be the best frontman in the world, then Brian had to be the finest guitarist, John and Roger determined to prove themselves an unrivalled rhythm section. It was that enormous self-imposed pressure that made Queen unique.'

For Brian May, the two nights they played at the Los Angeles Forum more than equalled their night at Madison Square Garden. Years before, he had gone along to see Led Zeppelin headline at the Forum and had wistfully wondered whether he would ever stand where Jimmy Page had stood. Each concert was a sell-out and left a lasting impression on Brian, even though the US critics tried to dampen things by running down Queen's performances while exalting Thin Lizzy with great reviews.

'We didn't take a lot out of that,' confesses Scott Gorham. 'Papers all over the place were saying that we were out there killing Queen, and it just was not true. Brian would come back to our dressing room after our set to say to me: "I feel you guys *are* killing us out there." I'd go out front when Queen were on and think: so what show's he lookin' at then?'

Just when the tour looked to be illness-free, as it entered its final stage in the second week of March Freddie's voice packed in. Again, strain was diagnosed and two shows were cancelled so that Mercury could rest. Brian headed back to San Francisco to look up some friends before the band regrouped for the last half-dozen Canadian gigs.

When Queen returned to Britain, it was to discover that their latest single, 'Tie Your Mother Down', had failed to break into even the Top 30. With the advent of the punk movement, bands such as the Clash, the Damned and the Sex Pistols ruled the charts. The Sex Pistols came to be universally considered to have single-handedly launched New Wave music in Britain, and the music press was quick to latch on to punk, to the exclusion of established bands like Queen. Perhaps particularly Queen, since they were the extreme antithesis of the punk philosophy. While some journalists were ready to pronounce rock as dead and Led Zeppelin, Genesis and Queen as passé, Brian viewed this latest movement with interest: new musical styles, however weird, intrigued him.

There was scant time to bother about new rivals, though, for Queen hit the road again, opening their European tour in May at Stockholm's Ice Stadium in Sweden, when Freddie Mercury appeared to go out of his way to offset punk's grosser aspects. He came on stage sheathed in a replica of an almost diaphanous costume once worn by the dancer Nijinsky. Not content with the impact that made, he took the final encore in a skintight silver leotard, so heavily sequinned that it blinded the audience as he shimmied under the huge array of spotlights.

After-gig parties had long since become the norm for Queen. Partly, they helped to dispose of the incredible levels of adrenalin still pumping after a show. To these shindigs flocked any showbiz celebrities who happened to be in the area, local stars and, more often than not, less salubrious gatecrashers. At one party held on board a yacht during this tour, the band were presented with thirty-eight silver, gold and platinum discs, a tribute to their enormous popularity in the Netherlands.

On their return to Britain, the UK leg of the tour began in

Bristol, ending in early June at London's Earls Court, where Queen played two consecutive nights. It was Queen Elizabeth II's Silver Jubilee year, which must partly explain the lavish expense the band allocated this time to their stage effects. Besides the familiar smoke bombs, fireworks and elaborate lighting, a specially designed rig in the shape of a crown had been commissioned at a cost of £50,000. Ascending dramatically from the stage, amid dry ice smoke, it was 25 feet tall and 54 feet wide and weighed two tons.

Such an ostentatious display at the height of punk was guaranteed to goad the critics. NME fired a salvo in an article claiming that: 'A rock gig is no longer the ceremonial idolisation of a star by fans. That whole illusion, still perpetuated by Queen, is quickly being destroyed and in the iconoclastic atmosphere of the New Wave there is nothing more redundant than a posturing old ballerina toasting his audience with champagne.'

The article, which included a lengthy interview with Freddie by Tony Stewart, was titled: 'Is This Man A Prat?' The gloves-off element in the headline was echoed throughout the entire spread. By the end, Freddie had clearly lost his patience and in reply to the observation that he only went to play the piano at gigs so that he could make another entrance centre stage, he bluntly rasped: 'The reason I go to the piano is to play the fucking thing!' The time would come when Queen would refuse press interviews altogether.

That year, the Sex Pistols' number 'God Save the Queen' topped the UK chart, despite having been banned from the airwaves; many distributors declined to handle the single. The band's manager, Malcolm McLaren, calls the number: 'The most English, angst-ridden toughest, mother-fucking rock song that has ever been written,' adding, 'that was to me, punk rock at its best.'

Queen and the Sex Pistols had met one day, in a recording studio. 'In 1977, after the Sex Pistols signed with A&M Records,'

Malcolm McLaren recalls, 'we all trucked off to Wessex Studios in north London. Queen were recording in studio one, and Chris Thomas, the Sex Pistols' producer, was in studio two. On entering studio one on his way next door, Sid Vicious got down on his hands and knees and crawled through Freddie Mercury's legs. That was the day the Sex Pistols had finished recording their second and most notorious single, "God Save the Queen".'

October saw the release of Queen's tenth single, 'We Are the Champions', a sturdy arm-locking anthem, written by Mercury. Its B-side was May's composition 'We Will Rock You'; according to Brian it was a song about mankind and the futility of violence. The single made number two in Britain and Elektra Records liked it enough to release it as a double A-side. They anticipated massive airplay and were rewarded by its huge success in America. 'We Are the Champions' found favour throughout Europe, too, holding on to the number one slot in France for twelve consecutive weeks.

When News of the World, the album from which the hit single had been selected, was released at the end of the month, it topped the charts in nine countries. Two years on, Queen were still reaping awards for 'Bohemian Rhapsody', but they valued most highly the one they received on 18 October, at a ceremony in Wembley Conference Centre, when 'Bohemian Rhapsody' tied with Procol Harum's 'A Whiter Shade of Pale' for the Brit Award for the Best British Pop Single of the Last 25 Years.

By now, plans were in motion for Queen to cut their last remaining tie with Trident. Financially, they were now in a position to buy themselves out of that clause in the severance agreements that had allowed Trident a one per cent share of six future albums, and they were looking forward to being finally free.

Unfortunately, they now found themselves facing a whole new set of management difficulties. Pete Brown explains: 'The problem was that Queen didn't feel that John Reid was able to give them enough of his time, and that did not suit them. When Queen were brought on board you have to understand that it was really the Elton John office. John Reid had been working at Tamla Motown before Elton picked him to handle his business affairs. He duly set John up with an office, and all the staff had worked for Elton for a long time already. So it must have been hard for them to share their loyalties. If Elton had a tour, that took priority, and with the different personalities in Queen, you can imagine how that went down!'

Queen relied on lawyer Jim Beach to find a way out that was acceptable to both sides. Dissolving the partnership with John Reid was not troublesome, as was exhibited by the informality of the arrangements. Says Pete Brown: 'It happened when the band were recording the video for "We Will Rock You" in Roger's enormous back garden. It was absolutely freezing that day. There was something like a foot of snow on the ground. Filming always means an awful lot of standing around and everybody was very touchy that day. Anyway, in the middle of about the millionth take, John Reid arrived and he, Brian, Roger, Freddie and John all piled into the back of Mercury's car to sign the severance papers. I think that they were glad to get in out of the cold, more than anything else!'

As a penalty for opting out of their contract in advance of the agreed expiry date, Queen had to pay a substantial sum of money to John Reid Enterprises, as well as signing over a sizeable percentage of royalties on existing albums. This latest severance with John Reid did not impoverish Queen, but it did leave them with the continuing headache of making the correct decisions concerning future management. After some discussion, they now decided to manage themselves, with help from, among others, Jim Beach, Pete Brown and their tour manager Gerry Stickells. Queen were convinced that they could make a good fist of the job.

7

DELECTABLE DEBAUCHERY

Queen's second US tour of 1977 began in Portland, and by the end of the year it was clear that this trek would mark the band's conquest of North America. They were to headline for two consecutive nights at Madison Square Garden in New York; for Brian, both shows turned out to be very special. He had invited his parents over, since they had never seen Queen perform abroad. Harold May jokingly refused to come unless they were booked on to Concorde. Much to Harold and Ruth's amazement, their son did just that and brought them over in champagne luxury style. May later reflected: 'I checked them into the Ritz Hotel and said: "Order room service, Dad," and they came to the show and after the show my dad said: "Okay, I get it now. I understand what was pulling you to music."'

This tour provided Freddie Mercury with the opportunity to scour the US gay scene rapaciously, but there are those who wonder just how contented he was with it. Says Thin Lizzy manager, Chris O'Donnell: 'Freddie demanded so much of people, so that at times they fell short of his expectations. He loved the adulation he received on stage but in his personal life, behind the scenes, I felt he wasn't really enjoying himself – not deep down.' If this is true, it was not something that Mercury cared to admit and with dangerous disregard for his health, and that of his countless one-night stands, he continued to behave recklessly for a long time. The AIDS spectre had not reared publicly, as yet.

In San Diego one night, John Deacon accidentally put his hand straight through a plate glass window. He needed nineteen stitches but still managed to play for the remaining gigs. It had been the first time Queen had taken on two major tours of America in one year, and by the time Brian flew back to Chrissy on Christmas Eve he was thoroughly worn out.

On the business front, it had become clear to Queen that managing themselves was not working out, so they turned to their new accountant, Peter Chant, for advice on setting up a proper management structure. After careful consideration, it was decided that Chant would be responsible for the band's business, accounting and tax. Jim Beach was persuaded to resign his partnership in a west London law firm in order to become Queen's manager, heading up the newly formed Queen Productions Limited. At the same time the band created Queen Music Limited and Queen Films Limited.

By now, Queen's earnings were so high that, in terms of UK income tax regulations, it was best not to spend more than ten weeks of the year in Britain. The answer was to play and record overseas. So after the release of the single 'Spread Your Wings' in February 1978, the band embarked on a spring tour of Europe. While in Berlin to play the Deutschlandhalle, Roger Taylor crossed Checkpoint Charlie into East Berlin. There, a piece of graffiti inspired the cover concept for their forthcoming album later that year; the tour wound to a close with a handful of British dates. Mercury's style, always flamboyant, was changing – now he favoured shiny black PVC. He once confessed: 'I rather fancy myself as a black panther.'

Taylor and Deacon almost immediately headed to Montreux in Switzerland to begin work on new material, while Mercury remained in Britain. Also in London, Brian needed to stay close to home, for Chrissy was due to give birth to their first baby any day. James May (Jimmy as he is known) was born on 15 June 1978. About a month later Brian celebrated his thirty-first birthday before flying to Nice in France, where Queen gathered at the Super Bear Studios to concentrate on their next album.

Songwriting inspiration can come to May from virtually any source, and 'Dead on Time', for the new album, would feature sounds he recorded during a ferocious thunderstorm. While everyone else huddled indoors, Brian dashed out in the torrential rain clutching a portable tape recorder. He was thought to be slightly crazy at the time, but he was happy with the results on record.

The annual Tour de France passed through the French Riviera when Queen were there, and the spark for the song 'Bicycle Race' had been ignited in Mercury by his appreciation of the sight of scores of hard-bodied Lycra-clad young cyclists crouched low over their handlebars. Simultaneously, May had been busy working on a number called 'Fat Bottomed Girls', about groupies. He later mused: 'Why does everybody love the idea of having casual sex with people that they, otherwise, would not want to be with?' It did not take too much thought to pair these songs up.

With ever more extravagant budgets for their videos, it was tempting to be risqué sometimes, and 'Bicycle Race', backed by 'Fat Bottomed Girls', gave them the ideal opportunity to indulge themselves. Deciding to stage a girls' bicycle race, Queen hired Wimbledon Stadium, sixty-five models and Steve Wood as director. There was one important detail: the girls were all naked. It was seen as a cheeky prank by those involved – except for Halfords, the company that supplied the bikes. They accepted the cycles back afterwards but not the saddles, leaving Queen to pay for sixty-five new leather seats.

When the single was released mid-October 1978, the sight of a naked rear on its sleeve brought accusations of sexism raining down on Queen. Brian was impatient with the pious uproar and retorted at the time: 'I'll make no apologies. All music skirts around sex, sometimes very directly. In our music, sex is either implied or referred to semi-jokingly but it is always there.' Eventually there was a reappraisal, and on later covers the offending rear end of the winning cyclist sported a superimposed pair of skimpy black knickers.

Yet another US tour kicked off later that month. Although it was punctuated with the usual shenanigans, this time a bash held on Halloween at The Fairmont hotel in the French quarter of New Orleans was extravagant enough to make the newspapers coast to coast in America and passed into Queen folklore. Their parties often lasted for days, but because they had a gig in Miami in early November, they made do with a 12-hour orgy of excess. This featured such exotica as a nude model served up hidden in a huge salver of raw liver, semi-naked girls cavorting about in bamboo cages suspended from the ceiling, as well as female mud wrestlers and topless waitresses, all for the delectation of the most bizarre cocktail of people imaginable.

Publicist Tony Brainsby remembers this party well: 'It was a pretty wild night. I took a party of press over. We flew from London to New Orleans, partied for twelve hours solid and stag-gered back to the airport, still not having been to bed. They had hired the huge hotel ballroom, which had been made to look like a jungle swamp. There were trees, masses of hanging creepy vines, dry-ice smoke pumping everywhere and snakes, not to mention strippers. All in all, a first-class party! I don't recall seeing Freddie take cocaine that night. Mind you, he was discreet that way and anyway, in those days, rightly or wrongly, doing cocaine wasn't really seen as taking drugs. It was more a trendy thing to do. I've got a photograph of Freddie signing his name on a stripper's botty as she bends over a table.'

The media dubbed such Queen parties 'Hedonism on an

industrial scale', and those journalists *not* present at these bacchanalian events were voracious for lurid details of all that went on behind closed doors. The band tended to take a discreet line by merely commenting: 'A lot of excessive things might have gone on, but we didn't see them.' But when pressed, once May revealed: 'It was all part of the experience and a worthy part. It wasn't just us enjoying it, but a whole team. I wouldn't make any apology for it. I thoroughly enjoyed some of it and we didn't hurt anybody.'

This Halloween shindig was considered an unofficial pre-launch for Queen's new album, *Jazz*, which was released in Britain in November. Still unrepentant over the bike race furore, the band had inserted a free graphic poster of the race participants. America, however, banned the poster, considering it to be pornographic. One week later, while the band were performing 'Bicycle Race' in New York, they arranged for the stage to be invaded by half a dozen naked ladies on push-bikes, defiantly ringing their bells. Perhaps aided by the controversy, the album survived in the charts for twenty-seven weeks, peaking at number two.

When the tour ended, Brian flew back to his wife and six-month-old son in time for Christmas, but there was to be no let-up in the constant merry-go-round and soon after the release in January 1979 of the new single, 'Don't Stop Me Now', Queen kicked off a two-month trek around Europe.

During this tour, personal manager Pete Brown was especially kept on his toes organising the band's comfort down to the last detail. He reveals: 'One of my jobs was to ensure that the accommodation I fixed up for all four of them was of the exact same size, quality and style. The idea was that no one person was to have anything bigger, better or fancier than the other. It was a good enough policy in theory, but in practice it was a different story. That tour, I could not seem to do anything right. Brian, I think for the first time ever, was very annoyed with me over the place I had fixed him up with. Another time, it was Roger with a list of complaints, but when we came to Paris, I managed to upset all four at the same time. It was a horrendous task, though, trying to find four suitable houses – not apartments, mark you – of precisely the same dimensions and standard to please them all. Try as I might, I could never develop a thick skin, and when they blew up at me it did hurt sometimes but I don't regret it. We had some good times.'

The tiring life on the road gave way once more to two months recording at Mountain Studios in Montreux. Brian adored working in that professionally stimulating yet aesthetically relaxing environment, and while there Queen were invited to write the music for a new feature film, *Flash Gordon*. Directed by Mike Hodges and starring the ex-American footballer Sam J. Jones, Max von Sydow and Topol, everything about the film version of Alex Raymond's 1930s' comic-strip adventure was intended to be lavish; the film's producers felt that a pounding rock score by Queen would be a perfect complement. It was a challenge that May, in particular, found extremely exciting.

Summer saw a rash of Queen releases, starting in June with *Live Killers* and the single 'Love of My Life', both recorded at recent gigs. Then, because EMI received the 1979 Queen's Award to Industry, the record company launched a 200-copy limited edition of 'Bohemian Rhapsody', pressed on blue vinyl. By now, Queen were busy writing material for a new album, this time at a new location – Musicland Studios, in Munich. Here, they began work on the film score and they first met record producer Reinhold Mack.

Queen had never lacked a strong sense of their own importance. Indeed, Brian May has stated: 'Part of you believes that the group is the most wonderful thing that the world has ever seen. We do not compromise with anyone else. It was pretty hard for anyone to sit with us as a producer or whatever, and the ones who managed it, managed it by having very strong personalities.' Known simply as Mack, Reinhold had no need to feel intimidated by Queen, having already worked with top groups including Led Zeppelin, Deep Purple and ELO. He was to become the first outside producer since Roy Thomas Baker to work regularly with Queen.

While in Munich, Mercury came up with an unusual song for Queen that would give them their first American chart-topper. At a piano, Freddie could conjure up melodies off the top of his head in minutes. Few can deny that Mercury was a one-off but he could also be an incurable mimic and 'Crazy Little Thing Called Love', the jaunty number he knocked together in record time, was a distinct pastiche of Elvis Presley.

When released in early October, the record quickly went gold. It also marked another first by featuring Mercury on rhythm guitar. May has been diplomatic: 'Freddie didn't have great technical ability on the guitar. He had it all in his head. You could feel this great frenetic energy bursting to get out.'

The following month, Queen embarked on what they called their 'Crazy Tour'. Brian felt that they had been playing 'the big barns' for too long. Although these gigs were enjoyable, he worried that Queen were losing contact with their core audience. He explained: 'Unless people can see you in their home town, it can almost seem like you don't exist. It's nice to be somewhere where people can actually see and hear you. The advantage of what we are doing this time is that, because our sound and lights systems are better than ever, we can really knock audiences in the stomach.'

The tour kicked off at the RDS Simmons Court Hall in Dublin, featured two Glasgow dates but was otherwise confined to England. On stage, Brian and Roger remained visually much the same in style but John, with a sober short haircut, took to wearing a conservative collar and tie, while Freddie was now never out of leathers and wore a leather and chain cap; at that time this image was closely associated with gay men's clubs.

In mid-December, in the final stages of the tour, Queen played a couple of nights at the Brighton Centre, and it was now that Mercury met the man who would become his first live-in male lover. The singer's weakness lay in well-muscled men, who looked like labourers and invariably had thick black moustaches. Still enjoying the gay scene to the hilt, after each gig Freddie would set off in search of local talent. On one such excursion, he found the Curtain Club and met 28-year-old Tony Bastin, who worked for a courier company. They hit it off so well that before Queen headed back to London, the two men had exchanged telephone numbers and promised to keep in touch.

As the seventies slipped away, May reflected on just how far he had come in the past ten years. At the close of the sixties, Smile were breaking up and he had been dejected and broke. Now he was wealthy, successful and famous; he was deeply involved with the challenge of creating the soundtrack for *Flash Gordon*, while also working on Queen's new album. He spent the first four months of 1980 in Germany, at Munich's Musicland Studios.

Back in Britain 'Save Me' struck out with the critics on its January release, but this was overshadowed by the continuing success of 'Crazy Little Thing Called Love', which now topped the charts in six countries. Working on two albums at once was at times a strain for everyone in the band, though.

In March, Freddie paid a flying visit to Britain to make a rare TV appearance as a guest on his friend Kenny Everett's zany show. Mercury's friendship with Everett survived into the mid-1980s, but tales surfaced later of their acrimonious split after a bitter row over drugs. In 1995 Kenny Everett died of AIDS, and his agent Jo Gurnett says: 'Kenny admired Freddie like mad and adored everything he did. They were very good friends. Their falling out is a bit of a grey area, but I know that it was a minor disagreement between them, after which they just seemed to drift apart. Freddie's career took him away a lot and certainly Ev's television work occupied most of his time, too. Kenny didn't see Freddie latterly. He would have liked to, but it was just one of those things. Then, Freddie was too sick and Kenny himself was too sick. I remember Kenny, in the late stages of his illness, when he knew he was dying, saying about Freddie and their lost closeness: "Oh, well, we'll all be up there together, and maybe then we will make it up."'

It was during this trip that Mercury purchased Garden Lodge, 1 Logan Place, Kensington, a 28-room Georgian mansion set in a quarter of an acre of manicured garden and surrounded by a high brick wall, though it would be a few years before he took up residence there.

In late spring, 'Play the Game' became Queen's latest single. It peaked at number fourteen in the UK charts, but on its video release many fans felt that Freddie personally wasn't playing the game. Their familiar Mercury was slipping away from them – replaced by a singer with cropped hair, no nail varnish and sporting a bushy moustache. Many of the faithful were further ruffled and let down when *The Game* followed at the end of June, because Queen had used synthesisers to create their music, something they had always boasted they did not do.

That summer, Queen undertook a strenuous tour of Canada and America. Kicking off at the PNE Coliseum in Vancouver, it climaxed in early October with four consecutive nights at Madison Square Garden, New York. Airtight security meant that they were cocooned to the point of suffocation, especially now that they travelled everywhere in private planes. Some hotels they stayed at were so security conscious that the windows were designed not to open, and May once remarked that he began to feel like a rabbit in a hutch.

Pete Brown certainly recalls: 'Brian got to the stage where he just did not want to use private planes any more. It was a case of arriving in a private plane on a private airstrip, being taken from the plane by limo to some sumptuous hotel, hotel to gig and back the same way. The rarefied atmosphere was driving Brian mad.'

Pete was aware of Brian's penchant for collecting things and remembers watching his boss flit blithely between tables in many of the world's top hotels, picking up little sugar bags to add to his collection. 'Part of what was wrong with him,' observes Pete, 'was that there are no gift shops to browse in at private airfields and Brian didn't like that. But seriously, what Brian missed dreadfully was normality. He used to say to me: "What can I honestly say I know about anything, living the way we do?" Eventually, he put his foot down and told the others that he wanted to fly commercial again. He told them: "I want to feel that I have been somewhere!"'

Everyone on the team felt the strain of Queen's hectic schedule. 'People imagine that it is a glamorous life,' explains Pete, 'but it is damned hard work. Someone would ask me how Boston was and I would reply: "Boston had orange curtains and a blue bedspread." They would look at me funny, but that really is what it was like.'

In August, John Deacon's 'Another One Bites the Dust' was released. Again, the song was a departure for Queen, but its throbbing, near hypnotic bass line overcame fans' initial resistance and it became the darling of the discos. It was universally a smash hit, selling 4.5 million copies in America alone, where it resided at number one for five weeks.

It did not, however, spell success for everyone, as Kent Falb, then head trainer of the Detroit Lions American football team, explains: 'Early in the 1980 season, defensive backs Jimmy Allen and James Hunter, along with tight end David Hill, heard

125

"Another One Bites the Dust" on the radio and decided to use the melody. They rewrote the words and made a recording of the song as a novelty tune, which was unofficially adopted by the Detroit Lions. However, at the time this was done the team had begun the season with four wins and no losses. As the season went along our fortunes declined, and unfortunately this tune ended up being used against us by numerous opponents!'

When the tour ended, Brian returned home to London looking forward to relaxing with his family, whom he had sorely missed. It was very difficult juggling the band with being a husband and father, since of necessity he was separated from Chrissy and Jimmy a lot. Time together became a precious commodity and, after completing work on the *Flash Gordon* film score, he tried to make the most of it before all too quickly he had to jet off to Zurich at the end of November to rehearse for Queen's European tour.

Days into that tour, 'Flash's Theme', written by Brian, was released in Britain, backed by Freddie's song 'Football Fight', also from the soundtrack album. The single made the top ten, outstripping Elektra Records' choice in America; 'Need Your Loving Tonight' languished at number forty-four in the *Billboard* chart. The purpose-built, all-seater Birmingham Exhibition Centre had newly opened when Queen became the first band to play there on 5 December, just three days before the soundtrack album *Flash Gordon* was released to astonishingly rave reviews.

The band's thrill soon evaporated when news broke that John Lennon had been callously gunned down in New York. Queen were getting ready to go on stage at London's Wembley Arena, and on learning of the tragedy Brian was devastated. Lennon had been one of his heroes and like every other rock star he suddenly realised with icy fear just how exposed and vulnerable they were. That night, though, Queen's thoughts lay with Lennon, and as a moving tribute they performed his 1975 hit 'Imagine'.

The circumstances of the former Beatle's murder seemed so unreal that it numbed most music lovers. On stage, Brian was inwardly so overwrought that he forgot the chords and got to the chorus too soon, which threw Freddie and put everything completely out of sync, but no one minded – the audience's distress was as real and raw as the band's.

By the year's end, Queen became the first band to enter the *Guinness Book of Records* – listed among Britain's highest paid executives. This achievement did not diminish their desire for new territories, and in Rio de Janeiro their manager was busy discussing arrangements with local promoters for a tour that would start in a few weeks' time. 1981 would mark the beginning of Queen's love affair with South America.

8

EMOTIONAL
DISTRACTIONS

Negotiations continued in Rio as Queen left London to play five sell-out gigs at the Budokan in Tokyo, Japan. The country that had started Queenmania had lost none of its enthusiasm, as shown by the annual polls in *Music Life* magazine. While Mercury and Deacon were voted top of their respective categories, May and Taylor took second place in their sections with Queen bagging the top award for best band. This recognition set them up for their first South American tour, which commenced in February 1981.

Queen were to play seven gigs, including three at the vast Velez Sarfield football ground in Buenos Aires, Argentina, and two at Brazil's Morumbi Stadium in Sao Paulo. The trip certainly proved unusual. Argentina's unstable political climate at that time made concerts by foreign artistes possible targets for terrorist hijackings; before Queen arrived, the Argentinian intelligence service had taken a close interest in the tour. President General Viola also contributed to the heightened sense of occasion by sending a government delegation to greet the group, and the fans' mass hysteria at the airport was televised live on the national news.

Two parties were specially laid on in Buenos Aires for Queen. At the first, held at the home of the president of Vélez Sársfield, the band met the country's soccer demigod Diego Maradona. By the end of the evening, May had swapped his Union Jack T-shirt for Maradona's football shirt. Then they were invited to meet General Viola at his official residence. May, Mercury and Deacon accepted this invitation in the spirit in which it had been extended, but Roger Taylor strongly disagreed with some of the General's political views and chose not to attend.

On opening night, on 28 February, Queen played to 54,000 people at Vélez Sársfield. Prior to setting foot in Argentina, Brian had realistically settled for Queen being received as a curiosity, at best. As Mercury said: 'Queen had no right to expect the works from an alien country.' May was astounded, therefore, to discover that the fans knew the words to practically every song.

The tour trundled from Argentina to Brazil, but it was a transition dogged by problems. Over one hundred tons of expensive equipment had to be road-hauled through dense jungle between the two countries. Logistically this was bad enough, but on arrival at the Brazilian border, with just three days to spare to meet their deadline, the road crew encountered overly bureaucratic customs officials. When the trucks were finally cleared for passage, just thirty-six hours remained before the next show.

Blissfully unaware of the drama, May relaxed with the others in Rio de Janeiro, a city with a rhythm that is redolent of the carefree Brazilian spirit, until they had to move down the coast to Sao Paulo for the gig. That performance at the Morumbi Stadium turned out to be before a crowd of 131,000 – the largest paying audience for one band anywhere in the world at that time. The tour itself also grossed approximately $3.5 million, making the prospect of returning later in the year very appealing.

On 22 May 1981, Chrissy May gave birth to a daughter, Louise. Once again, Brian was thrilled. While Queen's guitarist was immersed in domesticity, at the opposite end of the spectrum its singer was conducting a wildly different love life. Freddie Mercury now picked up where he had left off with Tony Bastin. On tour, the star had been fooling around with men and drugs, and Bastin was not naive enough to believe that Mercury had been faithful to him, but still their relationship continued to thrive. When he chose, Freddie could be very romantic and admitted to feeling intensely vulnerable when he imagined himself to be in love. He would lavish diamonds, luxury cars and substantial sums of cash on his man of the moment. Yet he was also prone to dramatic outpourings on the raw deal he believed he suffered in his affairs of the heart.

'Love is Russian roulette for me,' he once mourned. 'No one loves the real me inside. They're all in love with my fame, my stardom.' On the whole, he may well have been correct, but since he could commit serial infidelity from within a relationship, he contributed greatly to the emotional hollowness of which he often complained. That said, his passion for Tony Bastin endured for several months more.

By early summer, Brian had left his family at home in Britain to begin work on Queen's next album at Mountain Studios where David Bowie, a Montreux resident, began dropping by. One day, an impromptu jam session started. No one thought much of it until they realised that they were co-writing a song. 'Under Pressure' was finalised a couple of months later in New York and released in October. Bowie subsequently felt that with more work the single could have been even better, but his fans and Queen's loved it and it catapulted to the top of the charts.

Before that, Freddie celebrated his thirty-fifth birthday, on 5 September, in spectacular style. Although he had recently purchased a luxury apartment in New York, he took over an entire floor of the Berkshire Hotel in which to host the event there, and flew several of his closest friends over to America by

Concorde. Typically lavish, the birthday party went on non-stop for five days.

Queen regrouped mid-month in New Orleans to rehearse for their return trip to South America. With its first date at the Poliedro de Caracas in Venezuela the tour was called 'Gluttons for Punishment', which turned out to be apt. Touring the world inevitably exposes stars to unusual media experiences, but one appearance on a live Venezuelan TV show must rank, for Queen, among the strangest. The show featured a string of lookalike pop stars, and when Queen were announced there was confusion about whether or not they were the real thing.

Freddie Mercury had refused point-blank to appear and so May led the others on stage. He was already starting to feel like a prize prat when the show degenerated into farce as an excitable man rushed on camera, grabbed the microphone and announced that the statesman Romulo Ethancourt had died. A two-minute silence was ordered. Moments later, a second man rushed on and announced that Ethancourt had not died at all! As all this happened in rapid Spanish, Brian, Roger and John hadn't a clue what was going on and could only squirm with embarrassment.

More serious than being shown up on live TV was the fact that Romulo Ethancourt did die later that night, a development that plunged the country into mourning. Airports closed, stranding Queen, with their gigs cancelled, in the middle of a politically inflammatory situation. The country was ripe for revolution and it was easy to believe shady tales that people, particularly foreigners, were vanishing off the streets. There was great relief, therefore, when the airport reopened, allowing the band to hightail it back to safety.

With their nerves still jangling, Queen faced the three forthcoming Mexican dates, due to start in early October, with some trepidation. During the first gig at the Estadion Universitano in Monterey, the audience began pelting them with rubbish. Dejectedly, May concluded that the audience surely hated them. His height made him an ideal target and he spent the entire performance darting about to avoid being injured by the volley of shoes, bottles, stones and acid-filled batteries which were homing in on Queen with alarming accuracy. Fleeing the stage at the end of the show, it felt nothing short of the worst reception of their careers. They were astounded when gleeful officials rushed into their dressing room to congratulate them. Apparently, the crowd's behaviour was the traditional show of appreciation.

The band was ensconced in New York in time for the UK October release of their *Greatest Flix* video – a compilation of all their singles videos since 'Bohemian Rhapsody'. They felt it was fitting as the first in a series of special releases to mark the band's tenth anniversary. *Greatest Pix* followed, a book of photographs compiled by Jacques Lowe, then came the *Greatest Hits* album in November, and Queen rounded off their celebrations with two gigs at the Forum in Montreal.

By early December, Queen had returned to Munich, a city which became almost a second home to Brian right then. Accustomed to suffering from a continual sense of claustrophobia, he felt that the time spent in Munich was different. There was even time to get to know some of the locals and to visit night-clubs and discos like the Sugar Shack, which became a favourite haunt. Too many late nights, however, soon began to take their toll, and for a while May turned up at the recording studio each day tired. He later confessed that, during that spell in Munich, for himself and for Mercury the 'emotional distractions', as he called them, became destructive.

As ever, Freddie took things to the nth degree, plunging head-long into the so-called 'Bermuda Triangle' of the city's crowded gay scene, which he found appreciably more relaxed and open than in London. Mercury had taken an apartment in Munich and installed his retinue of attendants to ensure that his life ran smoothly. Personal assistants always accompanied him through the chaos of the heaving nightclubs and they witnessed, first-hand, the full extent of the star's unbridled indulgence. Relentless partying required a lot of stamina, and Mercury was using cocaine heavily, just to make it through each night.

The only woman, apart from Mary Austin, to occupy a special place in Freddie's heart was German actress Barbara Valentin, whom he met one night in a Munich disco. Herself a cult figure, known for her work with film director Rainer Werner Fassbinder, she was popular in gay circles. Says Barbara: 'I adored Freddie. We fitted together absolutely instantly, and we never separated for three whole days. He stayed at my house, I went to the studio with him, and we went out to the clubs together. We talked all the time and Freddie told me: "My God! Finally, I can talk to someone who understands the real me and what I want to do with my life." That was something he was needing badly. I loved him and he loved me. It was a once in a lifetime thing between us, so special.'

Cruising the Bermuda Triangle with Freddie, Barbara Valentin saw how many men, looking for rich pickings, homed in on the Queen frontman the second he walked through the door but Mercury was nobody's fool. He did nothing he did not want to do and he enjoyed stringing along a few men at a time. Later he would invite them back to his apartment where the tables turned as Mercury indulged in one of his favourite games. His groupies were to strip naked and parade before him in nothing but a selection of women's hats. He would ultimately select his bedmate and summarily dismiss the others.

By the end of January 1982, like the others, Brian May realised that there had to be a definite return to discipline, but he still found time to see other acts, and it was when the heavy metal band Def Leppard were playing in Munich that lead singer Joe Elliott first met May. Says Joe: 'It was backstage. Queen were working on their album *Hot Space* at the time. Def Lepp were supporting Ritchie Blackmore's band Rainbow, and Brian came along to see Rainbow, I assume. That first meeting was astonishing for me. The door of our dressing room opened and in walks this guy wearing a black jacket, black jeans and white clogs and he says: "Hi, guys. I'm Brian May from Queen," as if we didn't bleedin' well know! He was so very humble, genuinely humble. I mean, he wasn't making a great entrance or anything like that. He was introduced to everyone and spent ages talking to us and listening to us. He was really sincere. It's often made me laugh since. You get bands who are really nobodys and yet they get away above themselves, and here was Brian from Queen being like that. It was a good lesson in life to us. I reckon Brian has been a yardstick in that way.'

In spring, Queen embarked on the first of their touring commitments that would span the next eight months. By the time they arrived in France, their latest single, 'Body Language', had reached only number twenty-five in the UK charts. The fans' coolness was also reflected at performances. Perhaps too much time had recently been spent in Munich's clubland, for the band seemed unduly influenced by the unchallenging funky disco sound. Experimenting with rhythmic rock was the official line, but long-standing devotees were difficult to mollify. They could only be further upset when the album *Hot Space* finally emerged in May.

Gone was the familiarity of Brian's dominant hard rock guitar work, to be replaced by the unloved synthesiser. May was not terribly keen on the album; unusually, he publicly admitted as much, though he did defend Queen's decision to experiment with new musical forms. Possibly to boost this dip in their popularity, in mid-June, for the first time in five years, Queen appeared on *Top of the Pops*, performing their new release 'Las Palabras de Amor (The Words of Love)'.

Weeks later, the band embarked on another of those gruelling Canadian/US trips that involved playing almost every night, in nearly every state; it was punctuated with frequent wild parties. By this time, Mercury was freely admitting that he had begun to hate the tours. In contrast to his days of posturing in saucy leotards, his stage act had become much more energetic. For the entire show, he would rush around the stage, running up and down open flights of stairs – all of which was extremely draining. The financial incentive for the band, too, had gone.

Starting at the Forum in Montreal, the tour ended at the Los Angeles Forum in mid-September 1982. Little did they realise, but it was to be Queen's last ever American tour. Brian was bone weary, but with barely time to draw breath the band took off again for a six-date jaunt around Japan, culminating with a massive outdoor gig at Tokyo's Seibu Lions Stadium. Queen then returned to the UK to enter into protracted, though ultimately fruitless, negotiations with Elektra Records over the renewal of their contract. In December, as an interim measure, they signed all albums to EMI.

Splitting from the US record label coincided with Queen's decision to take a year off. Behind closed doors, it had been brewing for a while. Living and working so closely for twelve years had taken its toll, with serious arguments within the band becoming a regular feature. Individually they were exhausted, and their nerves were stretched to the limit. If they hoped to survive as a band, they needed a rest from each other. When it emerged that they would not be touring for the next twelve months speculation in the music press was rife that Queen were disbanding, but Mercury declared: 'It's got to the point where we're actually too old to break up. Can you imagine forming a new band at forty? Be a bit silly, wouldn't it?'

Stepping off the touring treadmill for 1983 was a smart move as far as Brian May was concerned; the opportunity to stand back and take a long look at themselves was invaluable. There had always been tension in the band. Often not one of the four liked the same things musically, and the resulting tussle to find common ground led to forceful disagreements that had grown worse during the making of their last album. May has admitted that, in these situations, he was perhaps the most stubborn one of them all. He knew that it was not the end of Queen. Even allowing for the strain, what they had was too precious. It was interesting to see, however, what opportunities could open up to him in the line of solo projects.

On that front, Freddie had booked time at Musicland Studios with Mack. He had nurtured aspirations of creating music without Queen for some time. While in Munich, Mercury also met producer Giorgio Moroder who invited him to collaborate on some music for a remake of the classic silent fantasy *Metropolis*. Generally living it up, at one point he attracted talk that he had been involved in a club brawl. These rumours were swiftly scotched, but when his jealousy was aroused, for all his foppish front, Freddie could be aggressive. His drug intake shoulders some of the responsibility for his violent tendencies, and it was becoming hard for friends to predict his moods. He was capable of flying into sudden uncontrollable rages, when he would demolish furniture and roar abusively at the top of his voice. Afterwards, he would remember nothing. Reports that once, in the grip of a drug-crazed sexual frenzy, the singer tried to strangle Barbara Valentin are not true, however. 'That just never happened,' insists Valentin. 'I don't know where that story came from.'

The rest of Queen preferred to lead less dramatic lives. John Deacon relaxed at last into steady family life. He had little inclination to make solo recordings, although he enjoyed occasionally jamming with friends. Roger Taylor, meanwhile, was busy making harmless mischief. As a way of livening up a brief stay in Scotland, along with his personal assistant, Crystal Taylor, the drummer tried playing tricks on Aviemore residents by posing as a door-to-door salesman, waiting to see how long it would take the house-holders to twig his true identity. The joke ended up on Taylor, for no one recognised him. Soon he quit the Highland ski resort for Switzerland, where Deacon later joined him at Mountain Studios to help lay down some tracks.

Brian and Chrissy had gone to Paris. It had been a while since they had been able to spend any uninterrupted length of time together, and the holiday went a long way towards uncoiling some of the tension that had been building in them both. Invigoratingly, too, May found ideas coming to him for a solo album, and the lure of the recording studio began to beckon. When he flew to America, Chrissy went with him. So too did his Red Special, which caused some problems at Orly Airport when he tried to take it on board the plane as hand luggage. Unwilling to deliver it into the clutches of the busy baggage handlers, and because it was too big to be stowed away in the overhead lockers, Brian had to pay for an extra seat for the unique guitar.

Soon after his arrival in Los Angeles, Brian met up with a friend, American vocalist Jeffrey Osborne. Osborne was in the middle of recording an album at the Mad Hatter Studios and asked May if he would guest on a couple of tracks. Brian features on 'Two Wrongs Don't Make a Right' and 'Stay with Me Tonight'; the latter single made it into the UK top twenty the following spring.

With his appetite whetted again for studio work, Brian rang around some friends who were staying in Los Angeles at the time to invite them to knock about some musical ideas. In late April, guitarist Eddie Van Halen, keyboard player Fred Mandell, bassist Philip Chen and Alan Gratzer, drummer with Reo Speedwagon, all turned up at Record Plant Studios to see what May had in mind.

Brian encouraged the guys to play whatever sprang to mind, be it jazz, blues or hard rock, while he kept tapes running. Once settled in, he channelled the melting-pot of talent at his disposal away from twelve-bar blues, towards something more specific. Brian had come up with his own arrangement of the theme tune to *Star Fleet*, his son Jimmy's favourite TV sci-fi series. As the day progressed the scratch band played this number, as well as a number of Brian's called 'Let Me Out', which he had written years earlier. Ending with a meaty blues jam, they had found the workout stimulating. May was not convinced that he had anything of note on tape but on the off-chance that he would like it later, before his friends left he secured their respective permissions to do a bit of work and future mixing on the tracks.

Not long after this studio jam, Brian flew back to Britain. Polydor Records had asked him to produce one of their newest signings, a Scottish group called Heavy Pettin'. May had co-produced Queen records, but had never produced anyone else. Nevertheless, he accepted the task and set to work at the Town House Studios in west London on the band's debut album, *Letting Loose*. He called in Mack, which gave him the scope to try out new ideas, secure in the knowledge that an experienced producer could step in if he got into any difficulties.

Although Queen had gone their separate ways, they remained in touch, and in July they got together at the instigation of manager Jim Beach. With links to the film world, Beach had a proposition for the band. A film of John Irving's novel *The Hotel New Hampshire* was in the works, starring Rob Lowe and Jodie Foster. Queen were asked to record the soundtrack. This prospect brought it home to all four how much they had missed recording together. The following month, Queen met at Record Plant

Studios in Los Angeles. They had never recorded together in America, and the novelty of this, combined with the break from each other, rejuvenated them.

While in Los Angeles, Brian got the chance to catch up with his friend Joe Elliott when he went along to see Def Leppard appearing at the Forum. This time, though, he joined the band on stage. Says Joe: 'Brian got up with David Lee Roth and a couple of others and jammed with us. It was great. That night he played the old Creedence Clearwater Revival number "Travellin' Band", and it was out of this world! Brian had actually brought his guitar and amp with him, yet when we invited him up he was a bit unsure at first, but we dragged him up by his curly hair, did a sound check and we were off!' May later said of Def Leppard: 'I was bowled over by them. Their show was one of the highest energy things I have ever seen. They just destroyed the place.'

Lately taking stock of his life, May had begun to wonder if he was capable of functioning outside Queen. In a way, that had been in his mind back in the spring when he had rounded up a few of his friends at Record Plant Studios. Now, the fruits of that experiment were to be tried out on the public as his first solo single, 'Star Fleet', a cover version of the song written by Paul Bliss, was released in Britain in late October. Despite the number featuring some powerful guitar work from both May and Eddie Van Halen, the disc received no daytime radio airplay; consequently it stalled at number sixty-five and remained in the charts a mere three weeks.

Work on the soundtrack for the film of *The Hotel New Hampshire* was also proving disappointing. Tailoring their music to the novel was not easy and their initial enthusiasm had steadily evaporated. Queen had faith in the material itself, so for a while were determined to persevere with the task, but, when it was obviously a lost cause, they regretfully pulled out of the project.

Brian's debut solo album, *Starfleet Project*, was released at the end of October 1983 in the UK. It was a mini-LP featuring just three tracks – the full eight-minute version of 'Star Fleet', 'Let Me Out', and an indulgent 12-minute blues jam now entitled 'Bluesbreaker', which Brian had dedicated to one of his guitar heroes, Eric Clapton. The album reached number one in the British heavy metal charts.

London's Capital Radio had meanwhile asked May to participate in a new series. Capital's Head of Music was Tony Hale, who recalls: 'At the time, we were recording what was called *Rock Master Class*. I presented and produced the programmes, which were to feature, besides Brian May, Rick Wakeman, John Entwistle, Steve Howe and Midge Ure. In essence, each programme was an extended interview with the artiste in front of an invited audience of about six hundred people in the Duke of York's Theatre. Answers were played, as well as spoken. As part of the show, two young players were taken through a piece with "The Master". For his programme, Brian chose a pavane. The two young guitarists were given tips and at the end of the show, along with Brian, they played the whole thing all the way through.' Brian's programme was broadcast live on 20 November 1983 and formed part of an all-round successful series.

Queen had recently signed to the US label Capitol Records and were concentrating on recording their new album at Musicland Studios in Munich, with a release date set for early in the new year. The first cut from the album was to be a Roger Taylor number, 'Radio Ga Ga'. On release in January it went in to the UK charts at number four, rising two places, but was ultimately denied the top slot by the Frankie Goes to Hollywood number, 'Relax'. It marked another milestone within the band, however, as now all four members had penned a top ten hit. This success was briefly marred a week later, though, with an incident in Italy during Queen's first live performance in fifteen months.

At the beginning of February, Queen headlined at an annual music festival in San Remo, at which a backstage row erupted between Brian May and Roger Taylor, almost resulting in a physical fight between the two friends. When later asked about this, Freddie Mercury described it as a 'very heavy scene' that developed from some tomfoolery. 'It was Roger squirting Brian in the face with hairspray or something,' he said. 'They nearly came to blows. It was a very tiny dressing room, very hot, and the whole thing just snowballed.'

Quick to recognise the potential gravity of the situation, Mercury leapt between the feuding men and mercilessly poked fun at them. Initially, neither May nor Taylor was remotely in the mood for Mercury's antics, which could have fanned the flames, but he was so relentless that they eventually dissolved into laughter, and sanity returned. Onlookers have since credited Freddie with more than rescuing the moment, convinced that, in fact, he had saved the entire future of Queen.

Out front, the crowd, oblivious to the carryings-on, had been enjoying a succession of bands throughout the evening and had now begun to chant for the headliners. The two thousand delirious Italians went berserk during 'Radio Ga Ga'. Keen to keep up the momentum, Capitol Records quickly released the song as their label's first Queen single. It made number sixteen in the US charts, and in nineteen other countries it seized the number one slot.

Having learnt the lessons of *Hot Space*, with their new album, *The Works*, Queen gave fans exactly what they wanted – lots of harmonies, a meticulous production and inspired musical arrangements. Above all, the material was far gutsier, mainly thanks to May's insistence; their reward came when in March 1984 it shot into the album charts at number two. Brian was thrilled, and even some of the reviews were good.

In particular, May's 'Hammer to Fall' came in for special praise for its powerful heavy metal sound – credit which Joe Elliott feels is well deserved. 'It is my personal belief that Brian was the big anchor of Queen,' he declares. 'I don't take anything away from the other three, but had it not been for Brian then I think they would have become a pop band and probably not as big as they are. Freddie, I feel, would have leaned more towards ballads and Roger to pop. "Radio Ga Ga" is a terrific Queen number, but very pop. The hard stuff is down to Brian. I think he kept a crucial and unique balance in the band.'

To follow on from 'Radio Ga Ga', the second single from *The Works* was 'I Want to Break Free'. So far, Queen's videos had been imaginative, often outlandish and certainly expensive, but on this occasion they wanted to have fun. *Coronation Street* is the longest-running soap on British television and Roger Taylor suggested that they should dress up as caricatures of the female characters from the show.

There were three separate sequences to the video. The first showed Queen in a crowd of moronic-looking futuristic miners. The second and main section was shot in a Battersea studio, and for this the band dressed up in drag. When asked later how he'd managed to persuade the others to dress in women's clothing, Freddie quipped: 'Darling, they ran into their frocks quicker than anything!'

Brian became a vision in a long pink nylon nightie, his hair a mass of curlers and beauty cream daubed all over his face. John chose the buttoned-up, disapproving granny look. Roger transformed himself into an alarmingly convincing St Trinian's-type fifth-form schoolgirl, complete with gymslip and stockings. Freddie burst on screen as a busty, brassy sort in a skinny-rib sweater and split-sided PVC miniskirt.

The final sequence involved Mercury working with Royal Ballet principal dancers Wayne Eagling and Derek Deane. Says Eagling:

'Freddie was inspired a lot by ballet. He had wanted for a long time to appear as a great dancer, and this was his chance, so we made him Nijinsky. Trying to choreograph for someone who is not a ballet dancer is difficult and it wasn't easy for Fred but he was determined to get it right.'

Deane picks up: 'Wayne had recreated the ballet *L'après-midi d'un faune* for Freddie, which had been made famous by Nijinsky. It begins with Freddie looking as if he is sitting on a rock but it's really made up of a pile of bodies, which one by one come to life. Later, there is a shot of Freddie rolling on his stomach on top of a line of rotating bodies along the floor. Now he *loved* that bit!'

The critics had fun, too, when the video for 'I Want to Break Free' was released in early April. It was obviously meant as a lark and Queen were not the first band to dress up for fun. The Rolling Stones had caused an outcry by doing it in 1966 for their rocker 'Have You Seen Your Mother, Baby', when Brian Jones transformed himself into a sexy blonde bombshell in uniform. Yet, eighteen years on, shouts of transvestism still rang out. Despite this, Queen's new single reached number three in Britain, was a big hit in Europe and went to the top in many countries. Some South American countries even adopted it as a freedom anthem.

It was a different story elsewhere by summer 1984, when Queen stirred up a hornet's nest by announcing that they intended to play at the Sun City Super Bowl in South Africa. This immediately antagonised the Musicians Union, anti-apartheid groups and the press. Brian plainly stated to the media: 'We have thought about the morals of it a lot and it is something we have decided to do. This band is not political. We play to anybody who comes to listen. The show will be in Botswana in front of a mixed audience.'

The *Works* tour started in Belgium in late August and welcomed among its session men newcomer Spike Edney, who had lately worked with the Boomtown Rats. Says Spike: 'I was introduced to Queen through Roger's personal assistant, Crystal, who said they were looking to replace Fred Mandell and asked if I was interested. Queen invited me to an audition in Munich and I went thinking there would be a queue of applicants, only to find I was the only one. I knew all their stuff anyway, so that was me in. I was more or less with Queen from that tour right through to Knebworth, two years later.'

In September, after Queen played a four-date stint at London's Wembley Arena, the hard-rocking number 'Hammer to Fall' became their twenty-sixth single and was redolent of what drives Brian May most in music. He has confessed that the heavy side of it is a release of emotion and that what he loves best about rock is its meaty sound. He had endeavoured to stamp good old-fashioned rock into *The Works* album and once revealed: 'The pressure has always been against me, because not everyone in the band is into the same stuff as I am. I get the most pleasure out of the things that I can hammer down and get some excitement out of. Basically, I'm like a boy with a guitar. I just love the fat, loud sound of it.'

It was while belting out 'Hammer to Fall' a fortnight later in Hanover, Germany, that Mercury slipped awkwardly on a flight of stairs. He carried on with the show, but when doctors examined him later it was clear that he had damaged some knee ligaments. He was advised against performing but, with a handful of dates remaining, he ignored their warnings and finished the tour. Five days later, Queen landed in Bophuthatswana.

Tickets for their dozen dates at the Sun City Super Bowl had sold out in a day. However, on the first night Mercury was scarcely warmed up, when his voice, which had lately been troublesome, threatened to seize up. Aware that he was in difficulty, the rest of the band tried to rally him, but his voice got worse. Spike Edney recalls: 'Fred was in agony and after three songs he walked off stage.' A specialist strongly advised Mercury to take a complete rest and the band had no option but to cancel the following four nights. 'It caused a big scandal because there was no time to reschedule dates, but it just could not be helped,' explains Edney.

Upset at the turn of events, Brian May decided to use the free time to go and talk with some black South Africans. He wanted to see life in this country for himself. In October, Soweto – the black township on the outskirts of Johannesburg – was where the annual Black African Awards shows were to be held. Brian accepted an invitation to attend and present some of the prizes.

That night made a lasting impression on him. It was muggy, and warm rain fell on his face as he stood on the bare stage in the open muddy field before an audience of thousands, handing out awards. For all the dire warnings over his personal safety pressed on him back at Sun City, he met with nothing but warmth and unmitigated friendliness. It moved him, and before he left he pledged from the stage that one day Queen would come back to Soweto and play for them.

Spike Edney recalls: 'We had all been very happy to have the chance to play South Africa and it was quite an experience. For one thing, it teaches you not to listen to people pontificating about something that they really know nothing about. Personally speaking, before I went there I was very sure about what I felt about South Africa. When I came home, I didn't know anything any more – the visit had altered my whole way of looking at things. For Brian and the others, it was definitely an enlightening experience.'

Not everyone, though, was convinced that Queen had truly understood the complex political implications involved. Mandla Langa, cultural attaché and an ANC spokesperson, says: 'People were infuriated. Queen came into South Africa at a time when we did not need any external influence that could lend respectability to the Pretoria regime. Sun City was always regarded as an insult to any right-thinking South African and to perform there, in the midst of poverty and rage, cannot be rationalised as Queen doing their bit to break down barriers. The people who attended those concerts were overwhelmingly white, and institutions such as the South African Broadcasting Corporation revelled at their new-found connection with the Western world and gave Queen maximum airplay. People here have long memories, and their music has never been embraced by black activists.'

Queen were placed on the United Nations blacklist of musicians who performed in South Africa – although their name was later removed – and in Britain the Musicians Union came down hard on them for flouting the rules. May went to face the Union's General Committee on the band's behalf and gave a lengthy and impassioned speech, detailing Queen's reasons for the trip and stressing how much he felt they had achieved. He also stressed that they were totally against apartheid but that they did not feel anything was achieved by just not playing there. Music, he maintained, should be the universal language transcending all barriers. By going to South Africa and speaking out against apartheid, they were trying to do something practical about the problem. The Committee was unmoved and fined Queen heavily.

With these problems behind them, Queen began work at Sarm Studios in London on their first attempt at a Christmas single. 'Thank God It's Christmas' was released in late November but failed to reach the top twenty. The battle for that year's Christmas number one was won as soon as it had begun, for 1984 was the year Band Aid emerged with their charity single, 'Do They Know It's Christmas'. In December, Queen released a batch of singles, all individual tracks from one album. Critics attacked them for exploiting their fans' devotion – all of which created a sour note on which to end their first year performing as a band again.

9

A SPARK IGNITES

In January 1985, 'Rock in Rio', a rock festival to be staged at a custom-built arena in the mountains at Barra da Tijuca, near Rio de Janeiro, was expected to outshine the famous Woodstock of sixteen years earlier. Queen were to headline the event and other guests on the star-studded bill included AC/DC, Ozzie Osbourne, Yes and Iron Maiden. Def Leppard were also due to appear, but had to pull out at the eleventh hour due to a horrific road accident on New Year's Eve in which their drummer Rick Allen lost an arm. For Iron Maiden's lead singer, Bruce Dickinson, the festival was a total eye-opener.

'The whole thing was an incredible circus,' he recalls. 'There were crowds besieging hotels, long-lens cameras poking into the poolsides and everything. The festival was run by a right-wing politician-cum-entrepreneur and there had been a succession of serious disagreements with the local socialist party over the event. That is why it had to be held outside the city, and the stadium was left to rot afterwards. A lot of money laundering went on during "Rock in Rio". Let's face it, with something like half a million people in a field, it is a great place to pass off dirty money.'

With a hugely energetic delivery, Iron Maiden's stage act was spectacular, with elaborate lighting effects to rival Queen's. Iron Maiden's single performance came directly before Queen closed the first gig in the early hours of 12 January. 'Everyone was helicoptered in to the site,' recalls Dickinson, 'but because of the opposition from town they were not allowed to fly at night, so it was, like, five hours getting back in traffic afterwards. Anyway, once there, we found a set-up like we had never seen. There were roving gangs of security guards, all of whom looked in really bad moods.'

The show was running behind time but, on top of that, Iron Maiden were fifteen minutes late in getting on stage. Dickinson explains: 'It was all pretty hairy. There was a furious row going on in the hallway, right outside our dressing room. Two gangs of security guards were going mental, waving pistols at each other, and their guard dogs were all snarling viciously and tugging on their leads. We were hiding like cowards, scared to step outside. Then, like something out of *Monty Python*, our own security guy eventually poked his head cautiously round the door and said: "Hey guys? Would you mind giving it a rest until we get on stage?" And they did! They all shut up, and we hurried past, but as soon as our backs were turned, it all started up again!'

When Queen followed Iron Maiden on stage Bruce watched their performance, which did not go according to plan. He says: 'Two or three of their numbers did not go down well with the crowd. Then, when they launched into "I Want to Break Free", they didn't really take to Freddie dressing up in women's clothes, but Freddie obviously didn't understand what was wrong.'

In Mexico, an audience had hurled rubbish at Queen as their show of appreciation but the rubble now rained down on them alarmingly. Hiding their confusion, Queen worked hard to ensure that they earned encores, but the apparent confidence with which Mercury strode the Brazilian stage belied his inner distress, as Bruce Dickinson reveals: 'When Queen came off stage, Freddie immediately broke down in tears. He just had no idea why the audience had reacted like they did. Someone quickly explained to him that "I Want to Break Free" was regarded as a freedom song there, and they had resented him sending it up, but he was very upset.'

It surprised Iron Maiden's singer that Mercury should have taken this negative reaction quite so much to heart. No band expects to be always universally adored, and in one important quarter Queen were already experiencing their popularity draining away. Says Bruce: 'There is a white, homophobic, bonehead bunch of people in the States, and there was a large minority who had kind of worked out that Freddie wasn't one of us, if you know what I mean? When that minority grew, it put the lights out for Queen in America for a time.'

Brian May does not disagree. He has stated of 'I Want to Break Free': 'It single-handedly ruined our career in America.' He recalled being on a promo tour of the US and the reaction the send-up video received from the producers at one TV station: 'Their faces went green and they took it off after about a minute saying: "Well, that's enough of that! Moving on . . ."'

When Queen closed the festival in the early hours of 19 January, there was not a false bust or tousled wig in sight. Spike Edney insists: 'The whole thing was treated as a holiday really, with loads of stars hangin' by the hotel pools and all that. What "Rock in Rio" did, though, was reaffirm Queen's standing as South America's top band.'

Shortly after Queen returned to Britain, Brian was approached by Michael Stimpson, guitar tutor at Roehampton Institute, who was writing a book entitled *The Guitar: A Guide for Students and Teachers*, which explained various techniques including classical, lead, bass, folk, flamenco and jazz guitar. He asked May to write a chapter for the book. Says Michael: 'I wanted to include a chapter on electric guitar because one of the main fields of my work was to encourage the acceptance and teaching of the guitar in a way which reflects its affinity with different musical genres.

In other words, it was well overdue that guitar teaching in schools and colleges was moved away from a purely classical approach.' To coincide with the book's publication in 1988 BBC TV made a short film, to which May also contributed, about Michael Stimpson's work.

In April 1985, Queen hit the road again. Their first tour date of the year was at Mount Smart Stadium in Auckland. May was excited by the prospect because they had never played in New Zealand before, but his anticipation was marred when Queen were harangued at the airport and outside their hotel by groups of anti-apartheid demonstrators. More noisy protesters were lying in wait for the band outside the concert venue. Having played in South Africa looked likely to haunt their career for a while to come.

However, while down under Queen received an intriguing invitation. Spike Edney recalls: 'I had briefly rejoined the Boomtown Rats between Queen's *Works* tour and them going to Australia and New Zealand, and Bob Geldof rang me up in New Zealand. He was going on about an idea he and Midge Ure had to follow up the Band Aid single with a massive rock concert, and he wanted to know if Queen would appear on the bill. He didn't want to officially ask them in case they said no, so he asked if I would speak to them about it.' Spike did, but although Queen were taken with the idea in principle, the project seemed unlikely ever to come to fruition and they refused initially. Says Edney: 'I know that Brian and Roger had been disappointed not to have been asked the previous year to be involved in the "Do They Know It's Christmas" single, so I wasn't surprised personally that their first reaction was to be all for it but when they thought about it, Queen were sceptical of this thing coming off, and who could blame them then?'

When Spike Edney relayed Queen's refusal to Geldof, he tempered it by saying that it might be worthwhile for him to approach the band personally. In the early stages of putting together the Live Aid show, it was not the case that every superstar was clamouring to take part. In the end, Queen said that they would appear if Geldof and Midge Ure did actually pull it off.

Days later Queen were in Australia, and between dates in Melbourne and Sydney, Chrissy arrived to join her husband. Together they flew up to the Great Barrier Reef where they tried their hands at scuba-diving. The couple relished being able to relax for a short while away from the spotlight. From Australia the band headed to Japan for a week-long visit, which would turn out to be their last tour of the Far East. Here Brian spent his spare time helping pupils with guitar techniques at the Aoyama Recording School.

Once back in the UK, in mid-May, all four went their separate ways. Taylor and Deacon each opted for a holiday, while Mercury shuttled back and forth between his beloved Munich and London. By now, Freddie was in a new relationship with a man named Jim Hutton, a barber who was working at the Savoy Hotel.

Meanwhile, May spent time at home with his family, occasionally meeting up with friends, among them Def Leppard's frontman, Joe Elliott. Says Joe: 'I had bought a house about twenty minutes walk from Brian's. Chrissy was from Leeds and my girlfriend was from Sheffield, which meant they found a lot in common. So the four of us would have dinner, the odd drink, or would just pop round to each other's for a chat. Brian is really good company. There's not any feeling of being threatened. There was none of the rivalry that can sometimes set in. One night, at dinner in a restaurant in Cobham, the wine had flowed particularly well. The later it got, the looser tongues grew all round and we very nearly set about making an album. The band was going to be Brian, myself and Rick Savage from Def Lepp, Jason Bonham [son of the late John Bonham of Led Zeppelin] and Spike Edney. Unfortunately, my manager wouldn't allow it to happen.'

By this time the Live Aid project had grown beyond all expectations. From a massive concert in aid of the Ethiopian famine held at Wembley Stadium in the summer, now a parallel gig was to take place at the JFK Stadium in Philadelphia. Bob Geldof had dubbed the event a 'global juke box' and Queen decided they were definitely in. Spike Edney confirms: 'Absolutely! By now, with his forceful personality, Geldof had got the BBC to agree to set up a satellite link to the States, and it was frankly just too good a thing not to be a part of.'

Queen's slot was to start at 6 p.m. With the satellite link-up, this meant that they would be the first band to be seen on live TV in America. On 10 July they holed up at the Shaw Theatre in Euston for three days of intensive rehearsal. Each band had been allocated twenty minutes, and to use this to best advantage Queen opted to restrict their showcase to their most famous hits. 'Later, such a fuss was made about how ingenious Queen had been, but to us it was the obvious thing to do,' Edney recalls.

Mercury, though, was proud of their strategy, as Radio One DJ Simon Bates remembers: 'I interviewed Freddie just prior to Live Aid, and he was particularly proud of the hard work that they were putting into the Queen set. He said to me: "Wait until you see it. You'll be blown away!" And, of course, he was right.'

Live Aid, on 13 July 1985, simultaneously broadcast live to over one billion people worldwide, was the first time a concert on that scale had been attempted. Consequently, nerves were fraught behind the scenes. It was a show that required state-of-the-art equipment, that included a revolving stage, split into three segments, one for the band in performance, one for the next band to set up their equipment and one for the band just finished to dismantle gear. Considering the logistics, it was surprising that six hours into the event, they were running only half an hour late.

Following David Bowie's set, with Wembley hooked up to the JFK Stadium in Philadelphia, Queen came on stage. The sense of occasion had threatened to paralyse May but all four played for all their worth, delivering a punchy, edited medley of their greatest hits, which got the Wembley crowd, Queen fans or not, rocking on their feet; undeniably, Mercury shone the brightest.

Like Brian, Freddie had been extremely nervous but he disguised it well as he blasted into 'Hammer to Fall'. During May's guitar solo, Mercury dug the end of the mike stand into his groin, pretending to play frantic lead guitar along its chrome rod. Quickly, he had begun visibly to enjoy himself. By the time they got to 'Crazy Little Thing Called Love' he was bathed in sweat, and the sheer magnetism of his performance had the audience eating out of his hand. Love him or loathe him, Mercury was untouchable that day, and the watching world knew it.

A fellow performer that day, singer Paul Young, concurs: 'I had always liked Queen, but that was the night I said to myself: these boys really are fantastic. The sound they managed to get was amazing. There was just the four of them on there, with none of their usual trappings and they *still* blew everyone away. Freddie also proved what a showman he was.'

When Queen quit the stage Mercury gasped: 'Thank God, that's over.' and was downing a double vodka in his trailer when Elton John burst in cheerfully yelling: 'You bastards! You stole the show!'

It was a sentiment echoed by almost everyone. Thin Lizzy's lead guitarist Scott Gorham states: 'Man, that was six hours of Euro wimp! Everyone was wondering, God, who asked them along? Then Queen came on, and there's Fred stickin' out his chest and daring the world not to like them. It was amazing, like the rebirth of Queen on the spot. When you'd seen those guys, who wanted to see the rest?'

Despite all the backstage plaudits, it did not actually hit Queen until some time later just how well they had gone down. Brian has admitted: 'It was the greatest day of our lives, although we only played a very small part in it. I think it's the thing I'll remember above all, out of all the things we have done. It was an amazing day.'

Live Aid's effect was far-reaching and the man responsible for it all, in a sense, was the BBC's foreign affairs correspondent, Michael Buerk, whose special televised report on the Ethiopian famine had moved so many. Michael Buerk says: 'When the whole Live Aid thing got going I was in South Africa, the one country which could not have cared less about the starving in Ethiopia. My original feeling, I must admit, was that it was a bandwagon thing that would die out in a week and wouldn't achieve anything in effective terms. I didn't see much connection with the pop world and dying people. Shows you how wrong I was.

'I didn't see the actual concert as South Africa didn't show it but it certainly increased the level of consciousness about the situation, which in turn placed pressure on governments and inter-governmental departments around the world, and that was a good thing. Two million people were estimated to be due to die in that famine and in the end 800,000 did, so Live Aid was at least, in part, responsible for saving over a million lives.'

After Live Aid, Brian was toying with the notion of recording a second solo album but, inspired by their triumph, Queen began collectively to think of going back on the road. They also desperately wanted to return to recording, so it was propitious when director Russell Mulcahy asked if Queen would create music for the Hollywood feature film, *Highlander*, starring Christopher Lambert and Sean Connery.

September saw Queen back in the studio. One track with all-round appeal quickly emerged and became their only single of the year. 'One Vision' was released in early November and, riding on the wave of their renewed popularity, it reached number seven in the UK charts. Critics sharply attacked the number, viewing its lyrics as a Live Aid cash-in, an accusation that hurt.

Another rub was the fact that the row over their Sun City gigs would not completely die away. Every so often something fanned the flames, and so at the end of 1985, Queen issued a press release reasserting their anti-apartheid stance, stating that they were not political and finally that they would never again visit South Africa. May was very upset at having to make this particular pledge because of his promise to the crowd in Soweto that one day Queen would return and perform for them. It seemed, however, the best way to quell the continued attacks.

Brian found a welcome distraction in the intensive work throughout January 1986 on the *Highlander* soundtrack. The songs were to be directly inspired by watching daily rushes from the movie and one day, while driving home, he began to hum into a tape recorder the strains of what would become the evocative ballad, 'Who Wants to Live Forever'.

May's reputation as a lead guitarist tended to overshadow his talent as a lyricist – something Brian has been modest about. He once revealed: 'I'm not a very prolific writer and I can never just sit down and write a song. There has to be something there and usually I get a couple of lines of lyrics and melody together. Then, the rest of it is really working very hard, searching the soul to see what should be in there.'

Joe Elliott believes: 'Brian's "Who Wants to Live Forever" should be like the Moody Blues' "Nights in White Satin" – a classic. It's got that feel. I remember when he wrote it, he presented it to Freddie as a demo and Freddie said: "Hey, that's good! No, no, I'll just come in second," – meaning he thought that Brian should take first lead vocal on it and that he would come in on the second verse. I thought Brian's early stuff was special – like "White Queen" and "39", which I've always felt sounded sort of like Lindisfarne. The thing about Brian is, he is never afraid to experiment.'

On the album's completion, Queen's UK and US labels differed over which single to release first. Capitol Records opted for Mercury's 'Princes of the Universe', while EMI preferred Roger Taylor's 'A Kind of Magic', which was also the album title track. Both accompanying videos were impressive in their individual ways.

For 'Princes of the Universe' *Highlander*'s star, Christopher Lambert, agreed to recreate his screen character to enjoin battle against Freddie Mercury. For 'A Kind of Magic', Mercury portrayed a magician who temporarily transforms three vagrants into rock stars. Its sophisticated animation guaranteed its unique appeal, and when 'A Kind of Magic' was released mid-March, it made number three in Britain and topped the charts in thirty-five other countries. The album release, to be backed by a major tour, was set for summer and in the intervening time again the band dispersed.

By now, Brian's home life was far from happy. For some time, he and Chrissy had known that things were not right between them and that they had both been papering over the cracks, neither willing to accept that their problems were multiplying. They had been married for almost ten years and had two children whom they both adored. Neither wanted to threaten their stability, if it could be avoided.

In some ways, it was a relief when Queen had to knuckle down to rehearsals for their forthcoming European tour but it was during a break in these, when May attended the London premiere of the film *Down and Out in Beverly Hills*, that fate brought him into contact with actress Anita Dobson.

Born in Stepney, London, in 1949 and trained at the Webber Douglas Academy of Dramatic Arts, Anita began her television career in the late 1970s. Her first starring role was playing Lois Tight in the 1983 situation comedy, *Up the Elephant and Round the Castle*, but by 1986 she had firmly established herself as Angie Watts, the feisty and emotionally battered landlady of the Queen Vic pub in the BBC TV soap *EastEnders*. She was dark-haired, petite, elfin-faced and extremely vivacious. Something clicked between Brian and Anita and, on impulse, he invited her to come and see Queen when they performed at Wembley Stadium in June.

At the start of that month *A Kind of Magic*, the soundtrack album from *Highlander* was released, entering the UK charts at number one. Days later, the band kicked off what would turn out to be their last tour. Called the Magic tour, it began at the Rasunda Fotbollstadion in Stockholm, culminating two months later with a massive outdoor gig at Knebworth Park in Stevenage; it proved eventful from beginning to end.

Much to May's dismay, regardless of the clear press statement they had issued six months earlier, when they arrived at the Stockholm venue for their first gig, Queen were confronted by a pack of chanting anti-apartheid protesters. A couple of days later their new single, the gentle, lilting ballad 'Friends Will Be Friends' was released in Britain. Brian, meanwhile, was spending a free day in a Dutch recording studio to prepare demos of two songs; one song was for Japanese singer Minako Honda and the other for Anita Dobson, whom he found was lingering in his mind. The tour then moved on into France.

It was in Paris that Fish, lead singer with the band Marillion, first got to know Brian. He says: 'Marillion had gone out to support Queen on the open-air gigs in that '86 tour, which in fact ended up being the last live dates that they would do, and, of course, Freddie was Freddie and kept himself very much to himself. Brian and I got talking. It's funny, because normally I don't get on with guitarists – not because I've got anything against them, but because of the personality types that guitarists normally are. Brian, though, isn't an egocentric guitarist who will sit and discuss pick-ups for two hours!

'Brian is a painful romantic and quite excruciatingly sensitive. He doesn't get angry. He gets hurt, very easily. He was hurting that night we first got talking. It was in a Paris nightclub and he sat and talked to me about South Africa and apartheid, all the pros and cons of playing Sun City which Queen were still copping an awful lot of flak for. Brian was deeply hurt by the furore. We both agreed that the straightforward blacklisting by the UN was out of order. That's what our talk revolved around for two hours solid and I was quite impressed at how much Brian had actually thought it all through, but then he's that sort of person. He churns things over in his head for hours and hours.'

Brian and Fish got along well, and to some extent it helped with May's personal problems, too. 'Yeah, his marriage was in trouble at this point,' Fish admits, 'and Brian was really going through it. We talked quite a lot about it during that tour. He was questioning: was it right, was it worth taking all this grief for? He was extremely tortured by it.'

After France, the tour trundled on through Germany and Switzerland to Ireland, then to Britain with a gig in the north of England before a two-night slot at London's Wembley Stadium on 11 and 12 July. Both were classic nights. Over the years, Mercury had dazzled fans with his stage-wear, antics that he once laughed aside saying: 'It's just theatre. I do love a nice frock!'

Ending the final encore with 'We Are the Champions', with the fans already in a frenzy, Mercury punched one fist triumphantly in the air, spun on his heels and careered off stage. He returned draped in a stunning red velvet silk-lined robe, trimmed with fake ermine and with a six-foot train. Cradling his sawn-off mike stand as a sceptre, he wore a jewel-encrusted coronation crown on his head. Naff maybe, but Freddie pulled it off and was proud to receive the fans' homage.

One special guest attending the first Wembley gig was Formula One motor racing champion Sir Jackie Stewart, who had been invited along by John Deacon. Stewart had known Queen since the mid-1970s. Says Jackie: 'It's a curious thing – music and motor racing. There always seems to be a link. George Harrison was a big fan of racing and Paul McCartney used to come to the Monaco Grand Prix, as did some of the Rolling Stones. Roger Taylor, of course, is mad keen on cars and had been to quite a few races. I'd always enjoyed Queen's music and had been to a few of their concerts.'

For Jackie Stewart, that night's performance at Wembley was exceptional, and to a great extent he feels this was down to Brian May. He says: 'What Queen created was an extraordinary thing, and there are no copies – nobody else was able to do what they have done. I call them sound merchants. They conjure up an individual sound instrumentally, and Brian's contribution to that is immense. He is so unique and very identifiable. I don't care which country you're in, you can always tell when you're hearing Brian May playing.'

Energised by their shows, Queen's post-Wembley knees-up at the Roof Garden above Kensington High Street carved its own place in the band's mythology. Over five hundred guests circulated in the roof-top restaurant, landscaped like a garden. Celebrity guests included Sir Cliff Richard, Spandau Ballet and Fish who were well acquainted with the band's reputation for laying on exotic entertainment. Anticipation was high, and no one was disappointed.

Sir Cliff Richard recalls meeting Freddie Mercury for the first time that night at the Roof Garden party: 'I have to say that previously, I had never been a fan of Freddie's in terms of his kind of vocals but I certainly admired his ability, including his skill on the piano and, of course, he was such an extrovert showman. Just the year before when Queen did Live Aid, although I myself couldn't take part as I was committed to a gospel charity gig in Birmingham, I managed to see snatches of the show and the second I saw Freddie launch into their act, it was obvious that Queen were going to steal the show. When they returned to Wembley during their Magic tour, I couldn't go to see them because I was on stage with Time but they invited me to their after show party. These kinds of parties are always the same – crowds of people, most of whom spend hours lining up to meet the star for usually no more than minutes, so it is not really conducive to getting to know someone.'

The European tour carried on. When Queen reached Hungary for a gig at Nepstadion in Budapest, they played to a capacity crowd with a huge number of ticketless fans hanging around outside the venue. May and Mercury had learnt a couple of verses of the traditional folk song, 'Tavaski Szel'. Much was subsequently made of this gig, with claims of Queen's performances making history as the first rock show behind the Iron Curtain. Certainly, their appearance there would have been historic in terms of their own careers – but not in rock music. Nineteen years earlier, the Rolling Stones had played the Palace of Culture in Warsaw.

What did become a landmark gig in Queen's career was the Magic Tour's final date on 9 August 1986 at Knebworth Park, Hertfordshire, before a crowd of about 200,000. Held in 247 acres of magnificent parkland, against the backdrop of the romantic castellations of Knebworth House, it was to be Queen's last live performance.

Spike Edney recalls: 'The demand to see Queen had been strong enough to have staged a third night at Wembley, but that couldn't be arranged.' Tour manager Gerry Stickells had suggested an outdoor gig at Knebworth and the band agreed, provided that they were guaranteed a sell-out crowd.

Several rock groups had performed at Knebworth, including the Rolling Stones and Led Zeppelin. Lady Chryssie Cobbold, whose family owns the estate, remembers Queen as being different from the others. She says: 'We have often entertained the groups before, during or after their concerts, but in the case of Queen, they were not interested in coming up to the house.'

Spike Edney recalls of the gig itself: 'It was an amazing day. We had never played to such a large audience in the UK before, and it was incredible. No one knew at the time, of course, that it would be Queen's last ever gig.' The party afterwards stands out, too. 'It was the usual Queen extravaganza, with everything from a fairground to female mud wrestlers.'

The band had been helicoptered in and out. Mercury, who had been especially uptight before this performance, was the first to leave. Lady Cobbold confirms: 'There was a backstage party after the concert, but Freddie left straight after finishing the gig.' He had closed Knebworth with the words: 'Thank you, you beautiful people. Good night, sweet dreams. We love you.' The fact that the tour was over came as a huge relief to him, privately.

In September, 'Who Wants to Live Forever' was released but when the lights had gone out on the Magic tour, although they had all enjoyed it, in some ways it had not come a day too soon for Queen. As at the end of 1982, friction and discord had been causing upheaval in the band and all four felt that they needed another break from each other. Brian once openly admitted: 'We did hate each other for a while. Recording *Jazz* and those albums we did in Munich, *The Game* and *The Works*, we got very angry with each other. I left the group a couple of times, just for the day. You know – "I'm off and not coming back," sort of thing. We'd all done that. You end up quibbling over one note.' It wasn't just with the band that trouble was brewing, though. For

Brian, coming home meant a return to his pressing domestic problems, which were compounded by the fact that Chrissy was pregnant again.

In early November, Iron Maiden staged a charity Christmas gig in aid of the NSPCC at London's Hammersmith Odeon. As one of the guest performers they had invited the spoof heavy metal band Bad News, which comprised four comedy actors: Nigel Planer, Rik Mayall, Adrian Edmondson and Christopher Ryan – then better known as TV's *The Young Ones*.

Says Nigel Planer: 'It was our idea to invite Brian to be part of our routine. As Bad News, on stage we would go mental with our guitars making all these fabulous noises, when it is really a guest guitarist hidden off stage who is doing all the work. For the Hammersmith gig, we had asked Jimmy Page as well as Brian. That night, Ade and I were doing our usual thing, then I switched on my amp and rushed to the front of the stage to fall to my knees and go through the big ecstasy thing, supposedly playing an intricate and absolutely fantastic lead guitar piece. The song was "Hey Hey Bad News", commonly known as "Fuck Off Bad News". On cue, Brian then walked out from behind the speakers, playing his guitar and showing me up. A big argument got up between me and him that he had been paid a fiver to stay hidden, which got clean out of hand. It was really funny and the audience lapped it up. So did Brian.' May had had such a fun time that he later agreed to produce the zany comedians' forthcoming album.

In reality, though, depression was swiftly setting in with Brian as his and Chrissy's marital problems worsened. By now, he had also agreed to be producer on some recordings for Anita Dobson, and through working together he was spending more time with her. As the divide between himself and his wife widened, he found himself getting closer to the infectiously bubbly actress.

Even before their affair actually began, journalists were swift to sniff out potential scandal. Anita Dobson's star was sky-high, playing one of the pivotal characters in Britain's top-rated TV soap. Up to now Brian May had been Mr Steady and Dependable, and the tabloid headline writers were growing impatient. Although both Brian and Anita issued emphatic denials, speculation began sprouting in press gossip columns. Brian worried how this would affect his children, whom he feared were being tormented at school. At times it was hard for him to understand how he had come to the place he found himself at. He had never envisaged this and now his entire world was upended.

It was a highly emotive time for both Brian and Chrissy, especially with their third baby due any day. Brian remained at home, although in his heart he perhaps knew that cutting Anita out of his life was something he could scarcely contemplate. That relationship itself could not have been plain sailing, considering the emotional triangle they were all embroiled in. Brian's single source of pure joy came with the birth on 17 February 1987 of his second daughter, named Emily Ruth.

10

BLEAK HOUSE

Brian left the domestic chaos behind him in spring 1987 and flew out to Los Angeles where, together with Meat Loaf, he began work on the theme song for the following year's Paralympic Games, ultimately penning 'A Time for Heroes'. Optimism was in short supply for May, however, as it also was for Freddie Mercury. The previous summer, Freddie had remarked on Spanish television that he would love to meet opera singer Montserrat Caballe. Now, while he was working on solo material with one of his closest friends, songwriter/producer Mike Moran, that wish came true.

Mike Moran recalls: 'We had left the studio late one night and gone home, when in the early hours Freddie rang me, very excited. He told me he had had a call from Spain that Montserrat Caballe wanted to meet him and that we were going over to Barcelona on Saturday. A little sleepy, I sat up and asked suspiciously: "What do you mean *we're* going to Barcelona?" He replied: "Well, I'm not fucking going by myself!"'

According to Mike, the prospect of meeting Montserrat Caballe petrified Mercury. 'He got himself worked into a right state,' he says, 'and was rushing about panicking. He kept saying: "First, I'll have to work out what samples of my work to take along. What can I take?" Eventually, I grabbed hold of him and said: "Freddie, you're famous! You don't need samples of your work," but he insisted that he did. In the end, he said: "I'll play her this thing", which was the B-side to "The Great Pretender".'

The meeting took place at the Ritz Hotel in Barcelona. 'We got there first,' Mike recalls, 'and Freddie was still fussing like a mother hen. He wanted the sound system set so that all he had to do was press a button. We waited, and then Montserrat swept in with an entire retinue behind her. The hotel staff were bowing and scraping, almost walking backwards before her, which made Freddie even more nervy, but she was really good fun and everyone, except Freddie, loosened up the more the champagne flowed.

'All of a sudden, at a break in the chatter, Freddie burst out to Montserrat: "Well, can I play you this song then?" The thing is, she got the wrong end of the stick because he somehow introduced the track by saying: "This is me, pretending to be you," and he played 'Exercises in Free Love'. As she listened, she glanced quizzically at Freddie and a few of us thought, what's she making of this? Then when the track finished, she asked: "You wrote this for me?" Freddie had now realised his mistake but made matters worse by saying: "If you want, you can have it." He turned and asked me: "That's okay, isn't it?"'

Confusion aside, Montserrat Caballe liked the track very much and less than a week later, in London, she visited Freddie for dinner at his home, Garden Lodge. Mike Moran recalls: 'Later, the three of us grouped around the piano as Freddie tried to teach Montserrat to sing gospel, which was a bit painful, but they became very good friends, and her parting shot was: "Do me a favour? I really enjoyed this. Would you and Mike write me a piece about Barcelona?" Freddie replied: "Oh, of course," and promptly forgot all about it.'

Montserrat Caballe was determined to ensure that Mercury kept his promise, though. Says Mike: 'She called Freddie from all corners of the world, asking how he was getting on with the song. Freddie eventually came to me and said: "Fuck's sake, we'll have to write this bloody song!" So we sat down and in pretty short order co-wrote 'Barcelona' and in between her opera engagements Montserrat whizzed over to London to record it.'

The strange alliance between the rock and opera stars became a talking point in music circles, and when a giant festival was planned in Ibiza for the end of May to celebrate Spain winning the bid to stage the 1992 Olympic Games, Freddie and Montserrat were invited to appear at it together. A favourite nightspot of Mercury's, the Ku Club, was the focal point of the festival and it was there, for a TV special, that he and Caballe publicly showcased their duet against the backcloth of exploding showers of spectacular fireworks. Behind the pizzazz, however, lurked a deadly and distressing time bomb.

Around Easter time, in the hope of allaying privately mounting fears over his health, Freddie had undergone a series of medical tests, one of which had involved the removal of a small piece of skin from his shoulder. When the results came back, he learned from the doctors that he had AIDS. At this early stage, Mercury confided in very few people; apparently only Mary Austin and Freddie's live-in lover Jim Hutton were told. Mercury's treatment began straight away, and Jim Hutton opted to remain with Freddie. Mercury desperately wanted to keep a lid on this devastating development, but that would prove difficult.

When Mercury and Caballe headlined at the Ku Club TV special, Spandau Ballet, Duran Duran and Marillion joined them on the bill. Marillion's frontman Fish recalls his deep shock when he came across Mercury here: 'I thought, I would go see him and say: "How ya doin?" you know, and he was like, really drawn. There were about three or four close friends in the dressing room with him, and it was like someone had fuckin' died! I thought, something really heavy is going down here and I'm not part of it. So I got out of there, fast. At the time, the people around Freddie were saying things like "he's got a kidney complaint or a liver problem" - stuff like that - but having glimpsed some of Freddie's excesses, it wasn't too hard to put two and two together.'

For those close to Mercury, indeed there wasn't much guess-work required. The signs of his illness had begun to show with the usual development of Kaposi's sarcoma, or KS, an otherwise rare cancer. It resulted in large dark red marks surfacing on the skin of his hands and face. Treatment for these early telltale marks is to neutralise them with special lasers. They fade, but usually leave blemishes, which are best covered by make-up, in itself a giveaway sign. At the Ku Club, Mercury had been unable to disguise these marks completely, as Barbara Valentin recalls:

'Freddie and I never spoke about his HIV and AIDS but he knew that I knew. It was in our eyes whenever we looked at each other and was a silent understanding between us. When I joined him in Ibiza for this TV special, I saw straight away that he had not been able to hide the marks on his face properly and so, before he and Montserrat performed, I said nothing but took Freddie away with me to another room and used my heavy profes-sional make-up on him to make him look better.'

As best they could, Freddie's friends maintained a seal of secrecy around his condition. Fish maintains: 'As with any band that develops to that stage, Queen had built such a strong perimeter fence that if they wanted to keep something inside it, they did. You *knew* that there was going to be no leaks.'

1987 would not be simply a year off roadwork for Queen. They would never tour again, though no one would admit it. Around this time, Brian May declared of the band: 'We're great friends. It hasn't always been that way. We have had some difficult times but we had a great night at New Year - just the four of us chat-ting about what the future could hold. I don't think we've got to the end of it yet.'

May continued to pursue solo ventures and had recently teamed up again with Bad News. To suggestions that the spoof rock band had to pester Brian to keep his promise to produce their album, Nigel Planer jovially protests: 'Not a bit of it. It was us who got begging letters from Brian, urging us to let him do it! Actually, it all started with Adrian [Edmondson]. He came up with the idea of us recording "Bohemian Rhapsody", and the next thought was: why not ask Brian to produce it for a laugh? From there, it went on to him producing our whole album.' In real need of some light relief, Brian was happy to get involved again with the zany comedians.

Nigel Planer admits: 'I have to say, it was a strange marriage, Brian being so very good and a proper musician on the one hand, and us a bunch of louts out to have a laugh on the other. Yet, recording comedy songs is much more difficult than you would imagine. If you carry the comedy too far, you lose the music. Carry the music too far and you lose the comedy. During the recording, we went into character. Mine was a bonehead called Den Denis, while Ade was Vim who had the biggest ego and was an incredible show-off. As Bad News, we would talk, swear and argue and all the time Brian had the tapes running. Once we started, we just improvised and, of course, it got way out of hand. Every time I looked up at Brian in the box he was laughing like hell, literally falling about.' The recording at Sarm Studios began in May, and the album was scheduled for an autumn release.

Before that, in early July, Anita Dobson's single 'Talking of Love', which Brian had also produced, was released. Her previous single, 'Anyone Can Fall in Love', to the theme tune of *EastEnders*, had charted at number four in 1986. 'Talking of Love' fell somewhat shorter and dropped anchor at forty-three. She and Brian still flew to Vienna to make a video to accompany the new single, continuing all the while not to get drawn into any detailed explanations on the rumours concerning their relationship.

By late summer, May's recording work with Bad News was drawing to a close. It had been an unusual experience and they had all become good friends. When the spoof band were invited to take part in the annual Rock and Jazz Festival at Reading at the end of August, the comedians asked Brian to join them. He agreed, with no idea of what was in store.

Bad News had played their first ever gig at Donington Park in Leicestershire before an audience of 60,000 and their reception had been volatile. While most had found their send-up of heavy metal hilarious, some dyed-in-the-wool metal heads had considered it offensive and showed their displeasure by bombarding the actors with rubbish. Amid all the debris littering the stage, they'd even found a sheep's eye. In his acerbic way, Rik Mayall invited those planning to attend the Reading festival to come and throw sheep's eyes at them.

Says Nigel Planer: 'It was a great day. Brian came with us all in the coach, taking his kids along with him. Everyone took their kids. It was more like a crèche than a heavy metal gig. The roadies and backstage helpers were more interested in goo-gooing at some baby than in seeing to us.' Of the performance, he recalls: 'The audience was just this seething horrible mass of pink! We did our usual act and Brian joined us on stage. We got pelted worse than ever that day. Plastic bottles of urine came flying at us by the dozen and enough sheep's eyes rained down on top of us to turn the air black but Brian was dodging away like an old pro, laughing his head off!'

In early September, despite his worsening illness, Freddie went ahead with plans to host a lavish party to celebrate his forty-first birthday, which he opted to hold at Pikes Hotel in Ibiza, owned by Tony Pike. Mercury was no stranger to this luxury complex, which enjoyed a worldwide reputation as an exclusive hideaway for the rich and famous.

Tony Pike had met up with Freddie earlier in the year at the

Ku Club TV special. 'By that time,' says Tony, 'rumours had begun circulating that Freddie had AIDS but then you don't ask a friend if he is terminally ill, and no one ever spoke about it. It was just not discussed. Those around him would have categorically denied it anyway.' Tony was happy to accommodate Mercury's wish for a birthday party to remember, but things almost went awry.

Pike reveals: 'Freddie's forty-first was originally going to be arranged in conjunction with Elton John's manager, John Reid. That was, until he and Jim Beach had a disagreement. Beach had been four hours late for their rendezvous, through no fault of his own – he and his family had been caught in a storm at sea – but Reid, unaware of the circumstances, was angry at being delayed so long. As a result, he cancelled the party. When Freddie found out, he called me and said he wanted a do regardless – just something for one hundred people instead of the previous two hundred and fifty. The story of the big bash being called off then somehow appeared in a UK newspaper, and when Freddie read it he was incensed. He told me that he wanted the biggest birthday party the island had ever seen, and I said: "But Freddie, there are only four days to go." He replied: "I know you can do it."'

Tony did not disappoint and, in the end, eight hundred people packed the place. Says Pike: 'I had arranged for a special cake to be made in the shape of the Gaudi Cathedral but when the plane it was in landed, the cake collapsed. It was a disaster, especially at such short notice, but we hurriedly made him a replacement cake, two metres long and decorated with the musical notes to "Barcelona". Six men dressed in white and gold uniforms carried it in, but nobody ended up having room for cake and as the high jinks began, my secretary at the time, a rather portly English lady in her best silk suit, ended up being thrown into it! Then there was the champagne. We opened three hundred and fifty bottles of Moet & Chandon in less than one hour. After I was dressed, I'd gone to check on the champagne only to find that the ice was in the vats but no bottles, and we all had to frantically empty out and start again. We just got it chilled in the nick of time.'

Tony Pike had hired a professional decorator from Barcelona and the hotel was hung with black and gold balloons, which had taken three days to blow up by machine. They were helium-filled and, in the middle of the party, there was a near disaster. 'There was this guy trying to impress the girl sitting on his knee,' Tony explains, 'and he thought he would put a lighter to the balloon above her head to make it pop, but instead the whole thing went up in a gigantic sheet of flame.

'The problem was, we had had extra electricity supplied and the massive overhead cables on the roof caught the blast and began to melt. It could have been catastrophic. I had been elsewhere, talking with Mike Moran and didn't know anything about it. As I returned to the party, someone anxiously asked what I was going to do about the fire and I replied that I would see to it tomorrow. I ended up with a "My God, that's a cool guy!" reputation that night.'

Having nearly missed out on his annual celebration, Mercury ended up with one of his best ever parties. He especially enjoyed the spectacular fireworks display that rounded it all off. 'He must have seen so many displays,' says Tony Pike, 'but he was like a little boy, seeing one for the first time.' That night, Mercury was the perfect host. He had allowed in no photographers, no hangers-on, and he appeared to be happy, going out of his way to personally greet as many guests as he could. No one could have guessed that his white cell count had dropped significantly, although earlier in the day at the hotel, friends had noticed with alarm some new and strange marks on the star's legs.

'Barcelona' was released in Spain in September 1987, and in

Britain a month later, where it peaked at number eight in the charts. The music press was polarised about it, with some critics damning Mercury as an out-and-out embarrassment to the rock world. Others deemed the song a brave and ingenious digression. Mercury's peers had varying views, too.

Abba's Benny Andersson believes: 'I think Freddie was amusing himself. I think he thought it would be fun, but it wasn't a musical experience for me.' While Bjorn Ulvaeus declares: 'Oh, I enjoyed it very much! I know people consider it schmaltzy but its strength, the theatricality and the grand scale of it all appealed to me.' And Sir Cliff Richard opines: '"Barcelona" was always going to have the stun factor, but our industry is so small-minded in that respect. It's the tall poppy syndrome. They can't wait to cut someone down who is doing too well. I just wish that they wouldn't automatically be non-supportive when someone makes a move in a new direction.'

Towards the year's end, it was Brian May's turn to have battles with the media, as he was still engaged in the increasingly fruitless effort of trying to douse the flames flickering in the tabloids about his romance with the *EastEnders* actress. Much of his time was occupied working with Anita Dobson on her album, but he was aware that he could not put off grasping the nettle indefinitely. It must have been a fraught Christmas in the May family household as he wrestled with his dilemma.

In January 1988, May rejoined Queen at London's Town House Studios to commence work on their first studio-recorded album for three years. For Brian, though, life was about to go from bad to worse. With his stress levels running high, he was already at a very low ebb when on 2 June his father died. Harold and Brian had been extremely close, had shared so much. To lose his father at any time would have been crushing but for it to happen right then, when he was so desperately unhappy, was almost more than Brian could bear emotionally.

This traumatic event loosened the very shaky grip he had on his life and family. Following Harold's death the rift between Brian and Chrissy split wide open and there was clearly no saving their marriage. At the same time, his relationship with Anita Dobson had now reached a stage where it would have been pointless to deny it. For Brian and Chrissy, one of their deepest concerns was their children. Brian could hardly bear the thought of leaving them. His physical and mental health had been suffering for some time, but now he descended rapidly into bouts of dark depression, plunging so low that no one could reach him as he struggled to work things out.

After wrestling with his conscience, his feelings and those of all the people most closely involved, it was decided that after twelve years of marriage he and Chrissy would part. More than a decade later, Brian talked of how aspects of life changed when Queen no longer went out on tour, and he seemed to be saying that only then did he and Chrissy come to realise that they had each, over time, carved their own separate position in life. Said May: 'When everything was over, we looked at each other and we didn't know each other any more – really, a tragedy.' He started a new life with Anita and it could only have worsened an already fraught time when the tabloids, which had smelled blood in the water for months already, now moved in and made the story front page news.

Brian revealed: 'The spotlight came squarely on us, and it was hell. The way the paparazzi treat people's lives is disgusting.' He later maintained that the first three years after leaving the marital home were filled with a great deal of pain. 'To contemplate not waking up with your kids is unthinkable. Anyone who finds themselves in that position can never forgive themselves, but I know in my heart that there was no other way.'

His new life with Anita Dobson was not a bed of roses either. It appears that the various tensions created around and within them led to arguments, some of which made their way into the newspapers. In October, one tabloid reported a blazing row between the couple after which Anita, it was claimed, furiously walked out on Brian, only for the couple to reconcile the following day. About this time Dobson was due to appear with singer/actor Adam Faith in a stage musical version of Faith's sixties' TV series *Budgie*. A soundtrack album was planned, and May was asked to guest on the track, 'In One of My Weaker Moments'.

That same month, Freddie and Montserrat Caballe were due to appear at La Nit, a huge open-air festival held in Barcelona, on the Avinguda de Maria Cristina, that would officially launch the four-year run-up to the 1992 Olympic Games. They sang with the Barcelona Opera House orchestra and choir on a stage situated in front of the illuminated fountains in Castle Square. This rock/opera star pairing continued to exercise the minds of the critics, but Mercury had a champion in one music heavyweight, lyricist Sir Tim Rice. Tim states: 'I thought "Barcelona" was absolutely wonderful. I don't think Freddie had an operatic voice. Obviously, his was more a rock voice, but then most opera stars could not get near a rock song. For instance, Montserrat Caballe couldn't sing a Pretenders' number. However, if Freddie had trained from childhood, he could very well have sung opera. He wasn't that far off it.' La Nit would mark Freddie Mercury's last live performance.

In November, Anita Dobson released another single, 'To Know Him Is to Love Him', which was a cover of the 1958 hit by the American band Teddy Bears. Her album, *Talking of Love*, which Brian had produced, swiftly followed. Since losing his father in summer, May had thrown himself into work as a means of keeping occupied. He was still writing some material for a possible second solo album, although to date his ideas had tended to be a kaleidoscope of musical styles and the lack of direction to the material was a problem. Solo work had to take second place to Queen projects, which included the album the band were currently concentrating on.

May also badly missed live performance; in many ways for him it was the most fulfilling aspect of being in a band. 'Suddenly life becomes simple again,' he once said. Queen had not toured for two years now, and although it was still not openly admitted, even among themselves, deep down Brian knew that they would never do so again. In a wider context, questions were quietly circulating as to why Queen had gone to ground. For May, Taylor and Deacon it was inevitable that when the time came to deflect media questions over Mercury, it would mean more pressure and some deceit.

In late 1988, May diverted his energies into guesting with a variety of artistes. He collaborated with the group Living in a Box on their single 'Blow the House Down', before working with Tony Iommi on Black Sabbath's album *Headless Cross*. Lead guitarist Tony Iommi is perhaps Brian May's closest friend and confidant, someone to whom May knows he can always turn whatever the circumstances. It is, on the whole, a very private friendship. Iommi agrees with the characterisation of Brian as having been the worrier in Queen. He says: 'Brian and I could relate really well on that one because we are very much alike in that respect. He was the one with most of the work to do, who would end up literally all day in the studio, holding it all together, no matter what happened.'

Regarding May's guest spot on Black Sabbath's album, Tony says: 'Brian would often come to my recording sessions, just as I would pop into whichever studio he was working at, and one day while working on *Headless Cross* I just said to him: "Bloody hell, come and have a play." He asked: "Really? Do you want me to?" and that was it. Except that Brian was, at that point, the only other guitar player we'd ever had play on any of our records.' Brian guested on the track, 'When Death Calls'.

It was the turn next of the all-girl group, Fuzzbox, to persuade May to lend his skills to their single 'Self', just before former Frankie Goes to Hollywood vocalist Holly Johnson asked him to contribute some guitar work to the single, 'Love Train'. Then ex-Genesis guitarist Steve Hackett wanted Brian to join their mutual friend Chris Thompson in singing backing vocals on his album track, 'Slot Machine'. It meant most to May, though, when he was approached by his long-time hero, skiffle star Lonnie Donegan, to write a song for inclusion on his forthcoming album. They shared vocals on the number, 'Let Your Heart Rule Your Head'; the song would show up years later on May's solo album.

This distracting flurry of activity took Brian through to December, when he attended a Bon Jovi gig at London's Wembley Arena. That night, the New Jersey rockers turned in a typically electrifying performance, and May, a huge fan of the band, was delighted when their lead guitarist Richie Sambora invited him up on stage for the encore. Richie recalls: 'Brian, Elton John and a whole bunch of guys came that night and so we just called them all up on stage to jam with us. We played the Beatles' 'Get Back' and a couple of other numbers. It was great.' As Brian had not anticipated this, obviously he didn't have his Red Special with him, but when he tried to opt out, Richie thrust one of his own guitars at him.

For Sambora, that night lit an important friendship between himself and Brian May. Richie reveals: 'It was one helluva jam and I'll always remember it, but what was really cool was something that happened after the gig. Brian gave Jon and me some really sound advice. This was right when our career was about to take off in a huge way, and Brian's advice to us was never to work our asses off to the point of burning ourselves out. You know – not taking time to smell the roses along the way, that kind of thing. That's what he felt he and Queen had often done, and he could not get it over strongly enough to us how important it is always to try to be there – to live the moment and savour it, because all too soon it will be over and you'll have missed clean out on enjoying it.'

As it happened, Bon Jovi *would* go on to burn themselves out, keeping pace with their massive success as the decade evolved, but at the time both Richie and Jon Bon Jovi appreciated the advice. It was made all the more special, says Sambora, because it came from Brian May. Richie explains: 'That night at the Wembley Arena was the first time I had met Brian in person, but I'd watched and admired him since the three nights I went to see Queen open for Mott the Hoople at the Uris Theater on Broadway back in 1974. I was knocked out. Queen were absolutely fantastic and Brian had made a big impression on me. I was just a teenager at the time, but I never forgot it.'

May's final guest appearance of the year was once more with Bad News, this time at London's Marquee Club. Hiding behind the speakers with him that night were Jimmy Page and Jeff Beck. Beck has referred to May as: 'The best pop-oriented guitarist there is,' maintaining that all aspiring guitar players desperately want to play Brian's licks, as once they used to want to play his. Nigel Planer maintains: 'That Marquee gig was very special for us. You don't often get the chance to play on one stage with three musicians like Brian May, Jeff Beck and Jimmy Page!'

Throughout 1988, Queen had been writing and recording material for a new album, but behind the scenes lay devastating heartbreak as May, Roger Taylor and John Deacon watched Freddie's gradual deterioration. His weakening condition was more and more being brought distressingly home to Mercury.

Mercury was a natural showman, and having been diagnosed with a terminal illness did not remove that overnight. He was not physically capable of performing any more and had bleakly been forced to acknowledge that, but he was not coping well emotionally. Leaving aside the reality that he was facing the prospect of a horrible and premature death, no one who had received so much adulation for so long – and who had derived such nourishment from it – could suddenly switch off. He said himself that performing live was so much in his blood that he would be vulnerable without it. His distress was causing stormy rows that shattered the illusion of tranquillity at Garden Lodge. Some of the arguments with his lover Jim Hutton and others were quite vicious and most ended in tears. The strain of keeping his condition to himself was clearly becoming too much for Freddie.

It had worsened matters, too, that he had severed all contact with some of his friends, only to miss them terribly. The closest friend he had been avoiding for months now was Barbara Valentin – the person he had once said he felt best understood his chosen way of life – but that was one battle he was about to lose.

'When Freddie suddenly quit living in Munich I knew he was worried that he had HIV,' says Valentin. 'I knew he went hurrying back to London to hide but there was nowhere to hide. Soon after the special concert with Montserrat in Ibiza, I began to see less and less of Freddie. I rang Garden Lodge often, but he would not take my calls. That Christmas I tried again, but this time was told by someone there to stop calling and I thought, okay, fuck this! But then, about eight months later my doorbell rang one day, and it was Freddie. He just stood there and said: "I can't stay away from you. I can't live without you in my life. Take me in and take care of me." And I did. He was in a lot of emotional pain and he *had* to work out a way to live with his illness, but it was very hard.'

By January 1989, Queen's album was finished. Because of past rows over money, the band had decided that it would be fairer to credit all tracks collectively to Queen and that the royalty earnings should equally be a four-way split. It was a happier arrangement all round. The release date for the new album had not yet been set but was expected to be late spring.

11

KEEPING SECRETS

With health matters very much at the forefront of his mind, in early 1989 Brian became involved with the British Bone Marrow Donor Appeal. The charity's aim at that time was to establish a register of people who had had their blood tissue-typed and were willing to donate some of their bone marrow to a patient whose type matched theirs. May had been touched that a young leukaemia sufferer, Denise Morse, had asked to have his ballad 'Who Wants to Live Forever' played at her funeral.

Malcolm Thomas, one of the charity's co-founders, who had lost his own daughter some years before to aplastic anaemia, contacted May. Says Malcolm: 'Denise was a remarkable woman. She had come out of remission and had brought Christmas forward for her family because she knew she would not be around for the real thing. It was in a lot of newspapers at the time and she appeared on the *Wogan* TV show. Although she was dreadfully ill, she worked really hard on the campaign. Denise died in March 1989 and I went to her funeral. It was the first time in my life that I had heard a record being played at a funeral, and it was a song called "Who Wants to Live Forever" by Queen. Denise had been a huge fan of theirs. Afterwards, the song kept playing over and over in my head, so I sent a letter telling them how this record had become the heart of the BBMDA. I didn't know then but, because it had been in the newspapers, at exactly the same time Brian's mother had been talking to him about the funeral and our charity.'

Malcolm Thomas was invited to Pinewood Studios where Queen were making a video; during the lunch break he and May talked in a dressing room. Says Thomas: 'I told Brian the whole involved story that went back to my initial search to find a donor for my daughter, and all that had happened along the way. It was also important to get across to him that the BBMDA was not one of those charities run by out-and-out businessmen, but that it consisted mainly of ordinary families who had either lost loved ones or, against the clock, were desperately trying to find a way not to. To my astonishment, Brian simply looked at me and asked: "Okay, what can I do?"'

Eventually, they came up with the idea to rerecord 'Who Wants to Live Forever' in a way that would generate maximum publicity. 'Because of Brian, we suddenly found ourselves doing a series of high-profile television interviews,' recalls Malcolm. 'On the BBC's *Daytime Live*, Brian and I asked for children to come forward to be auditioned to record the number, asking them to send in a tape of themselves singing. You wouldn't believe the incredible response we got – something close to 10,000 tapes poured in. People had gone to extraordinary lengths.'

It was far more than they had anticipated, but they split the tapes between them and set about listening. Malcolm admits: 'It was a Herculean task and the talent out there was truly amazing, but eventually we shortlisted it to sixty – half boys, half girls. Brian put together an arrangement of the song which was straight-forward enough for the auditioning kids to sing, and they were all invited to the Abbey Road Studios.'

It was debatable who were the more nervous – the children, overawed at being inside a recording studio, or their parents, gazing around Studio Two itself, the famous Beatles sanctuary.

The stellar line-up for the world premiere of *We Will Rock You* included Ben Elton, Roger Taylor, Robert de Niro, Brian May and Anita Dobson: Dominion Theatre, London, 14 May 2002.

The *We Will Rock You* musical proved a smash-hit worldwide. Outside the Koma Theatre in Tokyo, a three metre statue of Freddie is erected to mark the Japanese opening of the show.

Brian provided one of the defining images of the 2002 Golden Jubilee celebrations by playing the national anthem on the roof of Buckingham Palace.

As a devoted dad, one of Brian's chief concerns in life is always his children's happiness.

In the mid 1980s, behind the public smiles, Brian's marriage to Chrissy was in trouble.

The vital spark between actress Anita Dobson and Brian, pictured here in 1987, ignited a stimulating relationship that led to marriage in 2000.

It was a proud family occasion when Brian received his CBE at Buckingham Palace in December 2005.

Brian and Roger Taylor unveiled Queen's star on the Hollywood Walk of Fame in October 2002. Queen has joined the Beatles as one of the few non-US bands to be afforded this accolade.

Astronomy has always fascinated Brian, so he was thrilled to co-author *Bang! The Complete History of the Universe* with Sir Patrick Moore and Dr Chris Lintott in 2006.

Decades after starting it, in August 2007 Brian finally submitted his thesis to Professor Paul Nanda, head of astrophysics at London's Imperial College.

Sixty were eventually whittled down to two, Ian Meeson and Belinda Gillett, who were invited to Olympic Studios in Barnes for the actual recording.

The rerecorded version of 'Who Wants to Live Forever' raised over £130,000 for the British Bone Marrow Donor Appeal. Says Malcolm Thomas: 'Brian did an enormous amount for us in terms of getting us publicity, launching laboratories and raising public consciousness about what we do; because of that we have saved many children's lives. He was extremely passionately involved. Without Brian, quite simply, we would not have the organisation that we have today. His intervention at that early stage was crucial.'

Against this was the backdrop of Freddie Mercury's battle with AIDS, which created a densely unhappy state for everyone in Queen. The progression of his illness meant that the marks on his skin, where visible, were becoming harder to hide with make-up alone. So, to help his disguise, he grew a beard. He was still not ready to share his dreadful news with anyone apart from the two or three friends who were sworn to secrecy, but his band-mates were not fools.

The first single from Queen's new album was released at the beginning of May 1989, a hard rocking number titled 'I Want It All'. Its video had been shot in Pinewood Studios without an audience and was the first public recognition of how drastically Freddie Mercury was changing. He was dressed conventionally in a collar and tie and sported a beard, but this did little to distract from the shock of how much thinner he was – his face was gaunt and he looked haunted, even under the studio make-up. He sang as powerfully as ever, though, and despite being clearly much less energetic, his delivery remained defiant. The single charted at number three in Britain, Queen's highest entry to date.

In mid-May, *The Miracle* followed and starkly Brian has had this to say: 'I was in a complete state of mental untogetherness during most of the making of *The Miracle*. I always say that it's a miracle that I managed to play anything at all!' He had no real concerns over his actual playing, but he came to believe that his contribution to the material was not as good as he would have wished. It was a stylish album, however, complemented by an inspired sleeve design by artist Richard Gray, who had used computer graphics to create the striking effect of fusing the band's four faces.

Pushing on, Queen were working on material for their next studio album in Montreux, where one night they got together in a restaurant. That wasn't so unusual, but Brian found it hard to shake off a strong foreboding that Freddie was about to tell them the devastating truth. Perhaps Mercury *had* intended to confide in them that night, feeling the pressure of keeping his illness a secret, but although the singer admitted to his friends for the first time that he was unwell, he shied away from revealing that he had AIDS.

Soon after, for the first time in nearly a decade, Queen gave an interview – a one-hour question and answer session with BBC Radio One DJ Mike Read. When quizzed as to why Queen no longer toured, Freddie assumed the blame, saying that he wanted to break the cycle of album-tour-album-tour. It was an unsatisfactory reason for many and, as time passed, queries kept on coming from all angles.

Eventually, Mercury confessed to reporters: 'I can't carry on rocking the way I have done in the past. It is all too much. It's no way for a grown man to behave. I have stopped my nights of wild partying. That's not because I am ill, but down to age. I'm no spring chicken. Now, I prefer to spend my time at home. It's part of growing up.'

Although Mercury had not yet come clean to the band, inwardly Brian finally faced up to the truth that Queen would never tour again, and it was a blow to him. The fact that he could not get out on the road and expend his pent-up emotions and energies handicapped his ability to handle pressures in his own life, which in turn added to his acute sense of nervous tension. He was extremely restless and candidly confessed around now: 'Taking the touring side of things away messed up my life, without exaggeration. I feel it's taken the whole balance out of my life. I badly want to play live, with or without Queen. If we cannot come to some kind of arrangement within the band, I'll get my own project together, but I can't stand it much longer.'

Over the next six months, four further singles emerged from *The Miracle* – 'Breakthru', 'The Invisible Man', 'Scandal' and the title track. The first and last of these spawned unusual videos. For 'Breakthru', Queen were filmed performing the number on board a vintage steam engine hired from the Nene Valley Railway, near Peterborough. The private train was renamed 'The Miracle Express' for the occasion, and Brian White, then press officer with the Nene Valley, recalls: 'The filming itself took place over the full length of the line, which is chiefly set in water meadows. At the beginning of the video, you see the speeding train bursting through an apparently solid bridge arch. In fact, it had been filled with realistic-looking polystyrene bricks. The effect was brilliant, and it was filmed only the once.'

For 'The Miracle', in an effort to involve Freddie on screen as little as possible, child actor band look-alikes had been hired, who mimed to the song. The miniature Brian May had practised to perfection all the guitarist's idiosyncrasies and, with a Red Special replica hung around his neck, he threw himself into his role. Freddie's young double acquitted himself with such panache that at the end of filming Mercury quipped to the boy: 'How are you fixed for doing a tour?'

For most of that autumn, Brian toured the world, principally on PR duties for Queen but also promoting various charity projects. In between, he and Anita Dobson took a short holiday in

Los Angeles. Unfortunately, one sunny morning when fooling around with his son's skateboard, May fell off and broke his arm.

When Brian returned to Britain he began work with a friend of Anita's, Gareth Marks, who had been playing the lead role in the London stage musical *Buddy*. The actor wanted to make an album and May agreed to guest on the track 'Lady of Leisure'.

In November, Brian again guested with one of his all-time heroes when he joined Jerry Lee Lewis on stage at the Hammersmith Odeon, playing guitar on 'High School Confidential'. He was thrilled, but the experience only briefly blotted out the pressures. Late in the month, he joined the others at Mountain Studios in Montreux, although restricted by his broken arm, still in the process of mending.

The flow of singles from *The Miracle* kept Queen in the public eye, but behind closed doors the atmosphere was grim. Freddie was weakening at a faster rate now and could manage increasingly less time in the recording studio. He had been forced to give up smoking because of respiratory problems, and singing exhausted him. In December, Queen released *Queen at the Beeb*, an album of early recordings made for the BBC.

It was not the past the watching press was interested in, though, and they were on high alert. Media speculation about what ailed Mercury multiplied by the week and the strain on the band grew considerably. While Freddie's low-key existence helped him to avoid journalists, as May, Taylor and Deacon went about their business they were hounded by the press at every opportunity, and forced to lie and say that Freddie was fine.

It was a very painful time, as one of Freddie's closest friends, Mike Moran, recalls: 'Freddie showed immense bravery, and none of us really knew just how ill he was. He didn't want to be a burden to people and certainly did not want anyone to feel sorry for him. For about three years, it was awfully difficult for us but we coped by going into denial – the way you do when you don't want to face the fact that someone you love is dying. There were often times when we would say to each other: "He's looking a bit better today, don't you think? Maybe, right enough . . ." We would semi-convince ourselves that he was going to be okay. It was all a part of not wanting him to go.'

In January 1990, Brian continued work on the new Queen album. Relations during work on *The Miracle* had been more harmonious because the new arrangement had neutered the arguments and territorial infighting that had previously erupted over individually penned numbers. Though no one voiced it, it seemed highly likely that this could be the last album they would record as a band, and therefore strife of any kind was to be avoided.

Public appearances as a band were best swerved, too, if possible, but this year the British Phonographic Industry decided to honour Queen for their outstanding contribution to British music, which meant being presented with an award at their ninth annual cere-mony, held in February at the Dominion Theatre in London. In formal dinner dress the band received their award from BPI chairman Terry Ellis.

Queen were in a no-win situation. Had they turned up without Freddie, it would have fuelled the already rampant speculation about his health. Yet inevitably, when Mercury did walk on stage, keeping well to the rear and looking on as Brian delivered the acceptance speech, his hollowed features and gaunt frame were so marked that it sparked off a rash of new rumours anyway.

That night the band quickly quit the theatre, absenting them-selves from the official BPI dinner in favour of attending their own special party at the Groucho Club in Soho. They had cele-brated 1981 as their tenth anniversary. For the purposes of this party, they opted to make 1990 their twentieth. Mingling with over four hundred guests were celebrities and Queen employees past and present. Many people were privately shocked that night, barely able to recognise the once larger-than-life, fun-loving singer in their midst.

Freddie tired very easily now, and after a short time, looking drawn and not particularly alert, he tried to slip quietly away from the party. A press photographer lurking outside had been hoping for just such an opportunity and snapped Mercury leaving. Looking haggard and preoccupied, Freddie's picture was splashed across the front page of a national daily newspaper next morning. Fans and friends, already suspicious, became extremely anxious for him. Freddie tried to calm fears by maintaining publicly that he felt fine and denying that he had AIDS. He added, though, that he would not be touring in the foreseeable future and would instead be resuming work in the studio with the rest of Queen.

With Mercury's plight a constant dark cloud hovering over-head, it was very hard to be distracted, but about this time Brian received an unusual request from casting director Jane L'Epine Smith. She had newly embarked on an ambitious project that was to be her first theatre production as director. Jane recalls: 'When I decided I was going to do *Macbeth*, the main thing for me was to try to make it accessible to all sections of the public. Shakespeare tends to have a very stodgy image, and I wanted elements in my production that would be attractive to all walks of life so that they would come and see it and maybe move over to a new experience. I had always admired Queen and thought that Brian would be ideal to compose the music for the play.'

Jane approached May through the Queen office. 'I got a phone call from Jim Beach next day saying that he had given my letter to Brian and he was interested, so could I come along to talk about it. Director Malcolm Ranson came with me, but I was extremely nervous,' she admits. There was, however, an instant rapport between Jane and Brian and he agreed to take on the project. Says Jane: 'He didn't want to think about it or anything. I was thrilled, of course, but had to explain that I still hadn't raised all the necessary finance. That wasn't a problem with Brian. It was a case of when you're ready, I'll do it.' Jane left the Queen office elated. 'The fact that I could now tell potential investors that Brian May was doing the music was a huge plus,' she explains.

Over the coming months, Brian experimented with ideas in a recently installed home recording studio. He was excited, yet apprehensive about the project; worried that his interpretation of the Bard could be thought too radical and not what Jane L'Epine Smith had in mind.

Despite working on the theatre music and the new Queen album, Brian spent as much time as he could with his children. Jimmy, now twelve, was mad on computer games and in particular was drawn to the science fiction games marketed by Games Workshop. Father and son frequently haunted one of their stores and eventually the firm's projects manager, Andy Jones, learned of this.

Andy Jones remembers: 'I was told that Brian May and his son were in the habit of visiting one of our central London branches, so I left word for Brian at the shop that he and Jimmy would be very welcome to come and look around our design studio, to meet the artists and miniature makers. We had what was called Warhammer World, which included Warhammer novels and magazines. Jimmy arrived clutching a *White Dwarf* magazine. He was very excited at meeting the designers and went around claiming all the autographs he could. It was quite ironic, because the designers were all waiting with their Queen albums, hoping to get Brian to sign them.'

During the visit, May discovered that Games Workshop were about to expand. Andy Jones explains: 'I was telling Brian that we were setting up our own record label, Warhammer, and that we had signed our first band called D-Rok. He immediately said that he would love to come along and play on a couple of tracks of D-Rok's album. He was serious, even though Queen were in the middle of recording an album in Switzerland. So we sent Brian a tape of the band's songs and in days he got back to me to say that he would come along quite soon.'

D-Rok's lead vocalist, Simon Denbigh, was stunned when Andy Jones told him that Brian May was coming to record with them. Simon says: 'Well, you don't believe something like that, do you? We got the shock of our lives when Brian walked in. He was brilliant, certainly the nicest megastar I have ever met.'

The recording studio May reported to had been converted from a disused slaughterhouse at Driffield, near Bridlington on the Yorkshire coast. Says Jones: 'What struck me as being particularly nice was that when Brian arrived, he had taken the trouble in a very short space of time not just to listen to the tape but to learn all the songs. So he was genned up in a way none of us expected and he said right off: "Let's get into 'Get Out of My Way'." It was great for the boys in the band.'

Simon Denbigh picks up: 'We were all very nervous of meeting Brian but he was very understanding and really complimentary about our music. He liked our ideas and what we were trying to do, which was a real morale boost because we respected him so much. I also think he had been quite surprised when he listened to the tape, because he had agreed to come, even before he had heard us. I mean, we could have been useless. He was such a down-to-earth person to work with and very good-humoured. At one point, I even forgot myself and told him to tune up but he took it great. Our guitarist Chesley asked Brian if he could have a go on his famous Red Special and Brian actually let him!'

The young band were aware of May's reputation for experimenting with new equipment and were goggled-eyed at the device he turned up with. Simon says: 'It was a special kind of zoom, a little box you plug into and get all sorts of effects out of. It was a prototype, the only one, and did some fantastic things.'

To their amazement, before Brian left he casually offered to leave the band with it to try it out. 'We were delighted to be trusted with it,' Simon adds, 'but we never touched it. We never seemed to have much luck with our equipment and had blown up a couple of amps. One even melted! So we were scared stiff that we would somehow break his zoom which, apart from anything else, must have cost a packet!' Brian appeared on the track 'Get Out of My Way' on D-Rok's album *Oblivion*, which was released later that year on the new Warhammer label.

By July, work on the Queen album had switched to Metropolis Studios in London, but as Freddie's failing health created many breaks, Brian used these to develop the *Macbeth* music at home. The Queen album, to be named *Innuendo*, was scheduled for a Christmas 1990 release.

Macbeth was due to open in November. Although Brian had worked hard on the music, his confidence was at a low ebb when the time came to present his work to the theatre company. Jane L'Epine Smith recalls: 'Right from the start we had wanted a dangerous production, something exciting and startling which pulled on all the senses. The first time Brian brought the music to us, he was extremely nervous in case we didn't like it. Also, the equipment he had did not work and that got him all the more fidgety and uptight, but when we heard it through all of us quite individually stood up and applauded. It was absolutely wonderful.'

Brian was relieved. It had meant a lot to him to write this music, which switched in mood from dramatic and compulsive to hopeful and buoyant, showing how tuned in to the play he was. Jane agrees: 'Brian got very involved. He even came to the rehearsals and did the warm-up exercises with the cast. He took part in everything.'

By now, the strain of fielding questions from the press about Freddie's health had become severely wearing. Brian, Roger and

John wanted to do right by their friend, but it was now almost impossible to lie with any semblance of credibility. May later reflected: 'It was tough psychologically having to keep it from everyone else. I never told my family or anything.'

One day, ambushed by a determined press pack, Brian conceded that Freddie was suffering from strain and exhaustion and that the years of hard living had finally caught up with him. He said no more than that, except to categorically deny the rumours that Mercury had AIDS.

Next day, the *Sun* headline was: It's Official! Freddie is Seriously Ill. The story was supported with a picture that showed Mercury staring-eyed and haggard. When Freddie saw the tabloid, he was extremely upset. At Garden Lodge thereafter, Jim Hutton or one of Mercury's personal assistants vetted all newspapers before they got to him.

Brian managed to put things behind him for a while when, on 19 November, *Macbeth* opened at London's Red and Gold Theatre with Roy Marsden in the leading role. 'It had a five-week run,' says Jane L'Epine Smith, 'and Brian came practically every night to give the production his visible support. I think the project had come along at a time for him when he was needing something to take his mind off his problems. It was the right time, the right thing and the right chemistry.'

Of the music, Jane adds: 'The piece he wrote to be played when people were filing into the theatre was particularly startling. It starts quietly and builds up and up to a big bang, timed exactly for when the first scene bursts on stage with flashing lights for the fight sequence. The whole production had a very atmospheric, black and white cinema effect to it, and that is what came across vividly in the music.'

While Brian had been attending the theatre for those five weeks, the paparazzi had stepped up their stalking of Freddie Mercury, capturing him on camera at the end of November discreetly leaving the Harley Street premises of a top AIDS specialist. *Innuendo* had now had to be rescheduled for release early in the New Year.

With sadness permeating everything around him, Brian tried to find some solace in astronomy. In the early nineties, he had the opportunity to catch a solar eclipse in Mexico, albeit in less than comfortable surroundings. In California at the time, he dashed south and arrived at what was considered to be the best location to see this spectacle, only to find that there was literally no room at the inn. Undaunted, he roughed it by taking up residence in a corrugated iron hut positioned between two motorways. He recalled: 'I sat there among loads of poisonous spiders and cockroaches.' Closing his mind off to all else, he was thrilled to witness a perfect solar eclipse in an azure blue sky.

As a boy, Brian would rush outside his home just to gape wondrously at a universe so vast that it inevitably dwarfed life's problems. As an adult going through troubled times, he declared of the stars: 'They're old friends, up there. Your life can be falling to pieces, but you've still got friends up there.'

12

DEATH AND DESPAIR

In January 1991, 'Innuendo' became number one in Britain but when Queen gathered in Montreux the time for plain speaking had finally arrived. Freddie had decided to confide in his three friends that he was dying of AIDS. Typically, he invited no pity and said brusquely: 'You probably realise what my problem is. Well, that's it, and I don't want it to make a difference. I don't want it to be known. I don't want to talk about it. I just want to get on and work till I fucking well drop. I'd like you to support me in this.'

For those on the receiving end of this barrage of commands, it was hard to take. Brian later revealed: 'I don't think any of us will ever forget that day. We all went off and got quietly sick somewhere, and that was the only conversation directly we had about it.' Now that the 'secret' was out in the open among themselves, as they set to work in Mountain Studios, suddenly every day became intensely precious.

Soon after, May returned to London, where once again he became involved in charity work – this time producing the theme song for the Comic Relief campaign. That year, the song was to be performed by TV comedians Gareth Hale and Norman Pace. Pace explains: 'Producer Richard Curtis had asked everybody who had been involved in Comic Relief if they had any suggestions. Gareth and I came up with the idea of calling the whole day The Stonker, thinking we could write a song called "The Stonk", a silly thing that could perhaps become a dance as well. Richard liked the idea and asked if we would write it and sing it. Brian had apparently been in touch with Curtis some time before, saying that he liked what he was doing with Comic Relief and if there was anything he could do, he would be delighted to help.

'Gareth was on holiday, and Richard asked me to come along to an Indian restaurant and meet Brian May, who was interested in producing "The Stonk". This was like a thunderbolt to me. I had been a Queen fan for years and in particular a big admirer of Brian's talent, so of course I went like a bullet. This was the very day that "Innuendo" made number one in the charts, so Richard and I were sitting at this table in the restaurant, squinting every two minutes at our watches and saying things like: "Well, you know, Brian is bound to be celebrating. Maybe he won't show – understandable when you think of it." But suddenly he walked in and joined us.'

That evening, May invited the pair back to his house to listen to a tape he had made for them. 'I was amazed,' declares Norman. 'We'd written it as this honky-tonk type thing, but Brian had gone and put in Queen-like chords and added all sorts of sounds to it. My first reaction, I admit, was that it sounded a bit peculiar, but only because I was used to it as we had written it, but Brian was so enthusiastic. He heard possibilities in the song that we had never had any intention of creating. It was marvellous and we happily went along with the rewrite. Within two weeks of that Indian meal, Gareth was back from holiday and we were in the studios.'

They recorded 'The Stonk' at Metropolis Studios in London. Norman Pace recalls: 'It took five days in all and was a total education. When Gareth and I did songs for our shows, a band came in and played the backing track and we sang – that was it – but working with Brian was an entirely different experience. As a producer, he is very painstaking. It is all done layer upon layer. We had something like three drum layers. Brian had dragged in Roger Taylor, as well as his friend Cozy Powell. He even roped in Rowan Atkinson, who was also in the video, to play drums too, and Tony Iommi played guitar with Brian. For two days, Brian had been laying the bass line and piano and generally being in charge all round, and we just turned round and said: "Look, Brian, get your guitar out and play yourself!" which he did. I was stunned at how long he took to get his guitar right – something like two hours! Talk about being a perfectionist!'

May's way of working made a lasting impression on Norman Pace. He states: 'Two things I noticed. First, he has a brilliant musical ear. He hears things that no one else hears, but when he singles out the wrong note you say: "Yeah, I hear it now." The second thing is his incredible concentration over great long stretches of time – fourteen hours or so. His concentration never wavers for a second. It may sound a stupid thing to say, but Brian can even eat and still concentrate at exactly the same pitch. I was amazed at how much of himself he put into it.'

It was not a one-way street. Brian was grateful for the chance to relax and enjoy the company of the two live-wire comedians. May has a quiet, low-key sense of humour. He is not a practical joker or loud and brash. He has his own way of appreciating the lighter side of life.

Says Norman, 'We all got on very well together but for perhaps the first two days, Gareth or I would toss some off-the-cuff remark at Brian and he would look long at us and we'd think, aw God, I hope he's not offended! Then slowly a broad smile would cross his face and he would thump us on the back once he had worked out what we were getting at. He's not slow on the uptake. It's just a combination of our brand of humour and the fact that he analyses things so much. He would come in one day and pick up on a throwaway line from two days earlier!

'It's funny. Sometimes, when you get the opportunity to work with famous people you go into it with great respect for the guy and come out the other end feeling really let down. With Brian, my respect only grew. I'll never forget it, and it's unlikely that I'll ever top the experience either.' Released in late February, 'The Stonk' took the number one slot in the UK charts and raised over quarter of a million pounds for charity.

At the beginning of that month, Queen's *Greatest Hits* had re-entered the charts and the new album *Innuendo* was finally released, becoming an instant chart-topper. Brian rated this album as Queen's finest for quite some time, calling the song collection nicely complex and rewardingly heavy. In the circumstances, in the studio, they had opted for live takes as much as they could and had tried to curb any tendency to be obsessive. At the same time, like the others, May was aware of their fans' expectations. As he once put it: 'You can't create music in a vacuum.'

By 1991, May's favoured way of writing was to sing his ideas into a dictaphone, then develop the song on keyboards. He seldom wrote on guitar and it would be in the final stages before he reached for the Red Special. He had not lost his verve for the guitar, but this way he felt he could get a clearer grasp of what was going on in his head. It was difficult, however, to take much pride in the new album's success when the band filmed the video for the number, 'I'm Going Slightly Mad'. The experience was harrowing.

The song's lyrics centred on insanity; to reflect this on screen, all four band members were to portray differing exaggerated forms of madness. The shoot took place at Limehouse Studios and was directed by Hannes Rossacher and Rudi Dolezal. At one point Brian was dressed up as a giant penguin, Roger rode a tiny tricycle in circles, and Freddie in long winkle-picker shoes appeared with a bunch of enormous bananas on his head, but a dreadful sadness underpinned the filming.

Freddie was now so ill that a bed had been set up nearby for him to lie down on between takes. He looked skeletal – and that was with an extra layer of clothes under his suit. The marks on his face were so pronounced that to camouflage them, his make-up was caked on. To hide his very evident hair loss, he wore an outrageous wig.

The singer was also in excruciating pain. To the astonishment of the film crew, though, he continued to run through with them the storyboard he had worked out for one section of the shoot. They had been pre-warned that Freddie had muscle problems and a knee injury, but none of that really rang true. One scene where he crawled on all fours in front of Brian, John and Roger lounging on a settee was particularly painful for Freddie, although in the final cut he hid it so well that no one could tell. For those in the know it was very distressing. Journalists hung around outside the studio, hoping to catch someone off-guard as they left. Everyone, however, remained tight-lipped, and the official line was that Freddie had thoroughly enjoyed himself. 'I'm Going Slightly Mad' was released in early March.

Brian hated the utterly helpless feeling of having to watch the wasting disease take its relentless toll bit by bit on his friend. The previous year, at times like these, his answer had been to hole up in a studio and thrash out his feelings on gutsy rock numbers such as 'I Can't Live with You' and 'Headlong'; the latter was released in May as the third single from the new album. Now, to try to alleviate some of his inner trauma, he immersed himself in intensive songwriting. He was still working on ideas for a solo album, storing them up for the future, and it became a much-needed safety valve.

In late spring, Brian toured America and Canada to promote *Innuendo*. Taking occasional advantage of the radio airplay to test the water with a few ideas for his solo album, he found an encouraging response. When the tour ended, he flew to Montreux once more.

While Brian had been out of the country, the rest of the band had filmed what would be their last ever video for a poignant ballad titled 'These Are the Days of Our Lives'; May was filmed separately and his role integrated in the editing room. As in February, it was a distressing shoot, despite Mercury's continuing bravery.

DJ Simon Bates recalls: 'Brian told me that when Freddie was making their last two videos he was so desperately ill that he could hardly walk, yet his eyes still sparkled, and he would be saying: "Do it this way or that way."' Although almost cadaverously thin, in baggy trousers, loose silk shirt and waistcoat, Mercury managed to remain stylish and professional to the end.

In Montreux, Brian, Roger and John were only a phone call away and ready to record at a moment's notice. Their singer battled on as best he could. Mary Austin later said: 'I think that fed the light inside. Life wasn't just taking him to the grave. There was something else he could make happen.'

Mercury wanted to provide as much material as he was able, which could be worked on after he was gone. He repeatedly urged: 'Write me anything, and I'll sing it.' He pushed his tormented body to the limit. Sometimes, he was barely able to stand upright without suffering agonising pain. At his worst, he numbed that pain with shots of vodka to be able to sing. Roger Taylor reflected: 'Freddie knew his time was limited and he really wanted to work. He felt that was the best way to keep his spirits up.' His band mates never knew as he left the studio, drained and desperate to lie down, if they would ever see him again. In his last recorded interview, Freddie spoke of hoping to cram as much fun into life as he could in the years he had left. The truth was, time was now measured more in months.

In summer, Brian wrote the song 'Driven by You' for a Ford car advertising campaign, then agreed to take part in a massive guitar festival in Seville in Spain as a precursor to the Expo' 92 celebrations planned for the following year. The event aimed to showcase the best guitarists in the business, who were to perform live on the same stage for an evening.

Brian formed a backing band comprising some of rock's elite – including drummers Cozy Powell and Steve Ferrone, bassists Nathan East and Whitesnake's Neil Murray, together with Mike Moran and Rick Wakeman on keyboards. The vocals were to be handled by Paul Rodgers, formerly of the bands Free and Bad Company, and Extreme's Gary Cherone. Among the guitarists joining May were Joe Walsh of the Eagles, Nuno Bettencourt, Steve Vai and Joe Satriani – considered then to be the greatest guitarist in the world.

Joe Satriani himself is more modest. He recalls: 'I discovered that there was a shortlist with names on it like B.B. King and Paul Rodgers. I was very flattered to be included. I flew to rehearsals in London and that is the first time I met Brian. His job as musical director of this festival was a difficult one, but he put everyone at their ease at once. We rehearsed for three days and I can vividly recall feeling so thrilled that I was standing there with Brian May. My friend Steve Vai felt the same. In fact, there was one particular moment when Steve and I were standing shoulder to shoulder watching Brian get all these brilliant Queen sounds out of his guitar right there in front of our eyes and neither of us could believe it was happening. We looked at each other, just speechless with delight. After that we went to Spain and had just one day's rehearsal, then it was the show.'

The illustrious assembly took the stage on 19 October 1991. Joe goes on: 'It was a real big thrill for me, although I was very tense. I couldn't help but be aware that on stage that night were musicians from very different backgrounds. Some were legends in the business that go way back, like Paul Rodgers and Joe Walsh. Then there were the new guys, like me and Steve, getting our feet wet.'

The show's outstanding highlight was when Paul Rodgers, in better voice than ever, led the others in a nerve-tingling rendition of the Free 1970 classic, 'All Right Now'. Joe Satriani states: '"All Right Now" was a song I had grown up with, and here I was backing Paul Rodgers himself singing it. For me that was very special.'

According to Paul Rodgers, the honour, however, was all his. Paul had known Brian and Queen since the mid-1970s, their paths had crossed from time to time. Says Paul: 'Brian called me one day and asked if I would like to be part of this Guitar Legends night. It was very nice to be asked and I am grateful to Brian because, in a way, it was that night which got me back in the public eye. Joe (Satriani) is right. It was an incredible night, with an incredible on-stage atmosphere – backstage, too, as it happens. We were all rehearsing down in the dungeons below the venue and there was a great feeling about it. One minute, you were literally practising away, then the next you were thrust up top, out on stage. I think everyone there will remember that event for a long time.'

Inevitably, behind the scenes, life within Queen had, by now, drastically darkened. Mercury had tried driving himself hard and not giving in but more than ever he was now living on borrowed time. In the peaceful environment of a Swiss lakeside house he had sought solitude to reach some vital decisions, one of which was that he did not want to hang on longer than his body could stand.

Mike Moran poignantly remembers this painful period: 'A couple of months before Freddie died, I got a phone call from Phoebe (one of Freddie's personal assistants, Peter Freestone) asking: "Are you free on 5 September?" I said: "Yes. Why?" Phoebe replied:

"Well, it's Freddie's birthday" and of course we had never missed one, but we hadn't thought that he would be celebrating this year. However, a handful of us went to Garden Lodge, and Freddie was still the perfect host. He did not have long left and he knew it but he was very calm about it, very relaxed and very pleased to see his friends. We watched old videos, told old stories and laughed, and Freddie bravely stuck it out to the end, staying until he saw everyone off. He was amazing. After that, though, he didn't want people to see him because he was so bad. He and I kept in touch by telephone but if I suggested coming over, he would say to me: "No, you don't want to see me today, dear. I'm not looking very good."' Now a spectral figure, Freddie was so aware of his mortality that he began planning the details of his own funeral service.

In late October, Queen released *Greatest Hits Vol II*, just a couple of weeks after their fortieth single, 'The Show Must Go On', which is a favourite song of Brian's. He described its sound as 'very broad and lush', maintaining that while its lyrics were retrospective there was also an element in there of looking forward. Many missed that last sentiment for, as if the lyrics were not sufficiently haunting, the song's video, which was premiered on *Top of the Pops*, looked like an obvious farewell and only heightened speculation that the end was near. Officially, it was still denied that anything was seriously wrong with Freddie but by then half-written obituaries lay waiting in newsrooms around London, and in all areas of the music industry the consensus was that Freddie Mercury was dying.

Although Mercury's team of specialists did what they could to alleviate his suffering, his illness was a horrendous ordeal for Freddie. By early November, he opted to come off most of his medication. His doctors advised him against this, but he was suffering blind spells and night sweats. Plagued by mouth and skin sores, he eventually needed to use a breathing apparatus. Near the end, he would not be able to speak.

On top of his understandable distress, Brian had an added concern. He had earlier decided to take 'Driven by You' out as a solo single; the release date had been set for 25 November. Now, that seemed atrocious timing. Freddie was clearly not going to live for much longer and Brian was appalled. He talked with Jim Beach about stopping the single's release; Beach, in turn, spoke about it to Freddie. Although his strength was ebbing away by the day, Freddie's answer bounced back to Brian: he must go ahead because, if nothing else, just think of the boost to sales if he did die! Though shocking in the circumstances, the flippancy was vintage Freddie.

Freddie was serious, however. Joe Satriani recalls: 'Brian told me that Freddie was really insistent that he was to go ahead both with his single and his whole solo career. Freddie supported Brian literally right up to the end.'

By the third week of November, Freddie was existing on liquids alone and had almost entirely lost the use of his muscles. Brian's friend Joe Elliott recalls: 'Brian was in a very bad way, by now. I rang him to ask how he was coping and, as usual, he tried to hide it. He said: "Aw, well – okay, I guess." He said that Freddie had not got long left. Forty-eight hours later, Fred died.'

On Saturday, 23 November, outside Garden Lodge, Queen's PR officer, Roxy Meade, read out an official statement, in which she stated on behalf of Freddie that he had been tested positive for HIV and that he had AIDS. He felt it had come to the point at which he wanted his friends and fans to know the truth and he hoped everyone would join him and his doctors in fighting to combat the killer disease. The statement made headline TV news and filled newspaper front pages around the world the following day.

Sunday was a bleak day. Freddie's doctor had been in attendance on and off for hours. Mary Austin shuttled back and forth from her home nearby while Mercury slipped in and out of consciousness. An attempt tenderly to move his emaciated body for a change of bed linen had resulted in one of his brittle bones breaking like a dry stick. He needed help to stroke his favourite cat, which had sat sentinel all day with her doting owner.

In the past week, Mercury had felt himself fading. He realised that he would never again leave his house alive. Just days before, weighing very little, he had insisted on enduring the agony of being carried downstairs to take one last long look around at his beautiful home, packed with treasures, crammed with memories. After that, he never moved from his bed again and on Sunday, 24 November 1991, just before seven o'clock in the evening, Freddie died in his sleep.

After all the appropriate people had been informed, just before midnight the news was announced publicly. There was a brief statement that read: 'Freddie Mercury died peacefully this evening at his home. His death was the result of broncho-pneumonia, brought on by AIDS.' Brian, Roger and John issued a joint statement which talked of their overwhelming grief at losing Freddie, and of what a privilege it had been to know him and to have shared in his life, but privately each had to handle his own grief as best he could.

Joe Elliott again rang Brian. 'When our drummer Rick Allen lost his arm in a car crash, Brian was the first to phone,' says Joe. 'Again, when our guitarist Steve Clark died, he was first to call. I don't mean that it was some kind of weird race, and I did not want to intrude on his grief, but I was so concerned that I rang Brian as soon as I'd heard that Freddie had died. I have to say, Brian was a lot better than I'd expected, at least in one sense. Of course, he was extremely upset but he also felt a deep sense of relief. I could relate to that because of how I felt when Steve died. In Freddie's case, in the last week he suffered so very much that it took a bigger love actually to wish him gone for his own sake. There had been industry rumours about Freddie having

AIDS, they were rife, but it wasn't officially announced until the day before. Brian and the others, though, had lived with it for a long time. Having to lie and deny had added enormously to the strain of their personal pain. Brian was in a lot of pain anyway. He's a big guy, you know, but he has round shoulders. That's because he carries all the pressures for everyone else on those shoulders.'

When Freddie's body was removed from Garden Lodge and taken to a secret location in west London, the police provided an escort to prevent the more aggressive members of the press from tailing them. Reporters converged on Mary Austin at the first opportunity. Tearfully, she told them that Freddie had known that the end was coming, adding: 'But he kept his sense of humour right to the end. He told me, he had no regrets.' Distraught fans gathered in their droves outside Garden Lodge's high perimeter walls; floral tributes flooded in from mourners from all walks of life, and the Hammersmith Odeon – scene of many Queen triumphs – displayed the neon message FREDDIE MERCURY. WE WILL MISS YOU.

It had been Mercury's wish to be cremated. The 25-minute service took place three days later at the West London Crematorium in Harrow Road. It was a private affair on a raw day, with only a few special friends joining the star's family and relations. The ceremony was conducted in the ancient Avestan language, in accordance with the Zoroastrian faith, with both priests dressed in white robes, chanting traditional prayers. Adhering to Freddie's instructions, gospel music by Aretha Franklin was also played, as well as an aria from Verdi by Montserrat Caballe.

Several stars paid public tribute to Freddie, but his close friends said it best. Mike Moran confesses: 'Freddie was such a great loss to me that I found it very hard to get over. It was almost harder for me to get over Freddie dying than it was to get over losing my father. With parents, they're older and in some ways you expect it, but not with Freddie.' Wayne Eagling states: 'On stage, Freddie was so flamboyant but in private he was very quiet unless he felt very comfortable with you. I think he was always extremely brave in everything he did. He was never afraid to face up to the world and what was perceived as normal and conventional. It was a great shame that he had to go. You feel so cheated.'

During a TV interview a week later, Brian and Roger were invited to elaborate on a reference at the end of their joint press release – that the remaining band members hoped to plan a tribute to Freddie. All either would say at that stage was that it would maybe take the form of a live concert.

In early December, 'Bohemian Rhapsody' was rereleased, this time as a double A-side, along with the hitherto unreleased 'These Are the Days of Our Lives'. It went straight to number one in the charts to lodge there for the second time over a Christmas period. All royalties went to the AIDS charity, the Terrence Higgins Trust.

By the end of 1991, Brian felt emotionally battered. In the last five years, he had come through what felt like absolute hell. His marriage had run aground, he had lost his beloved father and now Freddie had gone. He had tried so hard to keep himself together for the sake of those who depended on him, but his ability to cope had been fragmenting at an alarming rate and now he had come dangerously close to breaking point.

He was trapped in a strange limbo where outwardly he saw himself carrying on apparently as normal, meeting people, talking, signing autographs, but all the while he felt he was breaking up into tiny pieces, haemorrhaging confidence, shattering irrevocably, and no one could see it, no one could help. He felt he didn't exist as a person any more and, on his own admission, he nearly drove off a bridge in a bid to escape his desolation and despair. At that point, he knew that he desperately needed peace and rest and that he had to get away from Britain. Before the year ended, he flew to Los Angeles to give himself a chance to get well, to regain control of his emotions and to mend his broken life.

13

ROAD TO RECOVERY

In February 1992, at the BPI Awards held at London's Hammersmith Odeon 'These Are the Days of Our Lives' won the trophy for the Best British Single of 1991. Along with Roger and John, Brian also accepted a special award for an Outstanding Contribution to Music made posthumously to Freddie Mercury. Emotionally, May maintained: 'If Freddie were here, he would tell me to put this on the mantelpiece. He would say: "Look, Mum, Dad – that's what I did, and I'm proud." We're terribly proud of everything Freddie stood for. We feel his spirit is with us.' Taylor then announced that they were to stage a huge concert in Mercury's memory on 20 April at Wembley Stadium, which would double as an AIDS Awareness Day. It had not been an easy decision and May later admitted to having had doubts about staging this tribute: 'We went through quite a while when we did not want to do it.'

Within hours of going on sale all tickets for this charity gig, already touted as potentially the biggest show since Live Aid, sold out. The task of inviting the guest performers devolved on the three remaining Queen members, and one of the first groups approached was Def Leppard. Joe Elliott recalls: 'Brian rang me and said they were organising this gig. They didn't have a British band, so we were real honoured. It was a proud moment for us and I couldn't believe that Brian was actually asking *if* we would appear. Blimey! I'd have swum over for it!'

Another act quickly roped in was heart-throb singer Paul Young. Says Paul: 'I knew the guys socially anyway, and one day Roger phoned me at home to say he was putting some names together with a view to staging a tribute concert to Freddie and would I be interested in taking part. I said yes, and a couple of months later it was confirmed.'

As each performer would take lead vocal on a Queen hit, with backing from the rest of the band, intensive rehearsals were required. At Bray Studios in Berkshire, May, Taylor and Deacon put Elton John, Robert Plant, Roger Daltrey, Liza Minnelli, Annie Lennox, George Michael and others through their paces. Most of these stars had never sung a Queen number before and in many cases the key had to be altered, as trying to emulate Freddie was difficult.

With over a dozen artistes to work with, it would have been impractical to have them all there at the same time. Paul Young explains: 'Brian, Roger and John were obviously there all the time, but we had our rehearsal times arranged in advance and just went along and got to work. In my case, it was a couple of hours on a couple of days. They showed me a list of the songs left for selection and I chose "Radio Ga Ga". The first day I turned up at rehearsals we started up the song with the drums, then Brian started playing, and suddenly it was Queen! Freddie was fabulous – there's no doubt about that – but for me, Brian is the real embodiment of the distinctive Queen sound.

'You know, once you become a celebrity it is very easy to find yourself distracted every ten seconds because there are always so many people trying to talk to you, to catch your attention in some way. That's the nature of the business, but you end up not being able to hold a conversation with anyone for more than a couple of minutes. Or if you do, you become edgy, itching to move on as if something's wrong. You can't help it. Your whole life is run that way. Brian, though, is different. He *takes* the time to communicate with people, and equally gives the time to listen. In this business, that is unique.'

Five days before the tribute gig, May and Taylor attended the Ivor Novello Award Ceremony at the Grosvenor House Hotel in London's Park Lane to receive the Best Selling British A Side award, again for 'These Are the Days of Our Lives'. Brian was also presented with the trophy for Best Theme from a TV/Radio Commercial for 'Driven by You'. At this ceremony, he and Roger handed over a cheque to the Terrence Higgins Trust for more than £1 million: the proceeds from sales of the single, 'Bohemian Rhapsody'/'These Are the Days of Our Lives'.

Easter Monday 1992 saw 72,000 people cram into Wembley Stadium. Many had camped overnight on the surrounding pavements to ensure getting in when the gates opened at 4 p.m. the next day. It was officially billed as THE FREDDIE MERCURY TRIBUTE. CONCERT FOR AIDS AWARENESS; on entry, each person was given a red ribbon to wear to symbolise their support for the fight against the disease.

While the crowds flooded in at the front, the artistes were already milling about the specially set up bar backstage. The pre-gig atmosphere was a strange brew, according to Joe Elliott: 'On the one hand, it was light-hearted and up – very positive – and people were in and out of each other's trailers all the time. Unusually, there were no hangers-on, only the necessary people were there, and there was a great feeling of the occasion. On the other hand, it was definitely sad, and later it all got a bit emotional which was understandable.'

It also meant a lot to Spike Edney to feel that everyone performing there that day was doing it for the right reasons. He explains: 'Live Aid was great, but over the years I had become very sceptical of events like this. It just seemed that anybody who didn't get on the Live Aid bill made bloody sure they appeared at any charity gig that came along afterwards, cynically seeing the exposure as a big boost to their careers, but it wasn't going to be like that this time.'

The show opened at 6 p.m., with Brian addressing the crowd: 'Good evening Wembley and the world. We're here tonight to celebrate the life and work of one Freddie Mercury. We're going to give him the biggest send-off in history!' Roger added: 'Today is for Freddie, it's for you, it's to tell everybody round the world that AIDS affects us all. That's what these red ribbons are all about, and you can cry as much as you like.' John then thanked all the artistes who had given their time and energy to pay tribute to Freddie, ending with: 'First of all, the show must go on.'

Metallica was the opening band on stage, followed by Extreme. Then Def Leppard appeared. 'Roger gave us a nice introduction,' remembers Joe Elliott. 'We had some technical problems with Rick's drums, but it didn't matter. It was a brilliant experience playing to 72,000 people in brilliant sunshine. The nice thing, too, although it escaped a lot of people, is that there were a lot of internal tie-ups at work that night. For instance, Liza Minnelli led the finale because Freddie had admired her so much and, of course, Ian Hunter and Mick Ronson were there because Queen had played support to Mott the Hoople before making it big themselves.' Spinal Tap, U2 by satellite, then Guns n' Roses kept up the emotional momentum until 8 p.m., at which point the celebrity section took over.

With a familiar explosion of smoke bombs May, Taylor and Deacon returned and plunged into the rocker 'Tie Your Mother Down', with Brian singing lead. A moment later, Joe Elliott joined him at the mike, taking over lead vocal and turning in a memorable performance.

As Joe hurtled off, Brian announced: 'I'd like to introduce you to an old friend of mine, Mr Tony Iommi.' Tony strolled on stage to play the distinctive intro to the Who's 'Pinball Wizard', which heralded the arrival of Roger Daltrey to lead the band in

'I Want It All'. Says Tony Iommi: 'I was really proud to play that night. It was a very raw experience. It had been building that way for weeks in rehearsals for the whole thing. That night, I think it showed just what Queen had achieved over the years.'

Thereafter, each turn came on, performed their chosen number and went off. Hollywood legend Elizabeth Taylor made a guest appearance in her capacity as National Chairperson for the American Foundation for AIDS Research to deliver an emotive speech about AIDS, despite a few hecklers, and there seemed to be something for everyone.

As the evening progressed, some people found it hard to contain their emotions. No one doubts that the event was well intentioned but for a few the concert fell flat. Bob Harris says: 'I thought it showed up terribly how all the acts struggled with Freddie's songs. The only person I enjoyed was Ian Hunter. He got me up in my seat, but the others were clearly in trouble.'

Simon Bates believes: 'It was very hard to take. They meant well, but it didn't come off. I felt it was more for the fans than anything else, but how do you do that? Do you make it a memorial or a wake? I was there, and the audience were not at all sympathetic. Elizabeth Taylor tried her best, but it was cringing, and Bowie was just awful.'

During his solo spot, David Bowie had announced that he wanted to say a prayer for a sick friend. Marillion frontman, Fish, echoes Simon Bates' feelings on the incident. He says: 'When Bowie dropped to one knee and began praying, it was really embarrassing. I cringed in my seat and thought, oh, my God! The tribute was very disappointing, yet it could have been something sparkling. I believe that the initial feeling behind it was genuine, so it was a great pity.'

Years later, when Brian May was asked what he thought about David Bowie delivering 'The Lord's Prayer', he cautiously replied: 'I remember thinking that it would have been nice if I'd been warned about that.' On the positive side, May selected George Michael as having given the best performance singing 'Somebody to Love'. There was a particular point in the singer's rendition that Brian called, 'pure Freddie'.

It had, nevertheless, been an evening to say a heartfelt goodbye to one of rock's greatest showmen, and over five hundred million viewers in close to seventy countries worldwide had tuned in. A touching moment came when after Robert Plant had felt his way through 'Innuendo' and 'Crazy Little Thing Called Love', Brian surrendered his guitar to sit at the keyboards. He wanted to sing a very special personal tribute to Freddie, and it was not a Queen number but rather one of his own compositions, never aired till now. He told the crowd: 'My only excuse for playing it is, it's the best thing I have to offer.'

He sang 'Too Much Love Will Kill You' and later said of the number: 'We worked on that song for a couple of days and I never went near an instrument. I never touched a piano to the point where we were going to put down a demo. By that time, the song was finished. It was obvious in my mind how it should go. The piano was immaterial. The only thing that mattered was getting the feeling across.'

Tony Iommi was amazed when he discovered his friend intended to perform the solo piece. 'It was one day at rehearsals. I had just turned up and heard someone playing a piano and singing "Too Much Love Will Kill You", and I thought it sounded good. In all the years we've been mates, we've jammed together a lot, sometimes playing non-stop while all the gear's being stripped down and packed away around us but I never saw Brian as lead vocal, I must admit. You don't, when someone is as good as he is on guitar and has only ever sung harmonies before, which is a different thing altogether. I stood there in the doorway behind Brian watching and listening to him and thinking: bloody hell! He can sing after all!'

When it came to the tribute finale, in a choked voice, Brian announced the Oscar-winning actress/singer Liza Minnelli on stage to lead the full line-up in a bluesy rendition of 'We Are the Champions'. At the end, she yelled: 'Thanks, Freddie. We just wanted to let you know, we'll be thinking of you!'

Publicly, they had said their goodbyes. Privately, the fallout was hard to bear. Tony Iommi reveals: 'Immediately after the show was over, it hit Brian very hard. It was so sad. John was just in bits. It was a case of: right, that's it over, final. I would be as well opening up a shop, or something. They had been very brave and it was highly emotional. There was this dreadful feeling of no more, it's finished. I felt it myself, strongly, had seen it lurking and building up all the preceding weeks and months. They had been so close, we'd all been close – all there together for Freddie. Then suddenly that was it – nothing but a terrible vacuum.'

Spike Edney adds: 'At the meal afterwards, a lot of people were going around patting each other on the back and everything, but the four of us just sat at the table staring silently into space, completely drained.'

Queen's music had spanned almost two decades. Soon after the Easter tribute came the announcement that they were to disband. Mercury had once declared: 'If I suddenly left, they have the mechanism in them, they would just replace me – not easy to replace me, huh?' Brian had already dubbed Freddie the fire and glue that held them together. So it was unsurprising when he stated: 'It would be wrong of us to go out with another singer, pretending to be Queen. Queen stopped at that point. I don't feel it in my bones that we should keep Queen alive. I don't think it would be right for Freddie.' It had just been made crystal-clear, anyway, that Mercury would be a hard act to follow; at least in the near future.

One-time *Old Grey Whistle Test* producer Michael Appleton agrees: 'You can assess Freddie Mercury's strength by that tribute concert. With the exception of George Michael, I think it showed, when the other artistes tried to sing those songs, just how incredibly strong Freddie had been. It also showed how one person in a band can be taken very much for granted, so much so that no one realises it until something happens to separate them. Freddie personally had incredible ability and charisma but still, in my view, Queen are not quite up there with the Beatles and the Rolling Stones. Those bands came in the first echelon and Queen came along later but I would definitely put them at the top of the second generation, along with U2.'

Hard though it was for May, after the demise of Queen he had to concentrate on building a bridge to a fresh future, one that would hold new challenges for him. He also needed to relax and to circulate once again. Fortuitously, about now Hank Marvin invited him to guest on his forthcoming album. Hank recalls: 'I've admired Brian's guitar playing since "Killer Queen". I remember the first time I heard it: I was driving along when it came on the radio, and I was struck with the expertness of its musical construction. Lots of Queen stuff is very grand, very showy, and Brian's guitar sound with these big power chords as well as the melodic solos balanced everything beautifully. It had to be big, to match Freddie's delivery.

'In the period immediately after Freddie's death, there was a lot of Queen music being played and it reminded me of how good they were. I thought it would be a nice tribute to their excellence to record some of their music, but then I sat on the idea for a while because I felt it might be cashing in on Freddie's death and I wouldn't have wanted that. Then one day my manager came up with the idea of me doing a duet with Brian May. From there, I thought I could combine that with my original idea, in that we could choose one of Freddie's compositions and donate the royalties to charity.' The number decided on was 'We Are the Champions'.

When the two men set to work, Hank could tell that Brian was still in a very raw state and that Freddie's death had brought back the heartache of losing his father, Harold. Marvin says: 'There was a lot of hurt there. Brian had been very close indeed to his dad. I picked up on that immediately because he talked of him a lot when we were together.' Of trying out the famous Red Special, Hank goes on: 'It is a fascinating instrument. Imagine playing a guitar that you made with your dad, that actually works! It's got woodworm holes in it and everything!'

Brian said of working with Hank Marvin: 'If someone had told me years ago that I would be duetting with Hank Marvin, I just wouldn't have believed them!' While enjoying their time together, Hank was weighing up his fellow guitarist. He reveals: 'Brian's a great guy, a deep thinker and very sensitive. At that time it seemed to me, too, that he was not overly confident and seemed genuinely in need of a lot of reassurance.' Hank Marvin's album *Into the Light*, which included this duet, was released later in the year.

For the first half of June 1992, Brian put the final touches to his album in his home recording studio. Recording solo after all the years of working as part of Queen had been stressful itself. At times, the mosaic of musical ideas made all the sense in the world to him, yet other times he would find himself sitting back at the end of a day wondering if anything on tape was really worthwhile. It was hard to be objective. The thought of going solo was an extremely daunting one, but he had invested so much of himself in each of the songs and he was keen to follow through.

Joe Elliott had been keeping in touch with Brian and concurs with Hank Marvin. 'Brian had invited me round to his house in March when he was working on the album. Cozy [Powell] was there, laying down the drum track for "Resurrection", and Brian was definitely tentative about the strength of his voice. He was playing me a fistful of tapes and kept saying he wasn't sure if he could nail it. He wasn't looking for an emotional crutch. He was simply worried that his voice would come over as weak, when it's not weak at all.'

Tony Iommi was not surprised that Brian should ask Elliott. He says: 'Brian was very worried about his singing and he asked Joe because Joe's a singer he respects. Okay, no one is going to turn round and say: "Hey, Brian, you're a crappy singer," but he needs genuine opinions and he knows where he'll get them. It wasn't all about whether he could make it as a lead singer, though. Brian was really nervous about going solo at all, because it is a huge step to go from being in a major band to going out on your own. After headlining all those years, you are back to playing support, and that comes into it as well, but he had to do it. After Freddie's death, on top of everything else, Brian very much wanted to do something of his own. He was so upset and it had been so very hard on him. They had had their ups and downs like anyone else, but it was still a terrible shock and Brian had been left with this frightening feeling: what do I do now? He had to get out there and throw himself into it.'

As to May's new material, Joe Elliott picks up: 'He had sunk such a lot of emotion in that album, but it would be a mistake to analyse every lyric and take them as an exact reflection of what was going on in his life. Whether it's clever or not, I don't know, but you can listen to some tracks and, while there is certainly a troubled cry for help in there, it does not have to be aimed specifically at his broken marriage. It can just as easily be attributed to losing Freddie. It's aimed, too, at any listener who can relate it to what is going wrong in their life. It was undoubtedly an enormous and terrible blow for him to lose someone he was so close to. Personally, I know it ripped the heart out of Brian but having said that, he was in great spirits after the album was finished. I remember us being in a car together around that

217

time. Brian played "Nothin' But Blue" on the tape deck and I couldn't get it out of my head for days afterwards. It was great.'

'Too Much Love Will Kill You', released from *Back to the Light*, charted at number five in September 1992. DJ Bob Harris, who twenty years before was one of the first in the music industry to recognise Queen, watched this rebirth with interest. He says: 'I think it was very brave of Brian. After being part of something as enormous as Queen, it would have been very easy to hide away.'

Supportively, Joe Satriani chimes in: 'After the tragic break-up of any band, it feels impossible to continue but I was really glad that Brian did launch a solo career. He had such a lot of music in him and a great deal more to give.'

May threw himself on to the PR merry-go-round, during which he revealed plans to take to the stage: 'Me, Cozy Powell, Neil Murray and some of the friends who guested on the album are going to South America to rehearse and do a few gigs. If we feel we have a good vehicle, then we'll come back and tour.' When pressed about making the mental leap from the side of the stage to the centre he was candid: 'Strangely enough, I'm up for it. I wouldn't have been a few years ago, but I've changed a lot over the last five years. I was working through all kinds of personal crises, a lot of which you'll find on the album in a way. It's very much a journey from someone who is locked in a very dark place, to someone who feels he can see a little bit of the light.'

October saw the formation of the Brian May Band. Joining Brian were Cozy Powell on drums, bass player Neil Murray, rhythm guitarist Jamie Moses and Spike Edney on keyboards, as well as backing singers Shelley Preston and Cathy Porter. Spike recalls: 'We didn't have much chance to rehearse before we were thrown right into performing, doing several shows supporting Joe Cocker and also the B52s in Argentina, Chile and Uruguay.'

Although Brian was a seasoned performer, the first few gigs

were something of an ordeal. He later admitted: 'I was nervous. I didn't know when I was supposed to be singing or playing at any one time, and combining the two was quite difficult. Then we were in Velez Sarfield, the same stadium Queen played. I was supporting Joe Cocker and something happened. The audience was incredibly pleased to see us.'

Spike Edney confirms these initial nerves: 'For a start, Brian didn't enjoy it at all. It was pretty much a shock to him, being out front and all that and it took a while for him to find his feet, but the South American audiences were great and very supportive of Brian. We played our first headlining gig in a club in Rio de Janeiro and the response he got was terrific, which was a great boost to his morale.'

Back to the Light peaked at number six in the UK album charts in mid-October and spawned four more single releases before the year's end. In the meantime, May made time to hook up with his friend, singer Paul Rodgers, who was recording an album called *Muddy Water Blues* as a tribute to the late blues great.

Paul Rodgers recalls: 'I did backing tracks of certain numbers together with vocals, then I wanted to invite particular guitarists to play on particular tracks. One day, there were a few of us in a room considering the song "I'm Ready", when someone said its walking bass line was reminiscent of the one on "Crazy Little Thing Called Love". I had been hoping that Brian would be able to play on my album anyway and this track seemed just right for him, so I rang him.'

May and Rodgers met up at the Power House recording studios in London in early 1993. 'It took us about four hours,' remembers Paul, 'which is quick, but Brian was right into it. Brian is not known as a blues guitarist and it was an unusual challenge for him but he proved up to it.'

Brian next got involved with Frank Zappa's son Dweezil on his latest album. Then support duties called; this time the Brian

May Band were to back Guns n' Roses. Their first date was in Austin, Texas, in February before a 15,000 capacity crowd, but not long into the tour an unforeseen spanner was lobbed into the works.

Spike Edney explains: 'Axl Rose suddenly had a few problems and cancelled some shows, which left us having to hastily arrange dates for ourselves to play as headliners. We already had some headlining gigs planned for New York and Los Angeles but now we had to fix up dates in Cleveland, Philadelphia and Baltimore too. It did not quite feel it at the time, but it was great experience for us. Brian's confidence this trip was very much up and down, depending really on how tired he was, but he was always convinced that he could make it work.'

In late spring, Brian again visited South America. On his return, he was saddened to learn of the death of former Mott the Hoople guitarist Mick Ronson from liver cancer. He had happy memories of Mick stretching back two decades and he was tired and pensive when he and Anita Dobson caught Concorde for New York.

The break was brief before he embarked on a solo UK tour, kicking off at Edinburgh Playhouse in early June. Hours before taking the stage in the Scottish capital, he confessed: 'It is every singer's worry: do I have a voice today?' He had worried about whether he was a strong enough singer, yet he had never considered enlisting a vocalist for his band. He was adamant: 'I wasn't going to let anyone else sing for me now. After Freddie, there just isn't anyone.'

In July, the Brian May Band rejoined Guns n' Roses for some European dates. 'Our last gig,' says Spike Edney, 'was in Paris. That gig was something else, but I think the highlight for everyone was when both bands were on stage at the same time playing Dylan's "Knocking on Heaven's Door"!

In mid-September, the band hit the road again, kicking off in

Winterthur, Switzerland. Says Spike: 'What was really special was the moment when Brian sang "Love of My Life" and stopped just like Freddie used to, and the audience sang the song right back to him. That meant a lot to Brian.' By the time they arrived at the Albert Hall in London in early December, May's confidence had strengthened. He said: 'The Albert Hall was a first, but it's a very tricky place sound-wise. My voice wasn't up to much because I had the flu. I thought it would stiff, but the audience was absolutely brilliant.' The tour wound up in Portugal a fortnight later.

Spike reflects: 'Throughout, it was very important to Brian to be one of the guys. On some of those European dates he was offered a limo while the rest of us were bunged on to a bus but Brian shunned the limo and got on the bus with us, saying he wasn't about to sit all alone when he would rather be where the fun is. A lot of people talk about Brian's great sensitivity and gentleness. They're right, but he also has a will of iron. He is very ambitious and works extremely hard to the point of sometimes making himself ill, but that's just the way he is.' In February 1994, the first live recording of the Brian May Band, *Live at the Brixton Academy*, was released and lodged at number twenty in the UK charts but, by now, solo endeavours had to be firmly relegated to the back burner.

14

FULL CIRCLE

May, Taylor and Deacon had promised Freddie Mercury that they would use the material he had struggled to record for them to complete a Queen album for release after his death, and while each was determined to honour that pledge, bringing this project together proved to be far more difficult than they had imagined. Come autumn 1994, May admitted: 'There are very real limits. We don't have the strong structure of the group to pull us together any more.'

When Brian had launched his solo career, Roger and John had started working on the tapes, requiring May to play catch-up when he came off the road. 'Because the others had begun without me, it started off in a fairly stressful way,' said Brian. 'It became an enormous task and it took literally two years out of my life, sitting in front of a computer trying to make the most of the scraps that we had of Freddie's vocal, or arranging and producing and performing to fill in all the gaps.'

There were rewardingly uplifting spells but largely it was a hard slog, not to mention emotionally tough at times. Getting over Freddie's death was not easy, and the trio were trying to make the album as if Queen still existed. May dubbed the finished article a kind of fantasy album, and there was certainly an ethereal quality to *Made in Heaven* which, when released in November 1995, topped the UK album charts. It went double-platinum and in contrast to the rough ride often given by critics in the past to Queen records, this work was praised as being the band's most poignantly personal album.

By the year's end, Queen also scored top ten hits with two of the spin-off singles – 'Heaven for Everyone' and 'A Winter's Tale'. The latter ballad struck a particular chord with May. It had been Freddie's last songwriting effort and it had amazed him that Mercury had had no bitterness in him. Living quietly at his house in Montreux, Mercury had managed to find a kind of inner serenity. Brian thought it a miracle that the AIDS-ravaged star had been able to express, lyrically, such an unblemished joy in a world that he had been tragically doomed to leave behind prematurely.

It was, in many ways, an unsettling time for Brian. Although his concentration on putting together the Queen album had been intense, beneath it all he had also found it deeply frustrating having to sideline, for so long, many exciting ideas he had for a new solo album. Yet at the same time, the endeavour had vividly reminded him of what a vibrant entity Queen had been. 'We were always on the run, working on the next project,' he reflected. 'Sometimes, I wish that I could go back and walk through it again. I miss that feeling of being connected to the main pulse of the world.'

Queen's fans missed the band, but had to make do with two further releases – *Ultimate Queen* and *Queen Rocks*. Of the latter, a UK number seven hit in November 1997, May revealed: 'The record company wanted to put out a compilation album and we thought it would be a good idea to encourage people to remember the heavy stuff that Queen recorded. I have always had a fondness for the rockier side of things.'

Five years on from disbanding, Queen continued to cast a long shadow over its surviving members, but May was itching to refocus his energies on his shelved solo career. Very specifically, this time, he did not want to make an introspective album. Rather, he sought new experiences, to revisit his roots and to revitalise himself by getting involved in a variety of projects. 'I travelled a lot of paths to gather all the pieces,' he said.

One such satellite project that proved stimulating was writing a song for the Sydney Pollack 1998 comedy-drama, *Sliding Doors*. He came up with a ballad, 'Another World', but it went deeper than that. He said: 'I realised that this film assignment had wrenched out of me, virtually in one night, the whole theme of what my new album should be about.' He now understood clearly that he wanted to express a yearning to find a better way of connecting with his surroundings, to find a better kind of truth, he called it. He confessed: 'I go through major crises every few months, but then I have great peaks of belief and creativity.'

The new solo album had been in the making, on and off, for about three years already, and May's initial aim had been to record a collection of cover songs. Although that idea fell by the wayside, he retained three cover versions – a Larry Williams number, 'Slow Down', and two songs by artistes he very much associated with his past – Mott the Hoople's 'All the Way from Memphis' and Jimi Hendrix's 'One Rainy Wish'. When Queen had supported Mott the Hoople on tour in Britain and America two decades earlier, Brian had watched the way in which 'All the Way from Memphis' would bring the house down every night. Explaining to the press why he had chosen to cover this rock hit, May was bullish: 'I damn well want to play this song live because I just love it so much. It's got all the right elements. It's got light and shade, changes of pace and suspense.' Of the Hendrix song, Brian declared: 'I chose "One Rainy Wish" because it was done really quickly by Jimi. It is something he put down in ten minutes and the lyric, I think, is genuinely a dream. That's the way I hear it. I've written stuff from dreams before.'

The bulk of May's third solo album would comprise original

compositions, and he quickly decided to make 'Another World' the title track. The movie *Sliding Doors* had centred on a 'what if fate had led me down this road instead of that road' scenario, and 'Another World' was a song that May strongly believed would hit the spot with the man and woman in the street, many of whom secretly feel that life could have turned out so differently for them, but for the hand of providence. An ambition of his, he maintained, was to compose a song that could solve people's problems; though that is a tall order for anyone to hope to satisfy.

Another new song related to the movie world was 'The Guv'nor'. The proposed film, a true story about a bare-knuckle boxer, unfortunately ran aground but May had his song 'The Guv'nor', into which he roped his friend, renowned guitarist Jeff Beck. Said May: 'In our world, Jeff *is* the guv'nor – the standard by which you judge yourself.' Somewhat nervous of asking Beck, May was thrilled when Jeff listened to and liked the track and agreed to play guitar on it. May conceded that when he and Jeff first recorded together, a degree of competitiveness naturally kicked in. When it came to the final mix, however, May considered Beck's input to be brilliant. Jeff Beck's lead guitar work, therefore, would dominate the number.

Beck himself was not too thrilled when he heard the first playback of this number and he asked if he could take it away with him, to work on it at home. Brian had half expected his friend to do this and agreed. However, it was almost a year later when, having heard nothing back from Jeff, he had to ask tentatively what stage he was at with 'The Guv'nor'. Unwilling to pressurise his friend, May waited anxiously as the record company deadline began to creep up on him. Beck made it on time, though, and May later recalled: 'The image of Jeff Beck is that he is unpredictable and spiky and spontaneous, but there is another side to him which is very much a perfectionist.'

Perhaps predictably, May strayed into the realms of science

fiction to come up with a song he titled 'Cyborg', which he composed on computer. *Guitar World* said of this number: 'May's blinding arpeggio work takes on the dangerous robotic perfection of the title character.' But largely, *Another World* was shaping up to be a heavier rock album than its predecessor, *Back to the Light*, and May's top priority throughout was the songs. He revealed: 'I try to capture the spontaneity of the moment and the rawness, the anger, the pain, and just do what is necessary to set it up. It's a weird thing. I'm sure painters went through the same sort of agonies.'

The recording sessions for *Another World* took place at May's home studio in Surrey, where he refused to compromise. 'I apply the same quality standards to my solo records as I did to Queen records, which is probably why it takes so damn long.' That said, May consciously avoided this solo album being connected in any way with Queen, and he believed that he had taken significant strides away from that chunk of his life, in order to feel that he was forging something separate and new with *Another World*.

May played many of the instruments on this new material himself but among those musicians he had drafted in were stalwart friends, bassist Neil Murray and drummer Cozy Powell. Shortly after the work was completed, on 5 April 1998, Brian received the shocking news that Cozy had been killed. The fifty-year-old drummer, who had been in hard rock bands Black Sabbath, Rainbow and Whitesnake, had been driving on the M4 motorway when, on the outskirts of Bristol, he had apparently lost control of his car and crashed into the central reservation barrier. He died of his injuries a few hours later in hospital.

May was rendered numb by the news. Often, Cozy had shown up at Brian's home, energised and eager to set to work in the studio; many a time the sheer force of Powell's personality had given May a much-needed added spark. Now his life had been snuffed out, without warning. Cozy had heard *Another World* in its finished state and had told Brian he believed it was brilliant. He could hardly wait, he had said, to go back out on the road with the Brian May Band to back the new album.

Said May of Powell: 'He was a pillar of British rock music and a hero of mine ever since we first met at a concert in 1976. It was always a dream to play music with him, and when he came out on tour it was a great thrill.' May credited Cozy with being someone who had always reminded him of where the true core of rock music lay. Emotionally, he told journalists: 'He was such an amazing guy, very down-to-earth. There was a thoughtfulness and a glorious oneness about him.'

Just weeks later, at the beginning of June, *Another World* was released; it dropped anchor at number twenty-three in the UK album charts. The rock music press saw *Another World* as an emotionally deep piece of writing. Some reviewers thought May was somewhat wearing his heart on his sleeve - yet it was not meant in a derogatory sense. May's wider vocal range was welcomed, and musically he drew plaudits both for having invested more meaning into his solo set pieces and for the impressive aggression of his fretwork.

Sustaining most of that fretwork was, of course, the Red Special - or the Old Lady, as the instrument has by now become affectionately known. Over the years, this famous home-made guitar had suffered a fair amount of wear and tear; unsurprisingly towards the end of making *Another World*, it finally screamed out for some restoration. It was a huge decision, and after careful consideration May enlisted master craftsman Greg Fryer to undertake the delicate work. There were replicas of the Red Special and it had been studied and its technical specifications meticulously logged long ago, but actually dismantling the instrument could near feel sacrilegious.

A single screw held the guitar neck on to the body, which had not been disturbed in thirty years and because Brian had not seen the inside of his precious guitar since he and his father had built it, he found it an incredibly moving moment seeing it being taken apart now. The Red Special is so intrinsically linked with Brian's late father, Harold, that it must also have made the restoration job rather nerve-racking for Greg Fryer.

There was scant time to be maudlin, however, for the tour planned to back *Another World* loomed large. Obviously, an unlooked-for dilemma was what to do now about a drummer. Just as it had crossed May's mind to cancel the tour altogether, so he had considered taking to the road without a drummer, but he swiftly realised that that was impractical. Initially, it was unthinkable to be replacing Cozy Powell, but someone had to pick up the sticks. That someone proved to be former Kiss drummer, Eric Singer, who had been recommended to May by Tony Iommi. In Singer, May found an explosive and gifted musician, able to articulate the heartbeat of his material. Eric Singer would be joining Neil Murray on bass, Jamie Moses on guitar, Spike Edney on keyboards and two backing vocalists to make up the Brian May Band this time around. May knew well that it would be strange to glance behind himself on stage and not see the familiar stockily built, dark-haired Powell pounding away on the skins, and he admitted that he had specifically constructed certain aspects of his style around Cozy; he had factored into the mix, when writing a song, how it would sound with Powell's power-packed delivery anchoring it.

Nevertheless, May geared himself up to go on the road in summer 1998, gigging around Europe before hitting the UK. In addition to playing London's Albert Hall in late October, he had dates in Nottingham, Bristol, Birmingham, Newcastle, Manchester and Sheffield. Brian knew that at any given gig, there would be dyed-in-the-wool Queen fans who wanted very much a replica of the Queen sound; when he performed classic Queen hits, he catered to that want. Yet he also needed to find something new on stage as a solo performer. It could be difficult striking the exact balance that would suit everyone, but when in Birmingham to play the National Indoor Arena he did not mince his words: 'As far as I am concerned, Queen is just about dead and buried. I don't want to live in the past.' Come November, May turned his sights on taking his tour to Russia, Japan and Australia.

Although May made it through the tour without his close friend, he still mourned Cozy. Powell had been a much respected figure in rock circles, but his death was never going to be marked with a big public send-off. Brian, however, wanted to stage a gathering at which various artistes and friends of the late drummer could come and pay tribute, and so a charity gig was arranged for 1 May at the Opera House in Buxton. Among those taking part were Chris Farlowe, Chris Thompson, Spike Edney and Neil Murray. Hundreds of hard rock fans came, and it was a bittersweet occasion as almost every turn had their own personal memory of the late musician to share with the crowd. When Brian closed the show, he spoke movingly of how Cozy's death a year earlier still seemed like just yesterday to him and of how he had battled with great sadness since. He said, however, that Cozy would be telling him to stop being maudlin and to 'Fuckin' get out there, rockin'.' 'He was a fantastic bloke to be with,' said May. 'He was like a brother, one of the true great spirits of rock.' The finale, led by Brian, included rousing renditions of 'All the Young Dudes' and the Beatles' song, 'With a Little Help From My Friends'.

1999 found May in a deeply reflective mood. Yet more cosmic events, including eclipses and the appearance of the Hale-Bopp comet in the earth's atmosphere, as well as taking trips with fellow astronomers to Mongolia, Chile and China, all renewed Brian's appreciation of how small mankind is within the context of the universe. On a more prosaic level, he now looked back on aspects of Queen's global success with a new eye. He did not deny that stardom had brought its rewards, and his pride in the band and its achievements was steadfast, but some of the experiences that had come along with that rollercoaster ride he was now ready to say had had a detrimental effect on him. 'I think it truly messed me up,' he maintained, 'and I'm conscious that I have not really recovered.' It was not only Freddie Mercury who had, at times, been out of control.

For such a private person, May can choose his moments to be soul-baring and in looking back at his bleakest period he frankly reflected on when he had been hit by the dissolution of his marriage and the deaths of Freddie and his father, Harold May. 'I really didn't want to live,' he now revealed. 'I felt wounded, depressed, brain-fried and the feelings of loss outweighed any of my achievements.' When Brian said depressed, he meant proper full-on depression – the sort that made him feel literally unable to function and filled him with a desire to hide away from the world. Poignantly, he described feeling mentally paralysed. 'Depression would clamp down like a black fog. I'd look up at planes and think, someone built that plane. I don't even know how to get breakfast inside me!'

When Brian had come to the tipping point in this crisis he had checked himself into a clinic in Arizona where he found himself alongside people with similar feelings of helplessness and also with drug and alcohol addicts and people battling eating disorders. At first, at this clinic, Brian did not want to take anti-depressant medication. Then when he gave it a try he believed that it exacerbated his problems. Mentally, he had felt dislocated from reality because of the medication, which also induced nausea. That iron will that his friends talk of kicked in and, quitting the antidepressant pills, he was determined to get well without that kind of chemical assistance. It had been a debilitating time, but he had pulled through.

By the new millennium, Brian felt a new person, someone who

had wiped the slate clean. One constant, however, remained Anita Dobson, whom May clearly considers to be his strongest pillar of support. Without this vivacious lady in his life, he has declared, no amount of therapy in the world would have helped him. Again, opening his heart to journalists he was once so wary of, he declared the depth of his devotion to the actress, talking of a kind of spiritual cord between them that may become stretched to the limit at times but could never break. Anita is, he has stated somewhat unscientifically for him, somehow a part of him.

That cord could conceivably have snapped, however, when in 1999 the couple, known for their lively volatility, had split up for a few months before repairing their fiery relationship. After more than a decade together, Brian then proposed to Anita during a romantic holiday, and on 18 November 2000 they married at Richmond Register Office in south-west London. It was a small private family occasion, followed by a reception at an exclusive Kensington restaurant before the newlyweds flew off to honeymoon in Venice. To May, marrying greatly strengthened their bond. He said recently: 'We came through every kind of battlefield and up to the point when we got married, it was always on and off. Now, my relationship with Anita is the same as my passion for music and astronomy – intense.'

With his personal life on an even keel Brian was happy and enthusiastic again about life, more able to enjoy that Queen were being recognised in a variety of ways. Freddie Mercury had once said: 'If we are worth anything, we will live on.' In the Channel 4 TV Music of the Millennium poll, Queen had been voted the second greatest band in music history. On 19 March 2001, alongside Paul Simon, Michael Jackson, Aerosmith and Steely Dan, Queen were inducted into the Rock and Roll Hall of Fame at a ceremony held in New York, just as news broke in Britain that there was to be a West End stage musical structured around Queen music.

Called *We Will Rock You*, the idea had been in the pipeline for a number of years. The Hollywood actor Robert de Niro ploughed money into the venture and Brian became heavily involved with the project. The story and script would be by comedian and novelist Ben Elton, and while at one point a biographical line had been considered, in the end the show's creators veered away from that. May maintained that none of the remaining Queen members were very comfortable with having even a version of their lives depicted on stage. Ben Elton's intention to set the story in a future where rock music is banned seemed to be the most exciting. May declared: 'Ben has written us a fantastic script.'

Director Christopher Renshaw was at the helm of the £7.5 million production and Brian threw himself into his role as one of the show's co-producers, immersing himself in every aspect of the musical, which would feature twenty of Queen's greatest hits. It was so hectic, he later recalled that he had hardly had time to swallow a mouthful of food. 'For five months, we worked with the actors in the theatre and it was one of the most creatively challenging periods of my life,' he declared.

The core cast of *We Will Rock You* featured Tony Vincent, Hannah Jane Fox, Sharon D. Clarke and Nigel Clauzel, and by March 2002 excitement was mounting. Robert de Niro enthused: 'It's an adventure. I have been involved in this for a long time. It went through a lot of stages and finally it's going to be terrific!' Brian could not help but be conscious of how incredibly thrilled Freddie would have been to see Queen's music living on in this particular way.

We Will Rock You opened at the Dominion Theatre in London's Tottenham Court Road on 14 May 2002, and that night earned an uproarious standing ovation, which May said gave him the shivers. It was an immensely proud moment for him. While some reviewers felt that diehard Queen fans would be thoroughly delighted with the musical, other critics were not so kind. *The Times* said: 'The script remains little more than two-minute blasts of knob gags and misplaced polemic between songs, and the musical numbers have nothing to do with the script.' The *Daily Telegraph* felt: 'Far from being guaranteed to blow your mind, *We Will Rock You* is guaranteed to bore you rigid.' Theatre-goers proved such critics wrong, however. The musical quickly began to break box office records and has recently been extended indefinitely. It has, so far, also been staged successfully in Spain, Australia, Germany, Malaysia, South Africa, Russia and America, and along the way has cultivated a new generation of Queen fans.

That June, Queen were inducted into America's Songwriters Hall of Fame. Four months later, the band were honoured with their star on Hollywood's Walk of Fame. Along with Roger Taylor, May unveiled what was the 2,207th plaque to be fitted to one of America's most famous boulevards. Queen joined the Beatles as one of the few non-US bands to be afforded this accolade. May appreciated the relaxed atmosphere surrounding an event that would have been far stuffier in Britain; that evening he was joined on stage by Steve Vai and other special guests at a party held in a Hollywood bar.

Brian believed that he had never had such an exciting and varied year; that was certainly true, inasmuch as back in the summer he had opened one of the biggest parties in the world when Her Majesty Queen Elizabeth II had celebrated her Golden Jubilee. As part of the lavish celebrations, the rock concert held on 3 June 2002 was dubbed the Party at the Palace. It was seen by 1.2 million people outside Buckingham Palace and by many millions of TV viewers live around the world. Brian had provided one of those historic moments in time when, dressed in white with a long flowing coat, he performed his own arrangement of 'God Save the Queen' on his Red Special standing on the roof of the palace. The concert itself, held in the garden at Buckingham Palace before 12,000 guests, featured music stars of all ages, and when May and Roger Taylor took to the stage they were visibly energised when the striking Tony Vincent from *We Will Rock You* hurtled on stage in a scarlet shirt, stuck his chest out in fine Freddie fashion and launched into his performance.

From music, the focus for Brian towards the end of the year swung to astronomy when in November he received an honorary degree from the University of Hertfordshire. After accepting the honorary science doctorate at a ceremony at the Cathedral and Abbey Church of St Albans, May addressed the 1,000-strong audience about his decision all those years ago to choose music over astronomy: 'It was very difficult at the time and I disappointed my parents, who wanted me to go along the academic route but I don't think I quite had the discipline to be an academic.' That he was thrilled by the honour was obvious. He said of the degree: 'It completes a great circle in my life.'

Queen's longevity became even more assured by the smash hit success of *We Will Rock You,* and the spotlight frequently fell on the three remaining members. Only now, increasingly, questions were being asked as to what had happened to bass player John Deacon, who was conspicuously absent from any Queen activity. When pressed on why Deacon had slipped so far off the radar, May simply maintained that John, who had always been Queen's quietest member, preferred to keep a very low private profile. According to May, Deacon was not at all negative about anything his ex-bandmates were doing. Brian stated that John had come to see the stage musical in London and had enjoyed it, although he had not wished to have anything to do with its creation.

In November 2004, Queen came fifth in a *Q* magazine poll of the 50 Biggest Bands Ever, beaten by Pink Floyd, Led Zeppelin, the Rolling Stones and U2, but ranking three places higher than the Beatles. That same month, Queen were inducted into the newly launched UK Music Hall of Fame, at a ceremony held at London's Hackney Empire. Performing during the show, Brian May and Roger Taylor were fronted by singer Paul Rodgers, who turned in gutsy, spine-tingling renditions of some of Queen's hard rock hits.

Six years earlier, May had publicly declared his view that Queen was just about dead and buried. For many watching the Hackney Empire set that did not seem so certain. Behind closed doors, between May and Taylor, too, the picture had been changing. The previous September, at the Albert Hall, Paul Rodgers had performed with Brian at the fiftieth anniversary celebrations to mark the creation of the Fender Stratocaster guitar, and it was on the strength of how well that had worked out that May and Taylor invited Paul Rodgers to front them on stage at the UK Music Hall of Fame appearance. Speaking of the trio's reaction to both of those performances, May said: 'We were so amazed at the chemistry. Suddenly, it seemed blindingly obvious that there was something happening. The UK Music Hall of Fame show went incredibly well and we got so many rave reactions from out there that we decided we would look at a tour together.'

The prospect of reviving Queen as a live performing entity was a big deal. By his own admission May had ploughed a lot of effort into his solo work, into putting clear water between the past and the present. Yet he had been a major force in creating Queen and now he had begun to question if he shouldn't stop trying to distance himself from that part of his life. In effect, he wanted to stop 'running away', as he put it, and having done so he could now contemplate Queen resurrecting and going out on the road again. May had come to class Queen as being in an odd place; whereas they were becoming increasingly recognised as a major force in British music, the death of their frontman had effectively stymied the remaining members from being able to get out and connect with live audiences. Subliminally, a notion had been lurking that there could be a frontman out there who would fit the bill and allow the Queen phoenix the chance to rise again.

In the music media, there was speculation at one stage that Robbie Williams could tour with May and Taylor, but that did not happen. May conceded, however, that having watched footage of Williams performing a gig at Slane Castle in Ireland, he had felt that the impish Englishman effortlessly exuded an infectious charisma that was similar to Freddie's effect on audiences.

From the youthful Robbie Williams eyes turned to the mature and experienced hard rocker Paul Rodgers, when at the end of 2004 May confirmed that Queen, fronted by the ex-Free vocalist, would kick off a UK tour the following spring. Said May: 'Paul Rodgers was a real hero to Freddie and a big influence. You can hear it on the early stuff.' Paul Rodgers knew that he would fall under very close scrutiny from Queen fans and the music press, and at the outset he made his position clear, that he viewed the tour as a chance to play music with musicians he respected. He was not, he pointed out, joining Queen. Paul stated: 'I am not trying to replace Freddie. I'm coming into this as myself, playing some of their material and some of mine.' The distinctive vocalist's musical roots lay in blues and soul music, and he had always been a far grittier rocker than the theatrically flamboyant Mercury, so the Queen song catalogue had to be closely studied to make up the best playlist for their upcoming performances.

The plan was to select songs that were Queen fans' favourites and songs from Paul's days with Free and Bad Company. In terms of Rodgers's own material, he would be revisiting numbers he had not belted out in decades. Asked if there were any Queen songs he would not contemplate performing, Paul singled out 'I'm Going Slightly Mad' as being too quirkily tongue in cheek for his style, while hard-rocking numbers like 'Hammer to Fall', 'I Want it All' and 'We Will Rock You' were right up his alley.

At the height of his game, on stage, Paul Rodgers had exuded his own arrogant power and presence as an impressive frontman, and he had the proven ability to draw the crowd into a performance, revving them up to fever pitch. He was, therefore, relishing the challenge to work his own kind of magic live with a Queen audience. Seeing how it was all shaping up, May was content. He admitted: 'It will never be the same without Freddie but it will be different.' Going back on the road together was not, on either Queen's or Paul's side, about making money. A creative spark had been inadvertently lit and they were eager to see if they could rekindle a flame.

In January 2005, it was announced that the upcoming shows would be billed as Queen and Paul Rodgers; John Deacon would not be participating. It would be nineteen years since May last went out on the road as Queen and the prospect both excited and alarmed him a little. He was conscious of a stunned feeling reverberating around the fact that this reunion was happening at all, and was aware that there would likely be those who were waiting to cut them down. Though he could do nothing about critics sharpening their knives, to anyone predisposed to dislike the new set-up his advice was blunt – don't come to the show then. May's focus on the upcoming tour was complete. 'It will take precedence over our lives,' he said. Joining Brian May, Roger Taylor and Paul Rodgers in the band were keyboard player Spike Edney, guitarist Jamie Moses and Danny Miranda on bass. The Queen and Paul Rodgers 26-date tour of the UK and Europe kicked off at London's Brixton Academy on 28 March 2005 and concluded in mid-May.

The following month, in the Queen's birthday honours list, Brian May was made a Commander of the Order of the British Empire for his services to the music industry. He said of receiving the CBE: 'I feel very grateful for the recognition. It is not something I have ever sought. The first thing that comes into your head is that you wish your mum and dad were there to enjoy it, but I am happy that my wife and kids will be able to enjoy it.'

Recognition of another kind came as he carried on touring fronted by Paul Rodgers throughout 2005 and 2006, taking in South Africa, Western Europe, Japan and North America. When the band played at the likes of the Meadowlands Arena in New Jersey, it was the first time Queen had faced a US audience since 1982. Commencing on 3 March 2006 in Miami, Florida, this trek wrapped up mid-April in Vancouver, BC, Canada.

That summer, off the road, May collaborated with Cliff Richard on re-recording the Cliff Richard and the Shadows' vintage hit 'Move It' for Richard's new album of duets, *Two's Company*, released in November, by which time Brian had a release of his own to cherish – the publication of the book *Bang! The Complete History of the Universe*, which he had co-authored with astronomer Sir Patrick Moore and Dr Chris Lintott, a co-presenter of the TV programme *The Sky at Night*. For Brian, it was another throwback – Patrick Moore's long-running show had practically single-handedly ignited his fascination with the stars, and he had been more than a little overawed when Moore had invited him to collaborate with him and Lintott on this book. Initially, May had also had reservations – uncertain that he felt qualified enough to be a valuable asset to this work. It turned out in the end, however, to have been immensely rewarding for him.

Talking of how Sir Patrick Moore had persuaded him to overcome his caution, May recalled: 'He said: "Look, you have to return to your other love at some point."' As to the weighty subject matter dealt with in the book, at its launch May reasoned: 'They are heavy concepts. They're not really difficult concepts, they're just unfamiliar ones.' What particularly pleased Brian was that the book was presented in a way that made it accessible to almost anyone. Readers were not required to have a fantastic grasp of maths or of complex astronomical matters to enjoy it.

His involvement in writing *Bang! The Complete History of the Universe* had gone a long way to stirring Brian's passion for astronomy to even greater heights than normal – to the extent, indeed, of bringing him full circle, for he decided to make a push at finally completing his doctorate; he was delighted when his alma mater, Imperial College, showed interest in his re-registering there.

Courtesy of his honorary science degree, technically speaking he is already Dr Brian May, but Brian wants the real McCoy, something he has genuinely worked hard for. He admitted: 'I have this terrible perfectionist thing. I have to do things to the perfect state.' At the end of 2006, he began looking into returning to his original PhD work, planning to rewrite everything. In August 2007, thirty-six years after first beginning it, Brian finally submitted his thesis to Professor Paul Nanda, head of astrophysics at Imperial College, London.

At the turn of the year, in a BBC Radio Two poll, Queen were voted the greatest British band of all time. Bands had been judged on songwriting lyrics, live performance, originality and showmanship. More than twenty thousand listeners had taken part and Queen had left their main rivals, the Beatles and the Rolling Stones, trailing well behind in the voting share.

Two years earlier, when May and Taylor had first hooked up with Paul Rodgers, apart from making live appearances, the trio had tentatively discussed that if all went well on tour there may be the possibility of one day also writing and recording together. In March 2007, it was revealed that May, Taylor and Rodgers were working on recording new material. It was very early days, but Brian said: 'We went into the studio to see what would happen and we came up with some tracks which I think are really great. They're different. They're unlike anything that we've done before, or anything Paul has done.' Fans waited to see if there were plans to take the new songs out for a spin on the road. The prospect of a new live stage act would appeal to May, because it would go beyond the boundaries of playing to nostalgia.

On 19 July 2007, Brian turned sixty, a major milestone in many men's lives when, beginning to look towards the twilight years of retirement, they often cast a wistful glance back at their younger days. Never a man to live in the past, however, although he has already achieved so much, Brian May retains an infinite appetite for embracing new challenges, for exploring different horizons. 'You have to let yourself be inspired,' he recently maintained. 'You can't be in a vacuum.'

INDEX